BOOKS BY PHILIP LEVINE

POETRY

THE SIMPLE TRUTH   1994
WHAT WORK IS   1991
NEW SELECTED POEMS   1991
A WALK WITH TOM JEFFERSON   1988
SWEET WILL   1985
SELECTED POEMS   1984
ONE FOR THE ROSE   1981
7 YEARS FROM SOMEWHERE   1979
ASHES: POEMS NEW AND OLD   1979
THE NAMES OF THE LOST   1976
1933   1974
THEY FEED THEY LION   1972
RED DUST   1971
PILI'S WALL   1971
NOT THIS PIG   1968
ON THE EDGE   1963

ESSAYS

THE BREAD OF TIME   1994

TRANSLATIONS

OFF THE MAP: SELECTED POEMS OF GLORIA FUERTES, EDITED AND TRANSLATED WITH ADA LONG   1984
TARUMBA: THE SELECTED POEMS OF JAIME SABINES, EDITED AND TRANSLATED WITH ERNESTO TREJO   1979

INTERVIEWS

DON'T ASK   1981

The Bread of Time

Toward an Autobiography

Philip Levine

The Bread of Time

Toward an Autobiography

New York
Alfred A. Knopf
1995

THIS IS A BORZOI BOOK
PUBLISHED BY ALFRED A. KNOPF, INC.

These compositions appeared in the following publications:
Gettysburg Review: "The Key" and "Mine Own John Berryman."
Michigan Quarterly Review: The second part of "Entering
    Poetry," under the title "Home Dreams."
New England Review: "The Bread of Time Redeemed," "Class
    with No Class," "The Holy Cities," "Living in Machado,"
    and "The Poet in New York in Detroit."
Ohio Review: "Fixing the Foot."
Townships, edited by Michael Martone, University of Iowa Press,
    1992: The first half of "Entering Poetry."
Zyzzyva: "The Shadow of the Big Madrone."

Owing to limitations of space, all other acknowledgments for permission to reprint previously published material will be found on page 295.

Library of Congress Cataloging-in-Publication Data
Levine, Philip, [date]
    The bread of time : toward an autobiography / Philip Levine. —
1st ed.
    p.   cm.
    ISBN 0-679-42406-7
    1. Levine, Philip, [date]   —Biography.   2. Poets, American—
20th century—Biography.
PS3562.E9Z462   1994
811'.54—dc20
[B]   93–22599
                                                        CIP

Manufactured in the United States of America
Published January 21, 1994
Second Printing, October 1995

In memory of Marie Louise Koenig

Introduction and Acknowledgments

This is a book about people and memory. My original intent was not to write an autobiography, for I agreed with Keats's remark contained in a letter written when he was twenty-two that the poet "is the most unpoetical of any thing in existence." I wanted to celebrate those "creatures of impulse" (to quote Keats again) who had served as my official and unofficial teachers. Some, John Berryman and Yvor Winters, for example, had become famous literary figures, but I found them misrepresented by their posthumous reputations. Others, who were even more important to me, I feared would be unsung and forgotten unless I captured them on paper. As the book grew to include not only my childhood and young manhood in Detroit but my middle and later years in California and Spain, I realized I was striving to account for how I became the particular person and poet I am. This episodic, unorthodox approach to autobiography allowed me to avoid the periods of teaching and writing I thought too ordinary to translate into either poetry or prose of interest to me or anyone else.

One of these pieces, "The Key," is largely a fiction. In another, "The Bread of Time Redeemed," I've taken great liberties with actual events, but in all of them my aim was to render the essential meaning of what I experienced and to pay homage to those people who shaped the way I've lived and thought. At first I was surprised by how much pleasure the writing of these pieces gave me, but I soon realized it was that pleasure that kept me writing. My hope for this book is that my readers will share that pleasure.

My thanks to my wife, who encouraged the writing of this book and served as my chief critic. "The Shadow of the Big Madrone" was written at her suggestion. My thanks to Terry Hummer, who appointed me "writer-at-large" for *The New England Review* for 1991–92 and for whom three of these pieces were written. My thanks to Richard Kelly of the University of Minnesota Library, who invited me to deliver the keynote address at the John Berryman Conference. My thanks to Christopher Maurer of Vanderbilt University and to La Fundación Federico García Lorca of Madrid, who invited me to participate in the fiftieth anniversary celebration of Lorca's *Poet in New York*. My thanks to Michael Martone, who invited me to contribute to his anthology *Townships*, on growing up in the Midwest. My thanks to Laurence Goldstein, who asked me to contribute to a special Detroit issue of *Michigan Quarterly Review*. My thanks to Bill Broder for his advice. My thanks to Harry Ford, who suggested I forge a single book out of these pieces and offered to publish it. My special thanks to José Elgorriaga, the Machado scholar, who worked tirelessly on my translations. (The errors are mine.) Finally my thanks to all those readers who wrote to convey their pleasure.

Fixing the Foot: On Rhythm

FOR LEJAN KWINT

Yesterday I heard a Dutch doctor talking to a small girl who had cut her foot, not seriously, and was very frightened by the sight of her own blood. "Nay! Nay!" he said over and over. I could hear him quite distinctly through the wall that separated us, and his voice was strong and calm, he spoke very slowly and seemed never to stop speaking, almost as though he were chanting, never too loud or too soft. Her voice, which had been explosive and shrill at first, gradually softened until I could no longer make it out as he went on talking and, I supposed, working. Then a silence, and he said, "Ah" and some words I could not understand. I imagined him stepping spryly back to survey his work. And then another voice, silent before, the girl's father, thanking him, and then the girl thanking him, now in a child's voice. A door opening and closing. And it was over.

AMSTERDAM, JUNE, 1974

Contents

The Bread of Time

Toward an Autobiography

Mine Own
John Berryman

I can't say if all poets have had mentors, actual living, breathing masters who stood or sat before them making the demands that true mentors must make if the fledgling is ever to fly. Some poets seem to have been totally self-starting, like the cars they used to build in Detroit; I'm thinking of such extraordinary examples as Emily Dickinson and Walt Whitman, who over a hundred years ago created not only their own gigantic works but the beginnings of something worthy enough to be American poetry, and they did it out of their imaginations and their private studies and nothing more. But, then, they had the advantage of being geniuses. And neither was from Detroit. I think also of those poets who *had* to be poets, whom no one or nothing short of death could have derailed from their courses—John Keats, Dylan Thomas, Arthur Rimbaud—and who outstripped their mentors before they even got into second gear. There are those who were lucky enough to find among their peers people of equal talent and insight to help them on their way—poets like

Williams and Pound, who for the crucial early years of their writing careers ignited each other. Though, of course, Williams tells us in the "Prologue" to *Kora in Hell* that Ezra benefited also from the scathing criticism of Williams's father, William George. Williams tells us that his father "had been holding forth in downright sentences upon my own 'idle nonsense' when he turned and became equally vehement concerning something Ezra had written: what in heaven's name Ezra meant by 'jewels' in a verse that had come between them. These jewels,—rubies, sapphires, amethysts and whatnot, Pound went on to explain with great determination and care, were the backs of books as they stood on a man's shelf. 'But why in heaven's name don't you say so then?' was my father's triumphant and crushing rejoinder." Pound himself showed Ford Madox Ford some early verse, serious stuff, and Fordie laughed so hard upon reading the work he actually fell on the floor and "rolled around on it squealing with hilarity at the poems." Pound said that Ford's laughter saved him two years of work in the wrong direction. Terrible conditions have driven others to take up the pen in an effort to write their way out of the deepest nightmares imaginable—Wilfred Owen in the trenches, Edward Thomas in his melancholia, Hart Crane in the slough of Cleveland. In some cases it worked.

As for those of us here in the United States of America in the second half of the twentieth century, we have developed something called Creative Writing, a discipline that not only flourishes on hundreds of campuses but has even begun to invade the public schools. It has produced most of the poets—for better or worse—now writing in the country. One can only regard it as one of the most amazing growth industries we have. Thus, at the same time we've made our society more racist, more scornful of the rights of the poor, more imperialist, more elitist, more tawdry, money-driven, selfish, and less accepting of minority opinions, we have democratized poetry. Today anyone can become a poet: all he or she need do is travel to the nearest college and enroll in Beginning Poetry Writing and then journey through the dozen stages of purgatory properly titled Intermediate Poetry Writing and Semi-Advanced Poetry Writing, all the way to Masterwork Poetry Writing, in which course one completes her epic on the sacking of Yale or his sonnet cycle on the paintings of Edward Hopper, or their elegies in a city dumpster, and thus earns not only an M.F.A. but a crown of plastic laurel leaves. Do I sound skeptical? Let me sound skeptical.

But I also must in fairness add that it is impossible for me to imagine myself as the particular poet I have become—again for better or for worse—without the influence of a single teacher, my one great personal mentor, and amazingly enough I found him at the head of a graduate class at the most unfashionable of writing industries, the much-maligned Iowa Writers' Workshop. He was, of course, John Berryman, not yet forty years old but soon to be so, with one book of poems to his credit and stuck with the job of teaching poetry writing—for the first time in his life and for the last.

I did not go to the University of Iowa to study with John Berryman; in 1953 his reputation was based on *The Dispossessed*, that first book, and it was no larger than it should have been. The poem "Homage to Mistress Bradstreet" had not yet appeared in the *Partisan Review*, though it soon would and would create shock waves through the then-tiny world of American poetry. The attraction at Iowa was Robert Lowell, whose second book, *Lord Weary's Castle*, had received the Pulitzer Prize, and whose singular voice had excited young poets as far away as Michigan. I among them journeyed to Iowa and enrolled in Lowell's writing workshop and audited his seminar in modern poetry; this was the fall of '53, America under Eisenhower ("Wide empty grin that never lost a vote," Berryman would later write) transforming itself into America under Joe McCarthy.

To say I was disappointed in Lowell as a teacher is an understatement, although, never having taken a poetry workshop, I had no idea what to expect. But a teacher who is visibly bored by his students and their poems is hard to admire. The students were a marvel: we were two future Pulitzer Prize winners, one Yale winner, one National Book Critics Circle Award winner, three Lamont Prize winners, one American Book Award winner. Some names: Donald Justice, W. D. Snodgrass, Jane Cooper, William Dickey, Robert Dana, Paul Petrie, Melvin Walker LaFollette, Henri Coulette, Donald Peterson, and an extraordinarily gifted woman named Shirley Eliason, who soon turned to the visual arts and became a master. I am sure there were others among the thirteen who were excited by Lowell as teacher, for Lowell was one to play favorites. No matter how much they wrote like Lowell, some of the poets could do no wrong; in all fairness to Lowell, he praised them even when they wrote like Jarrell. Needless to say, I could write nothing that pleased Lowell, and when at the end of the semester he awarded me a B, I was not surprised. Along with the B he handed me a little card with scribbled notes regarding my poems and then told me I had made more progress than anyone else in the class. "You have come the farthest," he drawled, which no doubt meant I had started from nowhere. "Then why the B?" I asked. "I've already given the A's out," he said. This was at our second and last fifteen-minute conference—which did not irritate me nearly as much as our first, when he accused me of stealing my Freudian insights and vocabulary from Auden. "Mr. Lowell," I had responded (I never got more intimate than Mister and he never encouraged me to do so), "I'm Jewish. I steal Freud directly from Freud; he was one of ours." Mr. Lowell merely sighed.

Lowell was, if anything, considerably worse in the seminar; we expected him to misread our poems—after all, most of them were confused and, with very few exceptions, only partly realized, but to see him bumbling in the face of "real poetry" was discouraging. The day he assured the class that Housman's "Loveliest of Trees, the Cherry Now" was about suicide, Melvin LaFollette leaned over and whispered in my ear, "We know what he's thinking about." His fierce competitiveness was also not pleasant to behold: with the exceptions of Bishop and Jarrell, he seemed to have little use for any practicing American poet, and he once labeled Roethke "more of an old woman than Marianne Moore." He was eager to ridicule many of our recent heroes, poets I for one would have thought him enamored of: Hart Crane and Dylan Thomas. Still, he was Robert Lowell, master of a powerful and fierce voice that all of us respected, and though many of us were disappointed, none of us turned against the man or his poetry. As Don Peterson once put it, "Can you imagine how hard it is to live as Robert Lowell, with that inner life?"

During the final workshop meeting he came very close to doing the unforgivable: he tried to overwhelm us with one of his own poems, an early draft of "The Banker's Daughter," which appeared in a much shorter though still-hideous version six years later in *Life Studies*. Someone, certainly not Lowell, had typed up three and a half single-spaced pages of heroic couplets on ditto masters so that each of us could hold his or her own smeared purple copy of his masterpiece. He intoned the poem in that enervated voice we'd all become used to, a genteel Southern accent that suggested the least display of emotion was déclassé. I sat stunned by the performance, but my horror swelled when several of my classmates leaped to praise every forced rhyme and obscure reference. (The subject was Marie de Medici, about whom I knew nothing and cared less.) No one suggested a single cut, not even when Lowell asked if the piece might be a trifle too extended, a bit soft in places. Perish the thought; it was

a masterpiece! And thus the final class meeting passed
with accolades for the one person present who scarcely
needed praise and who certainly had the intelligence and
insight to know it for what it was: bootlicking.

His parting words were unqualified praise of his suc-
cessor, John Berryman, not as poet but as one of the great
Shakespearean scholars of the age. And then he added
that if we perused the latest issue of the *Partisan* we
would discover the Mistress Bradstreet poem, clear evidence that Berryman was coming "into the height of his
powers," a favorite phrase of Lowell's and one he rarely
employed when speaking of the living. In fairness to
Lowell, he was teetering on the brink of the massive
nervous breakdown that occurred soon after he left for
Cincinnati to occupy the Elliston Chair of Poetry. Ru-
mors of his hospitalization drifted back to Iowa City, and
many of us felt guilty for damning him as a total loss.

How long Berryman was in town before he broke his
wrist I no longer recall, but I do remember that the first
time I saw him he was dressed in his customary blue
blazer, the arm encased in a black sling, the effect quite
dramatic. As person and teacher, John was an extraordinary contrast to Lowell. To begin with, he did not
play favorites: everyone who dared hand him a poem
burdened with second-rate writing tasted his wrath, and
that meant all of us. He never appeared bored in the
writing class; to the contrary, he seemed more nervous
in our presence than we in his. Whereas Lowell always
sprawled in a chair as though visibly troubled by his
height, John almost always stood and often paced as he
delivered what sounded like memorized encomiums on
the nature of poetry and life. Lowell's voice was never
more than faintly audible and always encased in his curiously slothful accent, whereas Berryman articulated
very precisely, in what appeared to be an actor's notion
of Hotspur's accent. His voice would rise in pitch with

his growing excitement until it seemed that soon only dogs would be able to hear him. He tipped slightly forward as though about to lose his balance, and conducted his performance with the forefinger of his right hand. The key word here is "performance," for these were memorable meetings in which the class soon caught his excitement. All of us sensed that something significant was taking place.

Beyond the difference of personal preferences and presentation was a more significant one. Lowell had pushed us toward a poetry written in formal meters, rhymed, and hopefully involved with the griefs of great families, either current suburban ones or those out of the great storehouse of America's or Europe's past. We got thundering dramatic monologues from Savonarola and John Brown that semester. For Berryman it was open house. He found exciting a poem about a particular drinking fountain in a bus station in Toledo, Ohio. Lowell certainly would have preferred a miraculous spring in that other Toledo—though, now that he was no longer a practicing Catholic, sainthood seemed also to bore him. Berryman was delighted with our curious efforts in the direction of free verse, on which he had some complex notions concerning structure and prosody. He even had the boldness to suggest that contemporary voices could achieve themselves in so unfashionable and dated a form as the Petrarchan sonnet. To put it simply, he was all over the place and seemed delighted with the variety we represented.

Their contrasting styles became more evident during the second meeting of the class. Lowell had welcomed a contingent of hangers-on, several of whom were wealthy townspeople dressed to the nines and hugging their copies of *Lord Weary's Castle*. Now and then one would submit a poem: Lowell would say something innocuous about it, let the discussion hang in midair for a moment, then move on to something else. Berryman immediately de-

manded a poem from one of this tribe. The poem expressed conventional distaste for the medical profession
by dealing with the clichés of greed and indifference to
suffering. (We later learned it was written by a doctor's
wife.) John shook his head violently. "No, no," he said,
"it's not that it's not poetry. I wasn't expecting poetry.
It's that it's not true, absolutely untrue, unobserved, the
cheapest twaddle." Then he began a long monologue in
which he described the efforts of a team of doctors to
save the life of a friend of his, how they had struggled
through a long night, working feverishly. "They did not
work for money. There was no money in it. They worked
to save a human life because it was a human life and thus
precious. They did not know who the man was, that he
was a remarkable spirit. They knew only that he was too
young to die, and so they worked to save him, and, failing, wept." (It turned out the man was Dylan Thomas,
but Berryman did not mention this at the time.) A decent
poet did not play fast and loose with the facts of this
world, he or she did not accept television's notion of
reality. I had never before observed such enormous can-
nons fired upon such a tiny target. The writer left the
room in shock, and those of us who had doubts about our
work—I would guess all of us—left the room shaken.

We returned the next Monday to discover that Berryman had moved the class to a smaller and more intimate
room containing one large seminar table around which
we all sat. He was in an antic mood, bubbling with enthusiasm and delighted with our presence. He knew
something we did not know: all but the hard-core mas-
ochists had dropped, leaving him with only the lucky
thirteen. "We are down to the serious ones," he announced, and seemed pleased with the situation; he never
again turned his powerful weapons on such tiny life
rafts. In truth, once we'd discovered what he'd accom-
plished, we too were pleased not to have to share his attention with writers we knew were only horsing around.

Now came the hard task for him of determining what we knew and what we didn't know. At least half of us were trying to write in rhyme and meter, and a few of us were doing it with remarkable skill. It was at this meeting that he asked each of us to turn in a Petrarchan sonnet so that he might have some idea how far we'd come on the road to grace and mastery in the old forms. (The logistics were simple: we turned in our work on the Friday before our Monday meeting, and John selected the work to be dittoed and discussed in class.) He presented us with two models, both recited from memory.

THE SIRENS *by John Manifold*

Odysseus heard the sirens; they were singing
Music by Wolf and Weinberger and Morley
About a region where the swans go winging,
Vines are in color, girls are growing surely

Into nubility, and pylons bringing
Leisure and power to farms that live securely
Without a landlord. Still, his eyes were stinging
With salt and seablink, and the ropes hurt sorely.

Odysseus saw the sirens; they were charming,
Blonde, with snub breasts and little neat posteriors,
But could not take his mind off the alarming
Weather report, his mutineers in irons,
The radio failing; it was bloody serious.
In twenty minutes he forgot the sirens.

Recited in Berryman's breathless style, it sounded like something he might have written; he had an uncanny knack of making a great deal of poetry sound like something he might have written. And who was John Manifold? An obscure Australian poet who fought in World War II, someone we should discover if we were serious, as he was, about poetry. The second sonnet was Robinson's "Many Are Called," which begins "The Lord Apollo, who has never died . . ." After reciting it, John went back to a passage in the octave:

> And though melodious multitudes have tried
> In ecstasy, in anguish, and in vain,
> With invocation sacred and profane
> To lure him, even the loudest are outside.

"Who are those multitudes?" he almost shouted. Petrie, a great lover of Robinson, answered, "The poets." "Exactly, Mr. Petrie, the poets. Certainly the poets in this room." It was perfectly clear he did not exclude himself.

Much to my horror, my Petrarchan sonnet was selected for discussion on that third meeting. (I believe the poem no longer exists; I had the good luck never to have had it accepted for publication.) Actually, it was not that bad: it was about food, which had been an obsession of mine for several months; I was running out of money and so ate very little and very badly. To be more precise, the poem was about my mother's last Thanksgiving feast, which I had returned home to participate in; since my mother was a first-rate office manager and a tenth-rate cook, the event had been a disaster. John discussed four poems that day. The first was not a Petrarchan sonnet, and as far as he could determine had no subject or any phrasing worth remembering. The second did have a subject, but John went to the board to scan its meter. "This is NOT iambic," he said. After getting through four lines, he turned and headed directly toward the cowering poet, suspended the page over his head, and finally let it fall. "This is metrical chaos. Pray you avoid it, sir." I was next. Much to my relief, John affirmed that, yes, this was a Petrarchan sonnet; it was iambic and it did possess a fine subject—the hideous nature of the American ritual meal become a farce. He paused. "But,

Levine, it is not up to its most inspired moments—it has accepted three mediocre rhymes, it is padded where the imagination fails. If it is to become a poem, the author must attack again and bring the entirety up to the level of its few fine moments." In effect John was giving us a lesson in how poems are revised: one listened to one's own voice when it was "hot" (a word he liked) and let that "hot" writing redirect one toward a radical revision. "No hanging back," he once said. "One must be ruthless with one's own writing or someone else will be." (I tried but failed to improve the poem. Even at twenty-six, I had not learned to trust the imagination.)

It was clear that, among those poems considered, mine had finished second best, and for this I was enormously relieved. What follows is the best, exactly in the form we saw it on that late February Monday in 1953:

SONNET *by Donald Justice*

The wall surrounding them they never saw;
The angels, often. Angels were as common
As birds or butterflies, but looked more human.
As long as the wings were furled, they felt no awe.
Beasts, too, were friendly. They could find no flaw
In all of Eden: this was the first omen.
The second was the dream which woke the woman:
She dreamed she saw the lion sharpen his claw.
As for the fruit, it had no taste at all.
They had been warned of what was bound to happen;
They had been told of something called the world;
They had been told and told about the wall.
They saw it now; the gate was standing open.
As they advanced, the giant wings unfurled.

After reading the poem aloud, John returned to one line: "As for the fruit, it had no taste at all." "Say that better in a thousand words," he said, "and you're a genius." He went on: "One makes an assignment like this partly in jest, partly in utter seriousness, to bring out the metal in some of you and to demonstrate to others how much you still need to learn. No matter what one's motives are, no teacher has the right to expect to receive something like this: a true poem." Class dismissed.

A week later a telling incident occurred. The class considered a sonnet by one of its more gifted members, a rather confused and confusing poem which Berryman thrashed even though one member of the class found it the equal of the Justice poem from the previous week. The tortured syntax suggested Berryman's own "Nervous Songs," but he saw little virtue in the poem and felt it was more in the tradition of Swinburne than any contemporary poem should be, writing that tried to bully its readers with rhetoric rather than move them with the living language of the imagination. "Write good prose diction in a usual prose order," he said, "unless you've got a damn good reason for doing otherwise." (It was clear he must have felt he had a damn good reason for doing otherwise when he wrote "Bradstreet.") After class, as we ambled back to the student union for coffee and more poetry talk, the same student who had defended the poem informed Berryman that the author had recently had a sheaf of poems accepted by *Botteghe Oscure*, then the best-paying and most prestigious literary magazine in the world. Berryman froze on the sidewalk and then turned angrily on the student and shouted, "Utterly irrelevant, old sport, utterly irrelevant!" He assured the man that absolute "shit" appeared in the so-called "best" publications, while much of the finest poetry being written went begging. (No doubt his own difficult early career had taught him that.) "You're stupid to have raised the subject, stupid or jejune." He paused a moment. "I'll give you the benefit of the doubt: jejune." John smiled, and the incident passed. He was incredibly serious about poetry, and one of us had learned that the hard way. In her gossipy *Poets in Their Youth*, Eileen Simpson would have us believe that all the poets in "the Berryman circle" ached to be the elected legislators of the world and suffered deeply because they were not among the famous and powerful. Everything I saw during that semester contradicted that view: the reward for writing a true poem was the reward of writing a true poem, and there was none higher.

In spite of his extraordinary sense of humor, the key to Berryman's success as a teacher was his seriousness. This was the spring of the Army-McCarthy hearings, the greatest television soap opera before the discovery of Watergate. John, as an addicted reader of *The New York Times*, once began a class by holding up the front page so the class might see the latest revelation in the ongoing drama. "These fools will rule for a while and be replaced by other fools and crooks. This," and he opened a volume of Keats to the "Ode to a Nightingale," "will be with us for as long as our language endures." These were among the darkest days of the Cold War, and yet John was able to convince us—merely because he believed it so deeply—that nothing could be more important for us, for the nation, for humankind, than our becoming the finest poets we could become. And there was no doubt as to how we must begin to accomplish the task; we must become familiar with the best that had been written, we must feel it in our pulse.

"Levine, you're a scholar," he once roared out at me in class. "Tell us how you would go about assembling a bibliography on the poetry of Charles Churchill." A scholar I was not, and John knew it, but he had a point: that poets had to know these things. The ignorant but inspired poet was a total fiction, a cousin to Hollywood's notion of the genius painter who boozes, chases girls, and eventually kills himself by falling off a scaffold in the Sistine Chapel. "Friends," John was saying, "it's hard work, and the hard work will test the sincerity of your desire to be poets." He rarely mentioned inspiration, perhaps because he assumed that most of us had been writing long enough to have learned that it came to those who worked as best they could through the barren periods, and this was—he once told me—a barren period for him. So we knew how to begin the task of becoming a poet: study and work. And how did it end? Here John was just as clear: it never ended. Speaking of the final poems of Dylan Thomas, he made it clear they were merely imitations of the great work of his early and middle period. "You should always be trying to write a poem you are unable to write, a poem you lack the technique, the language, the courage to achieve. Otherwise you're merely imitating yourself, going nowhere, because that's always easiest." And suddenly he burst into a recitation of "The Refusal to Mourn the Death by Fire of a Child in London," ending:

> Deep with the first dead lies London's daughter,
> Robed in the long friends,
> The grains beyond age, the dark veins of her mother,
> Secret by the unmourning water
> Of the riding Thames.
> After the first death, there is no other.

'Can you imagine possessing that power and then squan-
'ring it?" he asked. "During our lifetime that man wrote
oem that will never be bettered."

To doubt his amazing gift for ribaldry allowed him to
tate our poems without crushing our spirits, that
he recognition on his part that he too could write
dly at times. He made it clear to us from the outset
had often failed as a poet and for a variety of
lack of talent, pure laziness ("Let's face it," he
me, "life is mainly wasted time"), and stupid
here are so many ways to ruin a poem," he

said, "it's quite amazing good ones ever get written." On certain days he loved playing the clown. One Monday he looked up from the class list sent to him by the registrar and asked Paul Petrie why he was getting twice as much credit for the course as anyone else. Paul said he wasn't sure. "Perhaps," said John, "you're getting the extra units in physical education and home economics. I'd like you to arrive twenty minutes early and do fifty laps around the room and then erase the blackboard. You might also do a few push-ups or work on your technique of mixing drinks." He then discovered my name was not on the roll. (The truth was, lacking sufficient funds, I had not registered.) He asked me if I thought the registrar was anti-Semitic. No, I said, just sloppy. "You realize," he said, "that until your name appears on this list you do not exist. Tell me," he added, "does anyone else see this Levine fellow? Sometimes I have delusions." As the weeks passed my name continued not to appear on the roster, and John continued to make a joke out of it. "Levine, should I go see the registrar and remedy this hideous state of affairs?" I assured him it was unnecessary, that it was just a meaningless slip-up, and I wasn't taking it personally. "You're quite sure it's not anti-Semitism, Levine? These are dark times." Indeed they were for many Americans, but for the young poets in this workshop they were nothing if not glory days.

"Levine," he said on another day, "when was the last time you read your Shakespeare?" "Last week," I said. "And what?" "*Measure for Measure*." "Fine. I've noticed you consistently complain about the quantity of adjectives in the poems of your classmates." This was true. "Is it the number that matters or the quality?" I failed to answer. "Remember your Blake: 'Bring out number, weight, & measure in a year of dearth.'" I nodded. "'Thy turfy mountains where live nibbling sheep.' Two nouns, two adjectives. Any complaints, Levine?" I had none. "Who wrote the line?" "Shakespeare," I said. "What play?" Again I was silent. His long face darkened with sadness. LaFollette answered, "*The Tempest*." "Levine, do not return to this class until you have reread *The Tempest*. I assume you've read it at least once." I had. " 'Fresher than May, sweeter / Than her gold buttons on the boughs . . .' Recognize it?" I did not. "There is great poetry hiding where you least suspect it—there, for example, buried in that hideous speech from *The Two Noble Kinsmen*, Act III, Scene 1." Much scratching of pens as the class bowed to their notebooks. "We must find our touchstones where we can."

Knowing I had gone to Wayne University in Detroit, where John had once taught, he asked me if I'd studied with the resident Shakespeare scholar, Leo Kirschbaum, whom I had found a brilliant teacher. "Amazing fellow, Dr. Kirschbaum; single-handedly he set back Lear scholarship two decades." Little wonder I'd failed to recognize the line from *The Tempest*. While he was on the subject of Shakespeare, he required the entire class to reread *Macbeth* by the next meeting. " 'And yet dark night strangles the travelling lamp.' Hear how the line first strangles and then releases itself. Read the play carefully, every line, let it heighten your awareness of the extraordinary possibilities for dense imagery. You should know that Shakespeare had less than two weeks to complete the play. Why was that, Mr. Justice?" Don, well on his way to his doctorate, explained that the ascendency to the English throne of James VI of Scotland called for a play in praise of James's Scotch ancestry. Berryman nodded. "Took him no time at all to write it, and yet it would take half the computers in the world a year to trace the development of the imagery that a single human imagination created and displayed in a play of unrivaled power." So much for the School of Engineering. We were never to forget that men and women of the greatest intellect and imagination had for centuries turned toward poetry to fulfill their private and civic needs.

Certain classes were devoted to special subjects relating to poetic practices—prosody, for example. For two hours John lectured on the development of this study and how amazingly fragmented and useless the literature was. People of great learning and sensitivity had come to preposterous conclusions, and nothing in print was reliable. It was our duty to master this literature and discover what was useful and what was nonsense. "A man as learned as George Saintsbury, a man who had read and absorbed so much that in old age he took to studying doctoral dissertations from American universities just to keep busy, a man of that breadth of knowledge, gave us a three-volume study of prosodic practices in British and American poetry, and on almost every significant point he is wrong." Still, he urged us to read the work, for if nothing else it was a brilliant anthology of the diversity and richness of poetry in English. We, the hungry students, demanded to know to whom he went for "the scoop," another of his expressions. He laughed and pointed to his ear. There was no such book, and as in everything else we were thrown on our own. We would develop a prosody that would allow us to write the poetry we needed to write, or we wouldn't, in which case that poetry would never be written. And in order to do it right, we had to learn from those poets who had already done it—for, as John made clear, those who best understood prosody—Shakespeare, Milton, Keats, Blake, Hopkins, Frost, Roethke—had better things to do than write handbooks for our guidance.

"Let us say you are appalled by the society in which you live—God knows it is appalling—and you want to create a poetry that speaks to the disgusting human conditions around you. You want to mount a powerful assault, you want to be the prophet Amos of the present age. To which poet would you turn for aid?" Silence from the class. "You want to evoke your rage, your righteous indignation, in numbers that will express the depthless power of your convictions. To whom do you turn?" A voice from the class: "Robert Lowell." "Good choice, but there is a danger here, correct?" The voice: "Yes, I already sound too much like Lowell. I'm doing my best to avoid him." Berryman: "Indeed you are. When I first saw your poems I thought you'd borrowed Cal's old portable Smith-Corona. Why not go to Cal's source, the poet upon whom he based the movement and the syntax of his own work? And who would that be?" Another voice from the class: "Pope." "No, no, you're blinded by his use of the couplet. Milton, our great Milton." Affirmative nods from the class; how could we not know something so obvious. John quoted "On the Late Massacre in Piedmont," using his forefinger to mark the ends of the lines so we heard how powerful the enjambment was. "Bring the diction three hundred years toward this moment and you have one of Cal's early sonnets." More nodding of heads. "And the key to such rhythmic power is . . . ?" Silence. "Speed, achieved by means of a complex syntax and radical enjambment. Speed translates always into rhythmic power, and speed is unobtainable in a heavily end-stopped line."

Then he turned to me. "For the power you so dearly aspire to, Levine, you must turn to the master, Milton, the most powerful poet in the language, though you might do well to avoid the Latinate vocabulary. Have you studied Latin?" Levine: "No." "You might consider doing so; that way you'll know what to avoid when you're stealing from Milton. Do you have another favorite among your contemporaries?" Levine: "Dylan Thomas." Berryman: "It doesn't show, Levine, it doesn't show; you've done a superb job of masking that particular debt. How have you managed that?" Levine: "I didn't. I wrote through my Dylan Thomas phase and quit. It was impossible for me to write under his influence and not sound exactly like him except terrible." Berryman: "Levine, you've hit upon a truth. Certain poets are so much them-

selves they should not be imitated: they leave you no
room to be yourself, and Thomas was surely one of them,
as was Hart Crane, who probably ruined the careers of
more young poets than anything except booze. Levine,
you might go to the source of Dylan's own lyrical mysti-
cism, and who would that be?" Silence. "Mr. Justice?"
Justice: "Blake." "Exactly, you might go to Blake, who
is so impossibly lyrical and inventive no one in the world
has the talent to sound like him." In an unusually hushed
voice he recited all of Blake's early "Mad Song," ending:

> I turn my back to the east,
> From whence comforts have increas'd;
> For light doth seize my brain
> With frantic pain.

"Better to learn from a poet who does not intoxicate you,"
said Berryman, "better to immerse yourself in Hardy,
whom no American wants now to sound like. A great
poet seldom read." After class Henri Coulette said to me
that he'd passed over Blake's "Mad Song" a dozen times
and never heard it until John incanted it.

No one escaped unscathed. John advised Petrie to set
aside his Shelley and Elinor Wylie and leap into mod-
ernism. Coulette was told to loosen up his strict iambics,
to try to capture the quality of living speech. Strangely,
he underappreciated the formal elegance of William
Dickey's work. Neither Petersen nor Jane Cooper was
productive that semester; Jane later said she was put off
by John's sarcasm. Shirley Eliason's work he found wonderfully dense and mysterious; he wanted more. "Write
everything that occurs to you," he told us all; "you're
young enough to still be searching for your voice. You
certainly don't want to find it before you find your subject, and you're still young enough to accept failure." La-
Follette seemed the greatest enigma to him. "Yes, yes,

you have a genuine lyrical gift," he said one day in class, "but who encouraged you never to make sense, always to be opaque?" LaFollette eagerly revealed that he'd just finished a year's work with Roethke. "Yes," said John, "I can see the influence of Roethke, but Ted's best early work is remarkably straightforward on one level. Of course there is always the shadow of something more formidable, darker. Did Cal encourage this sort of obscurity?" LaFollette revealed he had also studied with Richard Eberhart. John's mouth fell open as he stood speechless for several seconds. "You let Dick Eberhart read your poems, and you are here to tell the tale. Amazing!"

He always wanted more work from Robert Dana, though, when Dana finally gave him a poem of ninety-eight lines, he mused over it for a time and finally noted two good images. His parting words were, "If you're going to write something this long why don't you try making it poetry?" Meeting after meeting produced the same advice: "Write everything that occurs to you; it's the only way to discover where your voice will come from. And never be in a hurry. Writing poetry is not like running the four hundred meters. Coulette, do you remember what Archie Williams said his strategy was for running the four hundred meters?" (Coulette, the resident sports maven, did not know. Williams had won the gold at the '36 Berlin Olympics.) John went on: "Archie said, 'My strategy is simple; I run the first two hundred meters as fast as I can to get ahead of everyone, and I run the second two hundred meters as fast as I can to stay there.' Now, that is NOT the way we write poetry, we are not in a race with anyone, but all of us are getting on in years and we'd better get moving." In other words, go as fast as you can but don't be in a hurry; we had a lifetime to master this thing, and with our gifts it would take a lifetime.

Even Justice got mauled. John found his "Beyond the

Hunting Woods" a bit too refined, a bit too professionally Southern. Those dogs at the end of the poem, Belle and Ginger, all they needed were a few mint juleps. And Levine? Levine got his. According to John, Levine's best poem that semester was "Friday Night in the Delicatessen," in which a Jewish mother laments the fact that her sons are growing away from her, becoming Americans, becoming—you should forgive the expression— *goyim*. At one point she describes them with "hands for fights and alcohol." "Hands for fights, yes," said John, "but hands for alcohol? No. We drink alcohol, Levine, as I know you've learned—we absorb it through the digestive system. The fact we hold a glass of whiskey in our hands is not enough. The parallel structure is false, but this is an amazingly ambitious poem." (I lived on that word, "ambitious," for weeks, even after a friend said, "He forgot to add, 'Ambition should be made of sterner stuff.'") Again I had finished second best. This poem was written to fulfill John's assignment for an ode, and the clear winner was "A Flat One," by De Snodgrass, a poem of enormous power that depicted the slow and agonizing death of a World War I veteran, and the vet's relationship with a hospital orderly who must kill to keep him alive. Even in this earlier "static semi-Symboliste version" (Snodgrass's description), it was a startling poem. (Although Lowell is generally credited for being the mentor behind the poems of *Heart's Needle* ["A Flat One" actually appears in De's second book, *After Experience*], De now claims that Lowell discouraged the writing of those poems, and quite forcefully. "Snodgrass, you have a mind," he'd said to him. "You mustn't write this kind of tear-jerking stuff." Berryman never found the poems sentimental; he tried to move De's writing further from traditional metrics toward something—as De put it—"more like his own experiments at the time . . . more like regular speech . . . less like the poetry being written at the time.")

A later class also began with a demonstration from the front page of *The New York Times*. "Allow me to demonstrate a fundamental principle of the use of language, which is simply this: if you do not master it, it will master you. Allow me to quote Senator McCarthy speaking of his two cronies, Cohn and Shine." Roy Cohn and David Shine were two assistants—investigators, he called them—of the senator for whom he had gained extraordinary privileges which allowed Shine, for example, an ordinary enlisted man in the army, to avoid any of the more onerous or dangerous work of a soldier. "The senator said the following: 'I stand behind them to the hilt.' We now know what Mr. McCarthy thinks we do not know, that he is about to stab them in the back, abandon them both as political liabilities." John was of course correct; within a few days the deed was done. "Because he is an habitual liar, Mr. McCarthy has blinded himself to the ability of language to reveal us even when we're taking pains not to be revealed. Exactly the same thing holds true with poetic form; if we do not control it, it will control us." He went on: "I do not mean to suggest that each time we enter the arena of the poem we must know exactly where we're headed. We have all learned that that is preposterous, for the imagination leads us where it will, and we must be prepared to follow, but— and this is the crucial point—should we lack the ability to command the poetic form, even if that form is form-lessness, toward which our writing travels, we shall be mastered by that form and what we shall reveal is our ineptitude." He then turned to a student poem in formal meters and rhymed couplets and painstakingly analyzed it from the point of view of how the need to rhyme and to keep the meter had produced odd and unconvincing movements in the poem's narrative, as well as needless prepositional phrases and awkward enjambments. "A poem of real fiber, a rhymed poem, will find its rhymes on sub-

jects, objects, and especially verbs, the key words of its
content." He then quoted a poem of Hardy's which ended:

> So, they are not underground,
> But as nerves and veins abound
> In the growths of upper air,
> And they feel the sun and rain,
> And the energy again
> That made them what they were!

Again with his forefinger he scored the key words, and
finally repeated that final line, " 'That made them what
they were!'—my friends, what they were! That is the
artist in command, that is triumph!"

Once again he seemed a walking anthology of poetic
jewels, and once again we learned how exacting this
thing with the poetry was. Later, in Kenny's tavern,
where many of us assembled after class, one poet recalled
that Ignacio Sánchez Mejías, the matador elegized in
García Lorca's great poem, had once remarked, "This
thing with the bulls is serious," and thus we produced a
catch phrase for John's class: "This thing with the poems
is serious."

What became increasingly clear as the weeks passed
was that, although John was willing on occasion to so-
cialize with us, he was not one of us; he was the teacher,
and we were the students. He had not the least doubt
about his identity, and he was always willing to take the
heat, to be disliked if need be. In private he once remarked to me that teaching something as difficult as
poetry writing was not a popularity contest. "Even a
class as remarkable as this one," he said, "will produce
terrible poems, and I am the one who is obliged to say
so." He sensed that the students had themselves developed
a wonderful fellowship and took joy when any one of
them produced something fine. Whether or not he took

credit for any of this I do not know. To this day I can recall Bill Dickey studying a Justice poem almost with awe. "Do you see those rhymes?" he said to me. "I'll bet this is the first time they've been used in all our poetry!" I shall never forget Don Petersen's welcoming me up the mountain of poetry—at that time Don seemed to believe he was the guardian of the mountain. He told me in his curiously gruff and tender voice that a particular poem of mine was in fact a poem, and though the class—including John—had not taken to it, it was evidence that I had become a poet. His words were welcomed and genuine. I can recall my own thrill on seeing a particular poem by Jane Cooper in which her portrayal of a nocturnal hedgehog came so vividly to life I shuddered. I expressed my wonder openly and knew she heard it. One day both Henri Coulette and Robert Dana took me aside to tell me they could scarcely believe how far I'd come in a single year. We were all taking pride and joy in each other's accomplishments.

This fellowship was a delicate and lovely thing, a quality that always distinguishes the best creative-writing classes. We were learning how much farther we could go together than we could singly, alone, unknown, unread in an America that had never much cared for poetry. I don't honestly know how large a role John played in the creation of this atmosphere, but I do know it had not existed during Lowell's tenure; his favoritism, his intimacy with some students and visible boredom with others, tended to divide us into two hostile factions, the ins and the outs. In John's class we were all in and we were all out, we were equals, and instead of sinking we swam together. In spite of John's willingness to be disliked, he clearly was not disliked. Of course he was a marvelous companion, and on those evenings he sought company we were all eager to supply it, but we never forgot that, come Monday afternoon, the camaraderie would be forgotten and he would get to the serious business of evaluating and if need be decimating poems.

Sometimes his seriousness could be more than a little intimidating. On one occasion over drinks, before going to dinner with a group of student writers and faculty, John began to muse over a remarkable poem by the Welshman Alun Lewis, "Song: On seeing dead bodies floating off the Cape." Berryman believed that Lewis was one of the great undiscovered talents of the era. He quoted a portion of the poem, an interior monologue by a woman who has had a vision of her lover's death at sea; then his memory failed him, and he apologized to the group. It so happened one of the poets present knew the poem and took up the recitation:

> The flying fish like kingfishers
> Skim the sea's bewildered crests,
> The whales blow steaming fountains,
> The seagulls have no nests
> Where my lover sways and rests.

His memory primed, John completed the poem, which ends with the woman lamenting the "nearness that is waiting in" her bed, "the gradual self-effacement of the dead." After a moment's silence John remarked, "The dead do not efface themselves; we, the living, betray their memories." John seemed lost in his reverie on the life and early death in war of the poet when another poet present, an enormous man who worked in town as a bartender and bouncer, began to praise one of John's own war poems which had appeared in *The Dispossessed*. Suddenly awakened, John shouted in the man's face, "We are talking about great poetry, do you get it, old sport, great poetry, and not the twaddle you have in mind. I do not appreciate bootlicking." A silence followed, and the moment passed. This thing with the poetry was indeed serious.

That semester Berryman conducted the most extraordinary seminar on other writers I've ever been a part of; again, for lack of funds, I was not registered, but I missed only a single class and that when the obligation to make some money took me elsewhere. The students were assigned a single long paper of considerable scope, the subject agreed upon by teacher and poet—for all the registered students were from the workshop. The papers themselves were never presented in class, but not because Berryman found them inadequate. Indeed he raved about their quality. The reason was simply that John felt he had news to bring us on the subject of poetry in English from Whitman to the present. The highlight of the semester was his presentation of the whole of "Song of Myself," which included the most memorable and impassioned reading of a poem I have ever in my life heard, along with the most complex and rewarding analysis of Whitman's design, prosody, and imagery ever presented. When he'd finished the reading, he stood in silence a moment and then from memory presented the final section again, concluding:

I bequeath myself to the dirt to grow from the grass I love,
If you want me again look for me under your boot-soles.

You will hardly know who I am or what I mean,
But I shall be good health to you nevertheless,
And filter and fibre your blood.

Failing to fetch me at first keep encouraged,
Missing me one place search another,
I stop somewhere waiting for you.

He stood for a moment in silence, the book trembling in his hand, and then in a quiet voice said, "Do you know what that proves? That proves that most people can't write poetry!"

When the semester began I was the only nonenrolled student attending, but so extraordinary were his performances that the news spread, and by the time he gave his final Whitman lecture the room was jammed to the bursting point. Crane, Stevens, Bishop, Roethke, Eliot, Auden, Dylan Thomas, and Hardy were also subjects of his lectures. These were not talks he gave off the top of his head. Far from it. He entered the room each night shaking with anticipation and armed with a pack of note cards, which he rarely consulted. In private he confessed to me that he prepared for days for these sessions. He went away from them in a state bordering on total collapse. It would be impossible to overestimate the effect on us of these lectures, for this was an era during which Whitman was out, removed adroitly by Eliot and Pound, and kept there by the Ironists and the New Critics, who were then the makers of poetic taste. In 1954 in Iowa no one dreamed that within a few years Williams would be rescued from hell, the Beats would surface, and Whitman would become the good gray father of us all. (John himself later claimed the Beats didn't know how to read Whitman and mistook his brilliant rhythmic effects for prose. "They don't write poems," is the way he put it.) I cannot speak for the entire class, but I know that Petrie, Jane Cooper, Dana, Coulette, Justice, Snodgrass, and I were convinced that "Song of Myself" was the most powerful and visionary poetic statement ever made in this country. Those lectures not only changed our poetry, they changed our entire vision of what it meant to write poetry in America, what it meant to be American, to be human. "There is that lot of me and all so luscious," I suddenly sang to myself, and I believed it, and thanks to John and father Walt I still believe it. Whitman had laid out the plan for what our poetry would do, and so large was the plan there was room for all of us to take our part, as, for example, Roethke was doing, that poet who according to John "thought like a flower."

It seems unlikely now that Berryman should have performed that task, for was he not an Eastern intellectual poet and part-time New Critic himself, a protégé of Mark Van Doren and R. P. Blackmur? Like so much that concerns Berryman, the answer is ambiguous. His reviews often sounded very much like what the New Critics were turning out, except they were far wittier and often more savage; in savagery only Yvor Winters could measure up to him. Who else would be bold enough to invent a poem that a poet might have written—nay, should have written—as John did in a review of Patchen, and then define Patchen's weaknesses on the basis of the poem Berryman and not Patchen had written? But unlike Winters and the rest of the New Critics, he was unashamedly Romantic at the same time as he was distrustful of the "cult of sincerity." He was, as in so many things, his own man and in a very real sense a loner.

Before we parted that semester he performed two more services for me. The day before he left for New York City—he was going east to teach at Harvard that summer—we had a long conversation on what a poet should look like. The Oscar Williams anthology, one of the most popular of that day, included photographs of most of the poets at the back of the book; John and A. E. Housman were the only exceptions—they were represented by drawings. John's was very amateurish and looked nothing like him. I asked him why he'd used it instead of a photograph. He claimed he wanted neither but Oscar had insisted, and he'd taken the lesser of the two evils. He thought either was a distraction, though the drawing did make it clear he was ugly enough to be a poet. I didn't catch his meaning and asked him to explain. "No poet worth his salt is going to be handsome; if he or she is beautiful there's no need to create the beautiful. Beautiful people are special; they don't experience life like the rest of us." He was obviously dead serious, and then he added, "Don't worry about it, Levine, you're ugly enough to be a great poet."

The next day, at the airport, he was in an unusually manic mood. "Think of it, Levine, in a few hours I shall be mine own John Poins." Not knowing Wyatt's poem written from exile in rural England to Poins in London, I asked him what he meant.

> I am not he, such eloquence to boast
> To make the crow in singing as the swan,
> Nor call the lion of coward beasts the most,
> That cannot take a mouse as the cat can. . . .

He quoted from memory. "Wyatt, Levine, Wyatt, his rough numbers would be perfect for your verse, you crude bastard." ("Crude bastard" was his highest form of compliment.) Before boarding he invited me to send him four or five poems in a year or so, and he'd be sure to get back to me to tell me how I was doing. Having seen an enormous carton of unopened mail in his apartment, I doubted he'd ever answer, but nonetheless a year and a half later I sent him four poems. His response was prompt and to the point, with X's to mark the lines and passages he thought a disaster and checks where he found me "hot," along with specific suggestions for revision; there was not a single line unremarked upon. There was also a brief letter telling me things were going well in Minneapolis and that he was delighted to know I was fooling editors with my "lousy poems." He looked forward to seeing me one day. There was not the least doubt about what he was in fact saying: our days as student and teacher had come to an end. We could not exchange poems as equals in poetry because we were not equals and might never be, and yet I had come too far to require a teacher. I felt the same way. I'd had one great poetry-writing teacher, I had studied with him diligently for fifteen weeks. From now on I had to travel the road to poetry alone or with my peers. This was his final lesson, and it may have been the most important in my development.

As the years pass his voice remains with me, its haunting and unique cadences sounding in my ear, most often when I reread my own work. I can still hear him saying, "Levine, this will never do," as he rouses me again and again from my self-satisfaction and lethargy to attack a poem and attack again until I make it the best poem I am capable of. His voice is there too when I teach, urging me to say the truth no matter how painful a situation I may create, to say it with precision and in good spirits, never in rancor, and always to remember Blake's words (a couplet John loved to quote): "A truth that's told with bad intent / Beats all the Lies you can invent." For all my teaching years, now over thirty, he has been a model for me. No matter what you hear or read about his drinking, his madness, his unreliability as a person, I am here to tell you that in the winter and spring of 1954, living in isolation and loneliness in one of the bleakest towns of our difficult Midwest, John Berryman never failed his obligations as a teacher. I don't mean merely that he met every class and stayed awake, I mean that he brought to our writing and the writing of the past such a sense of dedication and wonder that he wakened a dozen rising poets from their winter slumbers so that they might themselves dedicate their lives to poetry. He was the most brilliant, intense, articulate man I've ever met, at times even the kindest and most gentle, and for some reason he brought to our writing a depth of insight and care we did not know existed. At a time when he was struggling with his own self-doubts and failings, he awakened us to our singular gifts as people and writers. He gave all he had to us and asked no special thanks. He did it for the love of poetry.

The Holy Cities:
Detroit, Barcelona,
Byzantium

What follows is the story of a passion, or perhaps I should call it a faith, for anarchism is as much a religion as it is a political system. I'm not sure where the story begins. I suppose, like most of the stories which make up my life or which I make up out of the events of my life, it has no beginning or ending; rather, it has high points and low points, crests and troughs in the little seas of my awareness.

Let me begin with my growing up in the 1930s in the city of Detroit, a city choking on the ills of the Great Depression, though it was no worse off then than it is now, despised and avoided during the glory days of Reagan-Bush economics and racism. The first political event I recall with clarity was the presidential election of '32, which pitted the upstart Franklin Roosevelt against Herbert Hoover. My father, an immigrant from Tsarist Russia and a deserter from the British Army during the First World War, was then a partner with my grandfather in a small but lively automobile replacement-parts company located near the ballpark. He had also transformed himself into an ardent Republican. My grandfather had come to the U.S. during the first decade of the century in order to avoid military conscription for the Russo-Japanese War; his only politics were to avoid getting shot at protecting someone else's property. Since he could not read English he was unaware of the fact that the leading conservative journal of the day, the *Literary Digest*, had picked Hoover in a landslide. He and my father bet on the election. I don't know the size of the bet, but it was enough to arouse passion in Zaydee's heart. My grandfather's political intuitions were keen: "With a voice like honey you don't lose." (Years later he won a fortune betting against Dewey, who he knew could not win because "right after Hitler the American people don't elect a little schmuck with such a moustache.") The family sat at the dining-room table long after dinner listening to the returns come in as I played war with my lead soldiers under the table, hearing my father groan as each state reported the Republican defeat. My father was a good loser, and my grandfather generous in victory, so the evening ended without strain, although my father predicted bad times for business with this new president. Zaydee chuckled. "How much worse could they be?"

A year later, in an art class in kindergarten, I had my second political experience. We were assembling armatures for a sculpture the class was building, and for it we used wadded hunks of newspapers and paste we made ourselves out of flour and water. I was sitting next to a teacher's aide when I noticed an odd picture in the Sunday rotogravure section: men in uniforms bearing armbands and curious symbols on them were rounding up civilians. The symbols were swastikas, the men brown-shirts, a militia of the National Socialist Party of Germany; the civilians were Jews. The photograph and its caption froze me, and as I started to read the article below it the teacher's aide, who was a college student at Wayne University, covered the text with her hand. "You don't want to read that," she said. "Why are they wearing those things on their sleeves?" I asked. Slowly she pulled the paper away from me and repeated her ominous warning, "You don't want to read that." "Why are they doing that to us?" I asked. Immediately I recognized that she was far more upset by my discovery of the photograph than I; her hands were trembling, and she shook her head from side to side. "Please," she said, "you don't want to know any of this." Immediately I shut up, knowing I could get the truth from my mother.

Although I was born into the middle class, my father died before I was old enough to enjoy my station. My mother found work as a stenographer and, later, an office manager. Although she always provided for us, my memory includes a succession of moves from first a house to a series of ever-shrinking apartments. Something had been suspect about my father's life-insurance policy, and the company refused to pay the full value. Money became the chief topic of mealtime conversations, money and especially the lack of it. Curiously, my older brother seemed not the least fazed by our difficulties. Some days he would return from school, check himself out in the bathroom mirror, decide his shirt was dirty, and immediately change to another one even though he was going to do nothing except practice the piano or study his textbooks. When I questioned my mother about this, she merely informed me that he was the firstborn.

In the evenings my mother would return home from work exhausted but never dirty. I learned from Belle, my mother's younger sister, that this was significant. Once, before Belle took me on the bus downtown to buy a new pair of shoes for the beginning of the school year, she made me first take a bath and then change into my only clean knickers and of course into clean socks. I questioned her about the sense of all this preparation. "We may be poor," she said, "but at least we're clean." "We're poor?" I asked. She hedged. No, we weren't exactly poor, we just didn't have any money and that was why it was important to be clean, so no one would mistake us for the poor. Clearly it would be terrible to be mistaken for the poor. We had enough money, for example, to buy me a pair of shoes for the new school year. She held up the battered ones I'd been wearing all summer. "These are way too small for you, and look at them." She stretched the sole away from the rest of the shoe and let it slip slowly back like a fatigued spring. "People with money don't wear clothes that are falling apart, and they don't have to spend an afternoon going downtown to save a dollar on a pair of shoes." Later, at Hudson's Department Store, a massive structure that occupied an entire square block, Belle argued ferociously with a salesman who claimed that the sale did not include the shoes she wanted for me. Belle was fearless; she just kept pushing the ad clipped from the *Free Press* in his face and repeating, "It's right here in black and white." Finally the salesman relented and gave us the hideous brown, heavy "English" walking shoes at the sale price. On the way home she confided in me one of the principles by which she purchased: "The English make the best shoes." The little jerk of a salesman had been trying to pass off an American pair on her. I left the shoes in their box, afraid to wear them until the first day of school. I'd learned how quickly the gleaming surface of the soles could be eroded simply by sliding on the pavement, an exercise that was always tempting. A week passed before I took them from the closet; I discovered that the box clearly declared they'd been manufactured by union labor in Brockton, Massachusetts. Immediately I lost all affection for them, though I never revealed to Belle the profundity of her error.

Entering the second grade that year, I began to notice for the first time how differently we students dressed, and at the same time how many of us wore the same clothes. There were four boys in my class aside from me who wore sweaters which bore the figure of a stag knitted in white against a maroon background. It too had been on sale at Hudson's, the maroon a dollar cheaper than the navy blue. There was one boy who wore far more elegant sweaters in subtle hues of brown and fawn; even his checked socks were in matching colors. He was always neatly combed, his nails were never bitten down, and they gleamed as though they had been polished. I noticed too that my teacher seemed to defer to him, to call on him only when he raised his hand and clearly knew the answers to her questions, whereas she was continually trying to make fools out of the rest of us. This boy, Milton Journey, was always driven to school in a long white La Salle convertible, which I learned belonged to his older brother, who attended a nearby junior high school. On winter days, after school, Milton would wait in his long blue overcoat inside the main doors until his mother stopped and honked from her sedan. Milton would toss back his straight blond hair, shrug, and go out into the weather to accept his privileges.

Another boy, Fred Batten, disgusted me. When he spoke to me he had a habit of sticking his face as close as he could to mine, as though he were trying to swipe my breath; perhaps he truly meant to, for his own breath smelled awful. Unfortunately he had some sort of affection for me and constantly pursued me. One day I noticed that the skin behind his ears and around his neck bore dark smudges. I realized Fred Batten didn't wash; his hands too were always filthy. With a shock I realized he wore no socks, and often that winter the skin of his ankles was raw and swollen. One day he caught me staring at his bare ankles, and he turned away from me in silence. I began to notice several other boys and girls who bore these same "wounds" at wrist and ankles, and I did my best not to stare at them.

Winters in Michigan were fierce, but I never left for school without a warm jacket, socks, a cap that covered my ears, usually by means of some sort of hideous flap that fastened below the chin, gloves, and a scarf. Not once did I go off without a sacked lunch, nor were lice ever found in my hair, though weekly I had to bow for the health officer's inspection. Many of my classmates were not so fortunate and were taken off for their "treatment" and returned, heads bent and reeking of kerosene.

Lunchtimes grew particularly difficult, for many students had nothing to eat except the free carton of milk that was provided by the school. By the age of ten I'd decided that it was easier to walk the mile back to our apartment and eat my lunch in privacy than to bear the envious glances of many of my schoolmates. In autumn especially the tree-lined streets were lovely, and since my mother was unable to buy glasses for me until I was fourteen, in those early years I was walking through a city invented by an impressionist painter.

Often I'd make the walk home with a classmate, Martin Peters, who though shorter than I was actually two years older and lived with his family in a "halfer," a second-story apartment that was divided into two separate units both of which shared the kitchen and bathroom. Suddenly, during a particularly cold week in January, Martin stopped coming to school. I didn't see him for three weeks. The word was he was suffering from pneumonia, but when he returned to class he shared his secret. His mother had been keeping him home because he had no heavy jacket or coat. His father was out of work, the gas bill had not been paid, so the heat had been shut off. Martin had spent most days in bed, under the covers, listening to the radio. During those weeks he'd become an extraordinary source of the comings and goings of his favorite soap-opera characters, and now the need to return to class was depriving him of more of their adventures.

Something was very wrong with the world, and I was powerless to do anything about it. When my father died in his middle thirties I was assured that it was due to the rules of God: the good died young so that they could be close to Him. That did me and my family absolutely no good, for we were doomed to spend the rest of our lives deprived of this lovable man. Poor men came to our doors daily, and we had to turn them away for lack of anything to give them. To and from school I would walk past blocks of stately mansions. I experimented. In the back seat of my grandfather's Hudson, I would imagine myself equipped with a repeating rifle and opening fire on every Cadillac, La Salle, Lincoln, or Chrysler we happened across. This was my battle against the forces of injustice and greed. My bullets equalized nothing, but they made me feel better.

Meanwhile I was growing up in a viciously anti-Semitic community in a particularly anti-Semitic era. From Royal Oak, Michigan, a suburb of Detroit, the rantings of Father Coughlin were broadcast every Sunday, and those rantings blamed the Communist Jews for every social and moral problem and urged our expulsion. For reasons I still fail to comprehend, my family often tuned in to international broadcasts of Hitler's speeches. When the Italians invaded Abyssinia, when the Japanese moved into China, when Hitler annexed the Rhineland, I saw the motive as revenge against the Jews.

When I was seven my mother hired a hill woman named Florence Hickok to clean, cook, and look after us, especially during the summer, when we were out of school and my mother worked all through the season as a stenographer. Florence was one of those uncompromising Americans who believe in militancy, a fair wage, and the never-ending battle against the excesses of capitalism that all decent working people were obliged by God and common sense to carry on until their last breath. Tall, gaunt, weather-beaten, with a cigarette burning in the corner of her mouth, at the breakfast table she'd read through the morning *Free Press* muttering, "The bastards are selling us down the river." She hadn't the least doubt that the European "democracies" and America as well were run by and for the rich. By "us" she meant, of course, all those who had to work for a living, whose labor created the wealth that ironically imprisoned them. From the Black Hills of the Dakotas, Florence claimed to be of the same blood as Wild Bill, who she assured us was also a red. (In those days independent working Americans were proud of being red, which did not mean membership in the Communist Party: it merely meant struggling with the common people against the exploiters. No matter what you've been told to the contrary, we reds knew the difference between the totalitarian, brainwashed CP members, the professional Communists, and ourselves, the reds who wanted not to be encumbered with another hierarchy of bosses.)

Then occurred one of the epic events of my young life; I was eight years old during the summer of '36, when the generals rose up to overthrow the Spanish Republic. The American right-wing press called it a battle between the Nationalists and the Communists, but even then I knew it was the legally elected people's government versus the fascists, the ancient repressive forces of church, army, and the great landowners. Florence had no doubts, and when the United States, France, and England refused to sell arms to the Republic even though the Nazis and the Italian Fascists were sending men, tanks, and warplanes, she showed not the least surprise. "They're selling us down the river. You watch, Philip, France will be next. They'd rather lose to the Nazis than to the working people."

Immediately young men from my neighborhood were being recruited to join the Lincoln Brigade and fight for

the defense of the Republic. Before long one of my classmates told me that his parents had received a telegram
the night before saying that his older brother, whose
name was the same as mine, was missing in action. I was
puzzled by that expression, "missing in action," and asked
my friend exactly what it meant. "He may be a prisoner
of war," little Irv said, "but my uncle told me they aren't
taking prisoners, so I guess it means he's dead." Out on
the playground in the already chilled autumn air, we sat
on the bleachers just behind the baseball diamond while
Irv told us how scared he was to go home. His mom was
just wrecked by the news; she'd begged her oldest not
to go. To us Philip was a hero: in some curious way we
envied his sacrifice.

In those days baseball cards were not the only prizes
available with the purchase of bubble gum. You had the
option of choosing "War Cards," which until then had
featured the bombing of Abyssinians and the beheading
of civilians in Shanghai by hunks of plate glass blasted
from the windows of modern European-style hotels. But
now the Spanish Nationalists in their chic uniforms and
tasseled caps were attacking Madrid on one card and on
another holding out for over two hundred days against
the Communists, with the aid of Moorish troops. I never
saw it, but there must have been one that celebrated the
death of the commander of the anarchist Durruti Brigade, shot in the back on the road to Madrid. I don't
doubt that it existed in the lurid colors of the day, depicting a thick-waisted brutal man brought to a brutal
end; the friends of our enemies seemed to own every
avenue of communication except word of mouth, which
became the only one we trusted. Soon the cities with their
holy names fell to Franco, one after the other, Granada,
Málaga, Madrid, Alicante, Valencia, and lastly the great
outpost of our people, Barcelona. That was in the spring
of '39, and before that summer was over Florence's pre-
diction proved true: fascism was sweeping everything

before it. Poland was sliced in two by Hitler and Stalin; their nonaggression pact was sealed. The Nazis were one giant step closer to Detroit.

In D'Angelo & Ferrente's Dry Cleaning & Tailoring Shop, around the corner from where we lived, the two proprietors argued continually with each other and with their employees regarding the political truths of the day. D'Angelo was medium height, slender, and dressed with what he considered a studied elegance. It was a rare day on which he appeared without his suit coat; a lover of Verdi and Puccini, he considered himself several cuts above his squat little Sicilian partner, who never failed to assure me of his love for FDR and his loathing of Mussolini, who had plunged a knife into the back of his neighbor. They paid me a quarter for each delivery I made on foot, and while I waited for the parcels to be readied I often conversed with the tall, slender presser, whose name I have forgotten. Because of the heat he'd work in pleated trousers and a sleeveless undershirt which revealed his scars—a gift of his years of imprisonment for his loyalties to the anarchist cause. He and the Bulgarian tailor ("a whiz at trousers," Ferrente claimed) never spoke to or even acknowledged each other. Thick, gray-haired, and balding, the Bulgarian saw what was coming even in the winter of 1940 and legally renamed his sons Leonard and Stanley (they had been Lenin and Stalin). Because of his resemblance to another anarchist who shared his faith in the Spanish working people, I shall call the presser Cipriano. He was the first anarchist I met who knew he was an anarchist. He was by far the most reserved and self-contained member of this informal debating society. Perhaps because he had actually fought the battles in body and spirit, he seemed to have no need to carry on verbally, and his only response to the Bulgarian's Marxist rants was a silent shaking of the head. A tightly built muscular man with deep-set dark eyes and long black hair, he went about his work with an alarming suddenness, as though he were not a pants presser but an actor playing the role of one. I read in his movements not a disregard for this work but, rather, the affirmation that all work was worth doing with elegance and precision and that necessary work granted dignity to the worker. For me he was both a pants presser and the most truly dignified person I'd ever met, one of the unacknowledged legislators of the world. He never lectured me; instead he shared his views on the unending struggle for equality and independence that each of us must wage against the forces of government and private ownership, for it was only by owning nothing that each of us would come fully into possession of the gift of the self. In spite of all his defeats he was animated by an amazing optimism. "Someday this will all be ours," he said into my wide eyes, "someday you will see." Pared of all excess, he seemed to me the perfect embodiment of the human spirit.

During the summer of 1942 I was working in a soap factory on the outskirts of town, wheeling huge racks of sliced soap chips into the ovens, where they dried, yellowed, and curled until they resembled some rare, unworldly pasta. The heat was extraordinary, and I had to hop to it not to succumb, but for thirty-five cents an hour I did my best. (The ironies were lost on me; in '42 in Detroit we did not know about the other ovens or the transformation of Jews into soap.) I was saving for a good pair of trousers—hopefully created by the Bulgarian Marxist—in which I could return to school in the fall. On Saturday afternoons I'd stop by D'Angelo & Ferrente's and make whatever deliveries were needed. And one day Cipriano was gone, replaced by a short, wizened black man. No, he hadn't been fired, he hadn't called in sick, he hadn't even collected his last check. He had just vanished into America, and except for me no one seemed to care. I hoped that, wherever his life had taken him, he was sharing his vision with some other kid. Also, that summer Florence Hickok accidentally stumbled across her childhood sweetheart, Peg, at the zoo, where he fed and looked after the big cats. After a few weeks of spooning, they thought they'd try life together in the West, for Florence's lungs were bad after a lifetime of chain-smoking and a particularly severe bout of pneumonia the previous winter. My teachers were leaving, and I supposed it was time for me to become a man. I was thirteen, walking the avenues with eyes lowered, having discovered the sculptured beauty of women's legs and suddenly aware of the fact that every handsome woman knew I was looking.

That autumn I found poetry. After dark, ambling the deserted streets, I would speak to the moon and stars about the emotional revolution that was raging within me, and, true to their natures, the moon and stars would not answer. My most intimate poems were summoned by the promise of rain in the air or the odors of its aftermath. Night after night I spun and respun these poems—if poems they were—none of which I ever committed to the page. I was learning to love solitude and to discover the power of my voice to deprive it of terror; I was learning how to become one man in a sea of men and women who by some mystery came together to form a brotherhood and sisterhood of all those beings with souls. At that age I knew of almost no beings without souls; certainly trees had them, and the wildflowers that sprang up in the undeveloped lots and the tall grasses I lay down in for shelter. Even the hum of traffic on the distant Outer Drive had a kind of intelligence, as though it too spoke for some human yearning, as though each separate car were on some quest whose goal was love—for all I knew, love of me. Once the dark took over, nothing was impossible. Each night that I labored joyously at my new craft and art, I sang out to the city and the larger world beyond the city, and no one was the wiser.

*   *   *

The more I consider these events the more sure I become that I cannot write about the development in me of a faith or a passion. I don't actually understand why for so many years I lectured my friends on the virtues of anarchism and then suddenly stopped. I doubt that it had anything to do with my desire not to bore them. Perhaps some of my hesitancy sprang from the events that followed my being tossed out of the house my wife and I had been renting for fourteen years. That was 1973, a time when millions of Americans were intensely aware of the evils of the American state, and so many of the young were into a kind of rock or punk anarchism. All around me I perceived the truth of that basic anarchist tenet that property is theft. My wife and kids and I would drive into the nearby Sierra Nevada mountains for informal hikes only to be greeted by bullet-riddled signs announcing "No Trespassing," signs that made it clear that violators would be prosecuted or worse. All my growing up I'd been told about the immense wealth I'd inherited merely by being born an American, and now nothing was clearer than that my inheritance had been stolen. In my own life I was stealing nothing from anyone: I had clothes (two pairs of shoes now), a record player and records, a few hundred books I'd gathered over the years, a car, a house full of odds and ends of furniture. I had my poems also, but by its very nature a poem is something you hope to share with others, even to give away if need be. And suddenly our security was shattered by an order either to purchase a house we'd been living in for fourteen years or to hit the road. We chose to look elsewhere, but since rents were rising steeply and a poetry grant from the National Endowment gave me enough for a down payment, and since my wife happened across exactly the house she wanted—a small California farmhouse on an enormous lot dotted with orange trees and with room for a large garden—and since, walking through the place on a blazing July after-

noon, the thought came to me so clearly I declaimed it—
"I can write here"—and the price was reasonable, we
bought. I've never regretted that act, though it deprived
me forever of the right to say, "Property is theft." No
doubt all my friends were relieved, and in fact even I was.
My lectures ended, but though silent I did not stop believing the lessons I'd derived from my heroes.

So let this be a story of my heroes and the story of
how a particular poem grew out of the homage I tried
to pay to those heroes. And in the spirit of fairness to the
complexities of experience let it also become the story of
the poem I did not write and never will write, though all
the material is there, stored in my memory, textured
scenes I hope never to forget, peopled with those singular
individuals who enter our lives only on those days during
which creation has deemed us worthy of the highest gift,
the clarity inspiration gives us. This shall be the story
of the poem I wrote in 1978, "Francisco, I'll Bring You
Red Carnations," and the poem I did not write ten years
later, when I fulfilled the promise in the title of the
written poem.

For the sake of fullness let me return to an earlier me. In
the spring of 1965 my college, Fresno State, granted me
my first sabbatical leave. My sense of Fresno State is
that, as schools of higher education go, it's not much (my
best student once referred to it in print as "Wind & Dust
State"), although the student body represents the community far more accurately than most schools, certainly
far more than Yale represents New Haven or Harvard
represents Cambridge or the University of California
represents Berkeley. The overriding problem is the bu-
reaucracy of the entire state-university system as well as
our local administration. We teachers are required to
spend twelve hours in the classroom each week, usually
in four different classes, each with an average of thirty
students, for someone has to pay for the army of medioc-

rities we are saddled with, administrators with titles like Dean of Steam or Vice President of Nonacademic Affairs and Nonsexual Relations. These people with huge salaries and no function determine the priorities of the place, and they couldn't care less about the arts, the sciences, the humanities, the teaching of something so esoteric as poetry writing. The last time I saw our president in public he was on TV hawking private suites at our football stadium at thirty grand a year; we've gone into competition with the Dallas Cowboys.

A dear colleague urged England on me, reminding me how Frost's work took off during and after his English years. I seriously considered England. In April of '65 I took part in a writing conference at U.C. Santa Barbara; there I met the poet and fiction writer Jascha Kessler, who assured me that England was far too cold and too stuffy for my temperament. He'd recently returned from a year in Europe, most of which he'd spent in Italy. When I told him how much money I had, he said, "Spain, it's the only place you can afford." He described a wine he'd bought for ten cents a liter in a Spanish bodega near Málaga; the richness and delicacy of the wine were still with him, though he'd forgotten the name. "What about Franco?" I asked. "You don't bother him, he won't bother you." I returned to Fresno a few days later and presented the idea to my wife. In her youth she'd spent a large part of a winter in Paris and England, and she knew how cold Northern Europe could be; she was all for Spain.

She took up the study of the Spanish language while I began to grapple with Spain's history, both ancient and modern. I taught summer school and a writing conference in San Francisco and put aside as much as I could. Could a family of five make it for a year on less than eight thousand dollars? I was scared, but I was also excited to be making this break with teaching, with Fresno, and with the United States, now well into its exercise in imperialism in Southeast Asia. I wrote almost nothing that summer, but I read an enormous amount, and it was during a rereading of Orwell's *Homage to Catalonia* that I made the final decision. The book begins with a scene in the Lenin Barracks in Barcelona; it is December of '36, the anarchists are still in control of the city, and no one publicly says "Señor" or "Don" or even "*Usted*," Orwell tells us. They say "Comrade" and "Thou"; instead of "*Buenos días*" they say "*Salud*." Tipping is forbidden. "Practically everyone wore rough working class clothes. . . . All this was queer and moving . . . but I recognized it immediately as a state of affairs worth fighting for," wrote Orwell, some seven months later. But what moved me most in the book was what moved him most: an Italian militiaman he saw the day he too joined the militia. "He was a tough looking youth of twenty-five or six, with reddish yellow hair and powerful shoulders. His peaked leather cap was pulled fiercely over one eye. He was standing in profile to me, his chin on his breast, gazing with a puzzled frown at a map which one of the officers had opened on the table. Something in his face deeply moved me. It was the face of a man who would commit murder and throw his life away for a friend—the kind of face you expect in an Anarchist. . . ." I too knew that face, or at least one of its many million incarnations. I had not seen it in almost twenty-five years, I had not felt its singular power to rouse and inspire. I would search for it again in the capital of anarchism, in the streets of Barcelona.

Mid-September 1965. We entered the great city under a shroud of smog as heavy as any I had ever seen. In spite of the heat, we had avoided the coast road in order to save time. This took us through a dozen industrial towns which spilled into each other to form one seamless misunderstanding. We passed miles of cheap high-rise apartment buildings with that raw, unfinished look one associates with post-war Italian films or photographs of the third world. The truck traffic was extraordinary, and every time we got stuck behind one of the big diesels our windshield darkened with tiny spots of filth. And the noise! Scooters and two-cycle motorbikes weaved in and out of the stalled traffic, loudspeakers blared from every square as we crawled toward our new home. We had traveled halfway around the world to discover this Detroit of Europe. My wife and kids bravely accepted the fact: we would live here for a year, we would make the best of it.

The next morning I wakened early in a hotel room twelve floors above Barcelona's Rambla de Cataluña and descended by elevator into the streets to find someplace that served coffee and rolls. The air was surprisingly cool and fresh; it was before 7:00 a.m. and people were still on their way to or from work. I sat for over an hour in a bar watching the men in their blue coveralls embracing and chatting before going off to their separate jobs or their apartments. It was as though I'd known these men before I saw them, these men in their wool caps, smoking and hollering in their hoarse voices. Their faces unshaven, rough, spare, worn down but not worn out, these were the men of my boyhood and my growing up. In spite of or perhaps because of the decades of Franco's repression, their anger was palpable and fresh. Little wonder this city had become the birthplace and burial ground of one of the world's most daring experiments in self-government.

The beginnings of Spanish anarchism are usually traced to the arrival in Spain in the fall of 1868 of Giuseppe Fanelli, an Italian supporter of the Russian anarchist and theoretician Mikhail Bakunin, who had financed the trip from Geneva to Spain. His arrival there should have signaled a total fiasco; for one thing he spoke almost no Spanish, and for another he was constantly running out of money, but somehow wherever he went he was able to express his loathing of social injustice and the profundity of his libertarian ideals. (Those who write about anarchism have begun to avoid the very word, because the popular press has managed to transform it into a synonym for bomb throwing and assassination.) By January of the following year he had helped found an International Working-Man's Association in Madrid of twenty-some members. Urged to stay, he decided to leave, for, as he put it, these groups had to develop "by their own efforts, with their own values." On his way home he stopped off in Barcelona and there too made a few key converts. He returned to Italy and his life as a professional revolutionary, preaching his ideals in small villages, sleeping in railroad cars, impoverished, until his death eight years later of TB at the age of forty-eight.

What was "The Idea," as it was later called, that was now to spread throughout much of Spain, reaching its glory years in the 1930s? As Murray Bookchin, the historian of this era, writes, "anarchist ideals are difficult to fix into a hard and fast credo. Anarchism is a great libidinal movement of humanity to shake off the repressive apparatus created by hierarchical society. It originates in the age-old drive of the oppressed to assert the spirit of freedom, equality, and spontaneity over values and institutions based on authority. This accounts for the enormous antiquity of anarchistic visions, their irrepressibility and continual reemergence in history." Little wonder "The Idea" spread wildly in the rich, once Christian soil of Spain, for, as Bookchin notes, "The slaves and poor who flocked to Christianity saw the second coming of Christ as a time when 'a grain of wheat would bear ten thousand ears,' when hunger, coercion, and hierarchy would be banished forever from the earth." Throughout its history Spanish anarchism remained a people's movement. In spite of the most severe efforts to suppress it, it flowered in a country of the basest poverty and inequality, and not only in the industrial centers, but also in the mining country of the north and in agrarian Andalusia, though in each region it produced its own particular character. By the 1930s the largest trade union in Spain was the anarcho-syndicalist CNT (National Confederation of Workers), which had almost two million members.

The history of Spanish anarchism is also the history of terrible repressions under the monarchy, the dictatorship of Primo de Rivera, and even under the Second Republic. Perhaps the most famous was the "Tragic Week" of July 1909, which was touched off by the government's attempt to call up the military reserves to deal with the Riff uprisings in Morocco. There were very few workingmen who wanted to risk their lives to protect the colonial holdings of their employers. Workingmen of all persuasions banded together in what was largely a spontaneous uprising. As one observer wrote, "What is happening here is amazing. A social revolution has broken out in Barcelona and it has been started by the people. No one instigated it. No one has led it. Neither the Liberals nor Catalan Nationalists, nor Republicans, nor Socialists, nor Anarchists." After the army brutally put down the rebellion, one of those singled out for execution by the military to pay for his "crimes" against the state had absolutely nothing to do with the event. He was not even in Barcelona when the uprising began and had spent the previous month nursing his sister and caring for her daughter on his farm some fifteen miles outside the city. Francisco Ferrer y Guardia was famous not as a revolutionary but as the founder of what was to become the most influential school in modern Spain, the Escuela Moderna, which by today's standards may hardly sound revolutionary, but at a time when most young Spaniards were the students of clerics and were subject to terrible physical punishment and humiliation, he established a school that would promote "a stern hostility to prejudice" and create "solid minds, capable of forming their own rational convictions on every subject." His aim was to bring together not only the sexes—a thing unheard of in

Spain—but young people of all social classes so as to create a "school of emancipation that will be concerned with banning from the mind whatever divides men, the false concepts of property, country, and family." A man known for his gentleness and humility, Ferrer was none the less a marked man, and when the authorities got their chance at the end of the Tragic Week, they took it. After a farcical, rigged military trial of one day he was sentenced to death, and on the morning of October 13, 1909, in Montjuich Prison (which shares the Mountain of Jove or Mountain of Jews—there is disagreement on the source of the name—with the great cemetery of Barcelona), he was executed by a firing squad. It is reported that he faced his death calmly, and that as the soldiers aimed their rifles he cried out, "Look well, my children! I am innocent. Long live the Escuela Moderna!"

The other two historical figures, Buenaventura Durruti and Francisco Ascaso, were to become the two most famous Spanish anarchists, the central agents in the mobilization of the working class against fascist dictatorship and the ancient exploitations of church, army, and state. The biographer Abel Paz describes their first meeting in Saragossa in 1922. The two men were then in their twenties, and Ascaso had just been released from prison for his part in labor organizing, which was forbidden during the reign of Alfonso XIII. At the time, Ascaso was the better known of the two, having gained attention for his extraordinary courage, his shrewdness as an organizer, and also through his theoretical publications. Paz states that from the beginning the two were drawn to each other's person and thought. "The differences in their characters only brought out better the resemblances between the two men. Ascaso, small, thin, nervous; Durruti, athletic and calm. Ascaso with his strained and suspicious glance, seemed unlikable at first sight; Durruti on the contrary radiated sympathy. Icy calculation, rationality and mistrust in one; passion and

optimism behind an apparently calm exterior in the
other . . . Once a complete climate of confidence had
been established great projects were born from the
dialogue between the two revolutionaries."

The two men spent much of the rest of the decade in
exile, working together as organizers in Latin America
and Europe, spreading "The Idea." Once their activities
were discovered by the authorities, they were imprisoned
or forced to move on, and by the end of the decade there
was almost no country that would have them. The two
lived quietly in Brussels from 1929 until 1931, when a
general pardon was granted by the new Spanish Republic. Within a few weeks of their return they were speaking at anarchist rallies to enormous crowds, and before
a month passed Durruti was in prison on old, trumped-
up charges. Soon released, he threw himself with all his
ferocious nature into his work. The rest of the story is,
as they say, history. On July 19, 1936, the generals rose
against the Republic, and the terrible civil war began. In
Barcelona the workers, largely under the leadership of
the CNT, were able to seize the initiative, put down the
uprising, and declare a revolution in Catalonia. It was
on that day, July 19, that Ascaso died leading the charge
against the Atarazanas barracks in Barcelona.

There were many who saw in the death of Ascaso a
foreshadowing of all the disasters that were to follow,
the deep divisions within the left, the betrayal of the
revolution, and even the struggle against fascism by the
Communists. (As we know from eyewitness accounts,
Orwell's and others, the Communists did everything within their power to brand as pro-fascist all those on the
Republican side who refused to follow the commissars,
and they did not stop short of assassination.) One of the
most moving tributes to the particular gifts of Ascaso
and the beauty of his friendship with Durruti is found in
Robert W. Kern's *Red Years, Black Years*, a political
history of Spanish anarchism from 1911 to 1937:

Seen from our age, which is cynical about such things, their friendship can only be summarized as a revolutionary partnership, an incredible voyage by a pair of Spanish peasants through the politics and crime of Latin America, Western Europe, Africa, and Spain. In many situations there was something of the *picaro* about them, not in the sense of Lazarillo de Tormes, but more in remaining what they were, of not craving publicity or seeking a large following, of constantly working for a goal while staying very much as they always had been. Peasant rebels in an urban, industrial century, as political individualists representing the collective revolutionary dream of the countryside, unfettered by vanguardism or any of the other rigorous dialects of the modern Left, they had a certain roguish quality. One survivor who remembers Ascaso called him "one of the last nineteenth-century libertarians," a radical thrown up by the great upheavals of the early capitalist era when everything was much more black and white than in the 1930s.

Above all else, above even the sacrifices and the terrible martyrdoms, it was this friendship and the fellowship of working men and women it suggested that inspired my poem. In some way I cannot explain, I had chosen since boyhood to live vitally in the Spain of that era, to take part in the struggle for a new world.

Francisco, I'll Bring You Red Carnations

Here in the great cemetery
behind the fortress of Barcelona
I have come once more to see
the graves of my fallen.
Two ancient picnickers direct
us down the hill. "Durruti,"

says the man, "I was on
his side." The woman hushes
him. All the way down
this is a city of the dead,
871, 251, *difuntos*.
The poor packed in tenements
a dozen high; the rich
in splendid homes or temples.
So nothing has changed
except for the single
unswerving fact: they are
all dead. Here is the Plaza
of San Jaime, here the Rambla
of San Pedro, so every death
still has a mailing address,
but since this is Spain
the mail never comes or
comes too late to be of use.
Between the cemetery and
the Protestant burial ground
we find the three stones
all in a row: Ferrer Guardia,
B. Durruti, F. Ascaso, the names
written with marking pens,
and a few circled A's and tributes
to the FAI and CNT.
For two there are floral
displays, but Ascaso faces
eternity with only a stone.
Maybe as it should be. He was
a stone, a stone and a blade,
the first grinding and sharpening
the other. Half his 36
years were spent in prisons
or on the run, and yet
in that last photograph
taken less than an hour before

he died, he stands in a dark
suit, smoking, a rifle
slung behind his shoulder, and glances
sideways at the camera
half smiling. It is July 20,
1936, and before the darkness
falls a darkness will have
fallen on him. While
the streets are echoing
with victory and revolution,
Francisco Ascaso will take up
the hammered little blade
of his spirit and enter for
the last time the republics
of death. I remember
his words to a frightened
comrade who questioned
the wisdom of attack: "We
have gathered here to die, but we
don't have to die with dogs,
so go." Forty-one years
ago, and now the city stretches
as far as the eye can see,
huge cement columns like nails
pounded into the once green
meadows of the Llobregat.
Your Barcelona is gone,
the old town swallowed
in industrial filth and
the burning mists of gasoline.
Only the police remain, armed
and arrogant, smiling masters
of the boulevards, the police
and your dream of the city
of God, where every man
and every woman gives
and receives the gifts of work

and care, and that dream
goes on in spite of slums,
in spite of death clouds,
the roar of trucks, the harbor
straining the mother sea,
it goes on in spite of all
that mocks it. We have it here
growing in our hearts, as
your comrade said, and when
we give it up with our last
breaths someone will gasp
it home to their lives.
Francisco, stone, knife blade,
single soldier still on
the run down the darkest
street of all, we will be back
across an ocean and a continent
to bring you red carnations,
to celebrate the unbroken
promise of your life that
once was frail and flesh.

In the spring of 1988 we returned to Spain for the first time since I wrote the poem some ten years before. It was a very different Spain we found under the governance of the Socialist Felipe González, and a very different "Catalunya," as we found it spelled in Catalan, now one of the legal languages of the region, though banished during the reign of Franco. A hipper, richer, more swinging, more exciting Barcelona, though the city had never fallen as heavily under the thumb of fascism as the rest of Spain. One of my reasons for going to Barcelona was to fulfill the vow made in the poem, to bring to the grave of Francisco Ascaso the red carnations I felt were the least tribute I could pay him for leading a life dedicated to anarchist principles, a life I could not lead but which had inspired me for over twenty years.

I should explain that, though the poem is true to my feelings about my visit to the cemetery, it neglects to mention the most dramatic encounter I had with the three graves, which took place during my second visit. I went there in the company of my wife, my oldest son, Mark, and his friend Geraldine Pontius, an architect. Geraldine had brought to Europe an expensive rented 16mm movie camera, and for the previous few days she had been filming the work of the great Catalan mystical architect Gaudí. In order to find the graves we drove to a small office, a registry of graves, and there I asked for the location of the grave of Ferrer; I knew the exact date of his burial. A young woman looked up the date in an enormous and ancient tome, but she could find no Ferrer, nor could she give me any hint as to the whereabouts of the grave. Finally I told her that the three graves were side by side, Ferrer, Ascaso, and Durruti. *"Ah, los anarquistas!"* she said, and she summoned a uniformed official. He asked if we had a car. Fine, I could follow him. Noticing a 35mm still camera in my hand, he remarked that I must take no photographs of the grave. Did I understand that? I assured him I did. Two civil guards sitting in a corner seemed to take no notice of us but went on smoking and chatting. The man in the uniform mounted a motor scooter, and we followed up and down some small hills over very narrow roads that were more like cart trails than anything else. Less than a half mile later he motioned us to park in a small open area. Before us were the graves, overlooking a road below that led up to the main portions of the Catholic cemetery; beyond the road, in the haze, we could see the roofs of warehouses, industrial buildings, and beyond them blocks of tenements. Beyond all that was the sea. As I had been told by my friend Flavio Costantini, the Italian anarchist painter, the original gravestones had been removed, and before us were three large slabs with nothing incised upon them, but, as I note in the poem, the names of the dead heroes were written with chalk and marking pencils, and there were a few flowers and other objects left for decorations or tributes.

My son Mark is not a temporizer. He went immediately to the trunk of the car and removed the Bolex and its tripod and began to film the scene. Not to be outdone, I took a few photos of the gravestones, one of which appears on the cover of my book *7 Years from Somewhere*, the book in which the Francisco poem first appeared. I stood there musing on the sacrifices of these three men, on the fact that so few of us knew they had lived and died in titanic struggles to liberate the human soul and mind, when suddenly I heard the roar of motorcycles. Before we could gather our wits, the two civil guards from the registry office were upon us. As the men approached me, I noticed that Mark had dropped the Bolex in the tall grass beside a path that led downward to the road. Without removing his helmet, the taller of the two Guardias approached me. "You were told not to take any pictures." "Yes," I said. "And this?" he said, pointing to the tripod Mark had set up. "Yes," I said, "we were thinking of taking some pictures." He nodded sadly at my folly, and then he and his colleague began searching the area, and within a few minutes they turned up the Bolex. "And how did this get here?" he asked. "I put it there," I said, "when I heard you coming." I didn't know if he knew I was lying. "It was my fault." Then I offered to remove the film and give it to him. No, he did not want the film, of what possible use could such film be to him? No, the film was totally without value. Then he asked me a curious question: "Do you ever suffer from insomnia?" I wasn't sure my Spanish was up to it; I thought I must be misunderstanding him and asked him to repeat the question. "Do you ever suffer from insomnia?" This time I answered, "Yes, sometimes I cannot sleep." "Next time you cannot sleep, look at this film a few times, and it will put you to sleep." And then he and his sidekick roared with laughter. I was being let go, and there followed a stern warning, which—believe me—I took seriously. We were ordered to pack up and leave immediately, and we did so. We had lived in Spain during the Franco era and knew the limitless powers of the Guardia.

So it was on a Sunday morning in April of 1988 that my wife and I purchased a huge bouquet of red carnations on the Ramblas, the great boulevard of Barcelona, one of whose *ramblas* is the Rambla de Flores, where flowers are sold seven mornings a week. We decided that it would be most fitting to take public transporation to the great cemetery of Montjuich, and after much questioning and searching we located what we thought was the proper bus stop. The presence of several women carrying small bouquets of flowers suggested we'd found the right one. To make sure, I asked an old man in a heavy tweed suit if I could get the bus here to the cemetery at Montjuich. He told me which bus to take and then asked if we were going to the unveiling of the monument to Luis Companys (pronounced "comPANCH"), whom I knew to have been the first president of Catalunya under the Republic. I told him I had not known of the ceremony, and that my wife and I were taking flowers to some old heroes of ours. He asked if I had been a Brigadista (a member of the International Brigades that fought in Spain on the Republican side during the civil war). I told him I was too young to have fought in the war, which ended when I was eleven. He, it turned out, was a veteran, having fought on the Republican side. He had lived thirty years in exile in southern France before he had been allowed to return to Spain without fear of reprisal. A small, stiff, formal man, he spoke without bitterness, but, like so many older Catalans, he was very reserved, though also very considerate, for when we arrived at the cemetery he directed us toward the office of grave registrations. There I encountered a different young woman. This time I did not ask for the graves of Ferrer, Durruti, and Ascaso, believing it was better not to mention them so as to avoid any interference. Instead I asked for the location of the Protestant cemetery, thinking I could orient myself to their graves from that point. The Protestant cemetery turned out, however, to be far larger than we had remembered, and we wandered for almost a half hour without finding the least sign of the little alcove that housed the graves of our heroes.

On the upper border of the Protestant cemetery, I found two motorcycle cops. The larger of the two cops politely removed his helmet, saluted me, dismounted his bike, and asked if he could be of help. He was an enormous man by any standards, but especially large by those of Spain. (In 1965 I was informed in a clothing store in Barcelona that they had in stock nothing that would fit a man of my size, and I am under five feet ten and weigh 160 pounds.) No doubt his black boots and heavy leather jacket made him seem even larger. I asked him if he knew the location of the graves of the three famous anarchists. Yes, he did, he could tell us how to get there, but he could not lead us there because he had this other duty. "Do you see those people in the distance?" and he pointed across an open meadow to where a few hundred people were gathered in front of what looked like an enormous stone. "They are here for the dedication of a monument to the memory of Luis Companys, the first president of Catalunya. They are mainly old people, those who survived the war, and it is my job to protect them. I don't think there is any danger, but it is better to be careful, you never know. . . ." Then he told us how we must find a particular footpath and descend it, taking each turn to the left, and go all the way down to the end

of the path, and we would be there. Seeing our puzzlement, he said something in Catalan to his silent comrade,
who never lifted his eyes from the distant group. "Come,
I will show you," and he began to lead us in the direction
of the path, but every few strides he took a worried look
back over his shoulder to observe the distant group.
Finally he found the path. "I cannot go any farther," he
said, "but if you will descend, taking each turn to the
left, always to the left, until you get to the end of the
path, you will find them. Okay?" We assured him that
it was OK, and he gave us a wonderfully full and open
smile and shook our hands and hurried back. What a
Spain, with policemen whose main concern was ordinary
people. I wondered if he were merely human or some
magical presence out of the Spanish poet Rafael Alberti's
great book *Sobre los ángeles* (On the Theme of Angels),
the Angel of Protectors become a Spanish cop.

We did our best to follow his instructions, but after
descending to the end of the path we still had not come
upon the little alcove we were seeking. I decided to start
over—there was nothing else for it—and we returned
to the grave-registry office and this time asked for the
location of the graves of the three. The woman knew
where they were, she assured me, but even with the aid
of a cemetery map she had difficulty showing me exactly
how to locate them. She phoned for help, and a middle-
aged man with steely-gray hair arrived, dressed in casual
wear. Could I wait a few minutes? If so he would be
glad to drive us there. On a stone bench my wife and I
waited outside in the soft, dusty light, curious once again
what "a few minutes" might mean in Spain and growing
ever more impatient to complete our mission.

True to his word, he reappeared within less than ten
minutes and directed us to a state car. It was the same
ride we had taken years before behind the man on the
motor scooter. This very amiable man asked if I'd been

a Brigadista, and once again I answered that I had been too young to fight in the war. He remarked that I didn't look it, and I had the sense that he was merely being objective and meant no offense. There were, he informed me, many Brigadistas buried in the cemetery. Americans? I asked. Oh, yes, Americans, English, French, Germans, men from everywhere who had come to fight for the Republic and had given their lives for the people of Spain. Like many Spaniards, he seemed to have no trouble rising to a moment of eloquence in praise of courage. I was somewhat surprised how easily he made his sympathies known in the presence of strangers. I remembered that in 1965 the easiest way to stop all the busy voices in a bar was to ask a question about the civil war. And then quite suddenly we were there. He showed us the road below, which we could take to get back. "You are sure you can make your way back to the bus?" I assured him we could and thanked him, and after the formal handshakes he left.

Then came the laying on of the carnations. This time there were real gravestones, each bearing not only the names and dates of the man but also some small tribute. Ferrer was identified as one who had begun a school which long before its time was teaching the principles of liberty, and for this he had been persecuted and finally killed. Durruti's most famous quotation marked his stone: "We carry a new world here in our hearts. That world is growing this minute." Ascaso was identified as the great anarchist who had led the assault on the Atarazanas barracks during the first hours of the civil war, a man who had given his life for the working people of Spain. My wife fanned out a dozen carnations on the stone of Ascaso, and there were some left for the other two stones, which once again bore flowers and tokens brought by others. Then we stood back in silence. Below us, in the distance, was the same view I had described in the poem, the smog perhaps a little thicker, for now there were even more cars in Spain and much more commercial activity on a Sunday.

This was a day of celebration for Companys, who had once worked as a lawyer defending members of the CNT. It was he who, after the military uprising had been put down, had invited the anarchists along with the other parties of the left to take part in governing Catalunya and waging the war. Durruti accepted for the CNT, and thus the anarchists joined the government and for some months dominated it.

Before the year was over the Durruti column would distinguish itself in desperate fighting on the Aragon front and Durruti himself would die in the defense of Madrid. A half million people—one of every four citizens of Barcelona—would turn out for his funeral, which was an incredible jumble, since no one led the crowd and two bands played at the same time and in different tempos. The coffin, carried on the shoulders of men from his column, surged back and forth for hours. The cars bearing the mountain of wreaths had to drive in reverse. An observer wrote, "It was an anarchist funeral—that was its majesty."

Fifty-six years later, the noon sun falling evenly into the little incised gutters of their names, I wondered if the wounds ever healed, or if the wounded merely passed from the earth to be replaced by new generations of the wounded. I took a photograph of each of the graves to show my son Mark. We allowed ourselves the luxury of a long silence, and then hand in hand my wife and I descended to the road, returning just in time to catch the bus back to the center of the city. It was the same driver we'd had earlier in the day, and he smiled at us in recognition. Even then, on the ride back, I knew I would never write the poem of this day. For one thing I was no longer an anarchist. "Property is theft," I had said so many times I'd tired of hearing my voice. Now I owned a house. I even voted for the impossible losing candidates the Democrats presented us every four years. For another thing, this was all too improbable. These dark marble stones with their beautiful brief inscriptions topping the graves of my heroes were merely tokens of the incredible changes that had come over this country as it advanced on the road toward the twenty-first century. All day I had been meeting people who openly expressed their thankfulness to those who had died in the struggle against oppression. And the police were now my friends. Two nights before two cops had shown us the proper way to walk to our favorite restaurant so as to avoid the junkies who hung out in the Barrio Chino and preyed on tourists. We must be careful, they told us, the junkies are dangerous. What I had said to Ascaso was true, his Barcelona was gone, but so was mine, the Barcelona in repressed rebellion and fear under the thumb of Franco. This was a new world, though not the one Durruti claimed to carry in his heart, not the anarchist ideal. How certain he had been back in 1936 in the first flush of victory over the fascists. "We are going to inherit the earth," he had said. "We have always lived in slums and holes in the wall." Within a few weeks, he believed, they would be fighting and winning the crucial battles of the war, and they, the workers, could rebuild the palaces and cities that the bourgeoisie would blast and ruin before they left the stage of history. Had they not built them in the first place? They, the workers, would inherit the earth. "There is not the slightest doubt about that," he had said.

On a bright spring morning the roads heading south were clogged with BMWs, VWs, Seats (the Spanish version of the Fiat) loaded with Sunday crowds heading for the beaches at Castelldefels and Sitges and the new bedroom communities of Barcelona. I knew how packed the trains would be, having taken them on just such a day as this. The workers and their children packed in as tightly as the worst parody of a New York City subway train at rush hour, and because they were Spaniards, crazy and daring young men would ride outside the cars holding on to the frames of open windows with all their might and howling with mad fear and glee as the train raced through the black tunnels. And after an afternoon of sun, sea, picnic, and siesta, the whole process would be repeated on the way home.

Walking aimlessly on the Ramblas that afternoon, I found representatives of almost every Spanish and Catalan political party. Below their colorful banners the men and women sat at long tables pushing their pamphlets, buttons, bumper stickers, and membership forms. To my surprise there was even a table representing the CNT and FAI (Iberian Anarchist Federation), now fighting for legalized abortion, the rights of women and gays, an end to nuclear power, a new version of Spain's ecology. Two young anarchists smiled at me as I purchased a number of items to help finance their work. The younger of the two seemed utterly shocked to discover I was an American from the U.S.A. "Do not forget," I said to this slender woman still in her teens, "we have a great tradition of anarchist struggle in the U.S.A."

"In the United States of America," she said, shaking her head in total disbelief.

"Yes," I said, "it began in the nineteenth century and came to its greatest fruition before and after World War I. You must have heard of the Wobblies."

"Wobblies?" she said, mispronouncing the word.

"Yes, the Industrial Workers of the World, who organized all over the Western states of the U.S.A. They were especially effective among the miners, and they took hard stands on behalf of working people. This was before most of the major industries of America were unionized."

She looked at me in disbelief. "In the United States of North America the major groups of industrial workers have formed trade unions?"

"Yes, of course," I went on, "but even before that there were the Industrial Workers of the World, a truly international union of workers who saw that their cause involved all the workers of the world. Many of them chose prison rather than serve in World War I. They felt a solidarity with workers in other countries and none with the American state."

She turned to her male comrade, a young bearded Catalan; he was wearing a down vest and a baseball cap with a CNT logo stitched on it. Did he know there were once anarchists in the United States of North America and they were called Wobblies? A short, squat man of no more than twenty-five, he rose slowly from his folding metal chair to shake my hand. Like a character in a comic strip he seemed visibly to be thinking. At last he nodded sagely. This was certainly possible. After all, anarchism was a great ideal capable of inspiring men and women for centuries. "It is possible that even in the United States of North America people could awaken to the limitations of capitalism and the monstrosity of private ownership. Yes, this is possible, even in the United States of North America."

I assured them both that we in America had our martyrs to the cause of the anarchist struggle. I was thinking specifically of Frank Little, who had once organized a free speech demonstration in downtown Fresno and was later hanged for organizing miners in Idaho. "Yes, we've had our heroes," I said. "Men and women of the courage and dedication of Ascaso and Durruti." They both nodded without enthusiasm. I told them about finding the graves years ago and returning this morning with red carnations for the new gravestones I'd discovered.

"Why would you do that?" the man said. I told them I did it to fulfill a promise. "A promise to whom?" he asked. I explained it was a promise I'd made in a poem, a poem that dealt with the life and death of Ascaso.

Across the way the elderly well-dressed members of

the Communist Party of Catalunya were folding their tables and repacking their pamphlets. The day's politics were ending. Down the way the General Union of Workers were preparing to make their departure. "Ascaso and Durruti," the young woman said. "You know who they were? You know they were *pistoleros*, you know they believed in 'Propaganda of the Deed,' what now we call terrorism?"

"They were important men in their time," the bearded man said. "We do not dispute that. But you should also know they were willing to take part in the government. Durruti asked his followers to risk their lives for the government of Spain, for the Republic, the same government that had jailed him. He compromised all those members of the CNT, he spoke of fighting the war first and only when it was over resuming the revolution. He even urged his old friend Federica Montseny to take a Cabinet position." I knew the old arguments, how the anarchists had betrayed their principles by working for victory before revolution, how Montseny had defied her own father, had risked what he called "the liquidation of anarchism." "Once in power, you will not rid yourself of power," her father had told her, and, true anarchist that she was, she had agonized over the decision.

The shadows were lengthening along the Ramblas. The music of the Sardana, the ancient traditional dance of Catalunya—banned during the Franco years—drifted in from the great plaza. Another Sunday was coming to an end. Through the eyes of these two young workers for anarchism, I saw myself in the year 1988, a befuddled elderly man with powerful sentimental attachments to the past and—for a North American—a curious knowledge of their own history. Tomorrow morning the work week would begin again for all these, a routine I no longer took part in. We smiled at each other one last time and shook hands. "No doubt your Wobblies were sincere people, as were our *pistoleros*," said the bearded man. "No doubt they labored with great dedication." No doubt, I agreed. He offered me as a gift a bumper sticker which proclaimed in Catalan a refusal to employ nuclear power. These young, somber anarchists had an entirely new agenda. Their civil war seemed more a part of my history than theirs. What could I do but accept the gift and thank them.

Two years passed. In the spring of 1990, I went to the University of Massachusetts to deliver the annual Troy Lecture, which I was told should "go beyond the parochial interests of English Professors to interest the larger academic community." The year before I'd been invited to the Folger Shakespeare Library in Washington, D.C., to speak in a series concerned with "socializing the private vision," and I had not given a talk on the relationship between poetry and anarchism, which had animated so much of my writing life. Instead I attempted to make clear that living American poets did not need on the one hand elitist critics and on the other socially conscious, well-meaning, unimaginative drones telling them what to write. I had hoped to make clear that our obsessions and concerns came to us and not we to them, and that whatever poets are given to write should be accepted as a gift they can only regard with awe and modesty. Curiously enough, it was not my choice to repeat this lecture. At the Folger and on one other occasion I felt the talk was misunderstood, and I was tired of presenting it and tired of myself for not writing something new. But the essay had recently been published in a literary review, and I had been asked specifically to read it. And it gave me an opportunity to see my friend Paul Mariani, who teaches at U. Mass., and who surely arranged for me to be that year's lecturer.

Years before, in an academic setting, I'd given a talk that arose out of my obsession with the Spanish Civil War and concerned the translation of historical events into poetry. I'd chosen to examine the assassination of a hero of the Spanish working people, an event that led directly to the civil war. In doing so I'd made my politics clear to a group of "good old boys" at the University of Cincinnati, where I was that year's Elliston Poetry Professor. The exchange—it was not a talk, because before I could get under way I was interrupted several times by the outraged academics—took place in a marvelous house built by Frank Lloyd Wright. The more abrasive they got, the more radical I got, until I suggested their marvelous suburbs in which they took so much pride might better be turned over to the working people of Cincinnati. It ended with my silent host driving me back to my dim apartment and another solitary night in the retirement home in which the English Department had lodged me. For years I had thought it better not to repeat that mistake. Now I was not so sure.

The night before the talk Paul had met me at the Hartford airport, and, leaving the darkened terminal, I was amazed by how warm the night winds felt; even in the darkness I could tell there were still some scraps of snow on the ground, but at 11:00 p.m. the odor of the earth and its return to life were thrilling. I had left a California which seemed in perpetual spring and returned to the drama of my Midwestern boyhood. Before we retired that night, Paul asked me if I'd be willing to visit his modern-poetry class the next day, and I had agreed to do so. The poet under discussion was Yeats.

Awakening the next morning, I found what looked like the return of winter. At breakfast Paul did his best to make me feel I'd come to New England at the most glorious moment of the year. Outside his kitchen window a great variety of birds collected at the feeder, including bright tanagers and finches I never see in California. In

the fields beside the rain-slickened road from Montague
to Amherst he pointed out a little pale bloom of a crocus
dying of loneliness. I started to tell him about the overpowering perfume of orange blossoms that filled my
house two nights before, and then, realizing my rudeness,
I stopped. I recalled a good-natured argument between
my mentor Yvor Winters and that amazing critic Kenneth Burke. Burke had come west in the spring of '58,
and Winters tried to overwhelm him with the profusion
and variety of California trees. Burke countered by
claiming that nothing he'd seen in Winters's garden
rivaled in nobility his beloved Northeastern apple trees.
Winters, whose bent was toward the plain style in life
and poetry, had to concede.

In Amherst the huge campus hunkered down under
a cold wind and a leaden sky that promised more rain,
which was already arriving in little frozen spurts. Paul's
classroom was the usual: low ceiling, hideous artificial
lights that suggested a bus station, four rows of desks
facing the "business end" of the room, where Paul and
I seated ourselves behind the protection of a battered oak
desk. The students filed in, a friendly-looking crew of
all ages. Dressed as they were in gear suitable for hiking,
most of the men bearded or unshaven, none of the women
wearing makeup, they reminded me of the people I get
in my classes at Fresno State, the students I've grown
comfortable with.

Paul proved a skillful lecturer; without notes he moved
easily from one period of Yeats's work to another, bringing the relevant Irish history to bear. The students already seemed familiar with Yeats's cosmology and its
special vocabulary. After a muscular, impassioned reading of "The Second Coming" the class sat for some moments in silence. Paul was clearly waiting for a response,
and so I asked him, "Aside from the glory of the writing,
what do you think of the poem?" And of course he asked
me, "What do you think?"

I answered that I was dazzled by Yeats's ability in 1919 to forecast the rise of totalitarianism in Europe and the nightmare of World War II. But I was deeply offended by his notion that the best lacked all conviction while the worst were full of passionate intensity, then or now. For me the great lesson of the 1960s was that those who dared to stand in the way of America's war machine did so out of a genuine and passionate commitment to the deepest human values. Underneath all the commercially viable styles in music, dress, and drugs, I'd seen for the first time in my life millions of our young and no longer young willing to pay an enormous price for their beliefs. What was it that animated those who were able to face the batons of the police, the censure of their families and friends, and finally exile, prison, or worse? Perhaps through the flawed lens of my anarchist beliefs, I saw the old vision that the earth belongs to no one, that we all come for a little time to act as stewards of the place, obliged to do our best to leave it in as good shape as we found it. And why did so many Americans find it intolerable that these Asian stewards were being killed in their name? Perhaps they believed that we are all one being and as such the children of God, as anarchism teaches.

As for those lacking all conviction, I recalled a colleague and office mate who accompanied me to a protest march on campus; one moment he was beside me, and the next he had vanished. When it was over and none of us was hurt, though clearly our identities had been noted, I found him back in the office, immersed in the silent study of his books. Surely he was not the best among us. No religion puts the fence sitters in heaven.

I didn't mean to suggest that all self-styled anarchists are devoted to the well-being of the human animal; anarchism has its pure theorists. Back in 1980, when I was living in a small apartment in downtown San Francisco, two young anarchist thinkers came to interview me. One was very disappointed to discover that I had not worked in factories in Detroit to help form cadres of the working class; that my aim had been to make enough money to live on. Finally he interrupted a long spiel of mine on the heroism of Durruti and Ascaso to tell me that most young people would find my interest in those men "tacky." "Tacky?" I asked. "Why?" "It's just so extreme," he said, and I realized that he did not mean most young people, he meant himself. My tackiness was not really the point anyway. What he had discovered was that I was irrelevant, for I was far more obsessed with the men and women who had lived and died for anarchism than the theories that motivated them. He had discovered the truth: I was in love with those people and therefore untrustworthy.

Paul moved on to a discussion of "Sailing to Byzantium." Struck by the fact that I was the same age Yeats was when he wrote the poem, struck and humbled also, I felt it was ridiculous of me to be vexed by the poem (even the verb is Yeats's). Paul was fascinated by the presence of the Grecian goldsmiths and saw in them the image of the "artificer," the model for the poet Yeats aspired to be.

> Once out of nature I shall never take
> My bodily form from any natural thing.
> But such a form as Grecian goldsmiths make
> Of hammered gold and gold enamelling
> To keep a drowsy Emperor awake;
> Or set upon a golden bough to sing
> To lords and ladies of Byzantium
> Of what is past, or passing, or to come.

"Once out of nature," Yeats chose to entertain the master of a slave society so rigid that no one escaped the station of birth. He would sing to the lords and ladies of the place, perhaps for his supper, if golden birds eat; he would sing to the very people who in real life I would like to strangle. Once out of nature, I knew I would be nothing or at most a remembered voice, hopefully the voice of my poetry, and if that poetry proved worthy, perhaps a voice as authentic and powerful as the voice of my lost Cipriano, who seemed even in his living flesh to be pared down to the essential. No one else I'd ever known either in his physical or spiritual presence came so close to being "out of nature." He dared each day to live for the sake of "The Idea" and if need be for the sake of it to surrender the little that was left of him. In a poem written years before I had implored him to return to me and rekindle my faith.

> Come back, Cipriano Mera, step
> out of the wind and dressed in the robe
> of your pain tell me again this
> world will be ours. Enter my dreams
> or my life, Cipriano, come back
> out of the wind.

Of course for a poet there is something wonderful in Yeats's notion of being transformed into a magical bird, one who might sing with the perfection denied the living writer. But why sing to the courtiers of a vanished world? In his poem "Winds of the People," the great Spanish poet Miguel Hernández also imagines himself transformed into a singing bird. He accepts his death in battle against the tyrannical forces of Franco's army but asks to remain an inspiration to his comrades,

> for there are nightingales
> above the rifle fire
> there where our fight is, singing.

Before he moved on, Paul noted how original it was of Yeats to choose Byzantium and to avoid Rome and Jerusalem, the traditional holy cities of European poets.

A young, studious-looking man directed a disturbing question at Paul and me. For the sake of the poem had Yeats deliberately avoided those aspects of Byzantine culture which did not suit his purposes? I started to answer that that was exactly what he'd done—though a hierarchical society would hardly have offended Yeats the way it would offend most young Americans—and then it struck me that I was simplifying what I had no right to simplify, for like Yeats I'd chosen a holy city and my allegiance to it was far more powerful than anything I'd managed to express in my poetry. I'd made my pilgrimage to Barcelona over and over and unquestioningly accepted all its lessons. I'd made certain of its heroes the high priests of my life. I needed my Barcelona, I needed to uncover somewhere in the history of the failed attempts of men and women to create a decent society an experiment that worked, and, having half-found it in the violent struggles of Spanish anarchism, I'd clung to it no matter what, no matter that Ascaso probably assassinated the archbishop of Saragossa, no matter that he and Durruti robbed banks to fund their exploits, no matter that Durruti's "discipline of indiscipline" was a military disaster, no matter that "Propaganda of the Deed" was terrorism. I recounted for the class a passage from Hugh Thomas's monumental history of the Spanish Civil War in which Thomas describes the anarchists of Barcelona killing "as if they were mystics" in order to crush the material things of this world, choosing indiscriminately anyone who displayed a bourgeois past. Victims were trucked thirty miles down the coast to be shot overlooking the dazzling Bay of Sitges. "Those about to die," wrote Thomas, "would pass their last moments on earth looking out to sea in the marvelous Mediterranean dawn. 'See how beautiful life could have been,' their assassins seemed to be saying, 'if only you had not been a bourgeois and had got up early and had seen the dawn more often—as workers do.' "

The class was stunned by this fragment of anarchist history as well as by my allegiance to such a movement. Of course the centuries of violence done to these workers had to produce an equal violence. The students were unconvinced. A hushed atmosphere invaded the room. I was no longer a sixty-two-year-old "smiling public man." In recounting the events, I felt a portion of my old pride in the worthiness of the anarchist vision and the totally uncompromising behavior of its adherents. Had I apologized for anything, it would have been my failure to live as an anarchist, having so long ago discovered "The Idea."

The time has come to bring this tale to an end, but since, as I wrote earlier, most of the stories that make up my life have no beginning or ending, I shall have to compose one. So let the class turn their attention back to the poetry of Yeats, this time to my favorite poem of his, "Lapis Lazuli." Let the students bow their heads to attend to their texts as Paul reads aloud with serenity and passion. Let all those present, teacher, students, guest, allow the words to enter their minds and hearts, let them be momentarily overwhelmed as the poem sings to its extraordinary ending.

> Every discoloration of the stone,
> Every accidental crack or dent,
> Seems a water-course or an avalanche,
> Or lofty slope where it still snows
> Though doubtless plum or cherry-branch
> Sweetens the little half-way house
> Those Chinamen climb towards, and I
> Delight to imagine them seated there;
> There, on the mountain and the sky,
> On all the tragic scene they stare.
> One asks for mournful melodies;
> Accomplished fingers begin to play.
> Their eyes mid many wrinkles, their eyes,
> Their ancient, glittering eyes, are gay.

Somewhere bells sound the noon hour. The students file out in silence and, once released from this odd encounter, resume their usual lives. Now their good-natured chatter echoes down the halls. Paul packs up his books and papers. The guest stares out the window. The sky is lifting, and high above, the sun seems for a moment about to peep through. All their adult lives these students of poetry have climbed between heaven and earth and, wearied, have stopped to look down "on all the tragic scene." Let the guest realize that no matter what he has climbed toward he has never left the world below, that tangled mess he would escape only at his own peril. And what has he climbed toward? Perhaps a "lofty slope where it still snows," perhaps a sky unsullied by our human blunders, perhaps the holy cities of the world and of the imagination, Detroit, Barcelona, Byzantium, stained with our blood.

Entering Poetry

Not until my thirteenth year did I fully discover the pleasures of solitude; this was at the same time I also began to discover the magic and variety of the natural world. That seems a little late in life, but I grew up in a city, one I liked, and my elders were seldom called upon to take me away for more than a day trip to a nearby lake or amusement park. At the age of eight my twin brother, Eddie, and I were sent to a dilapidated summer camp for several weeks. The food was so tasteless and meager we scarcely ate, and the evening we returned to town we greedily devoured my grandmother's heavy cooking only to spend a long night vomiting by turns in the bathroom. The next morning the family doctor was sent for, and my mother's fears were calmed when he informed her that such eruptions were general throughout Detroit as boys and girls returned from their various summer outings. Thereafter Eddie and I remained in town during the long summers.

As the years passed I began to find dinner increasingly

difficult. It was the only time the family assembled, and thus it often became the arena for the resolution of daily grudges. I was as much at fault as anyone. I frequently ate in as slovenly and loud a manner as I could command, as though I intended to drive my mother and brothers away from the table. Only my fingernails were filthier than my language. It did no good to race through the meal. My mother was doing her best to bring us into harmony, and we were required to remain until the last morsel was consumed. Eddie was a very elegant eater; he no longer switched his knife and fork from hand to hand as I did. He ate slowly, methodically, and with great satisfaction, and he ate a lot. I envied his style and patience. Even after dinner, in the room we shared I found little peace. Although we were no longer addicted to torturing each other, as in years past, no true fellowship had replaced our rivalry. It should have, for we were both preoccupied with gaining revenge from all those who belittled or insulted us, from Adolf Hitler to our shop teacher. "I'll give no quarter and I'll take no quarter," Eddie stated with typical gusto. (He'd already discovered Sir Walter Scott.) I'd seen him fight and knew he was serious. When he got another boy down he would kick him with all his considerable might. Only the tallest and toughest of the Episcopal boys at our new school called him a dirty Jew.

The year was 1941. My mother had just purchased a house near the outskirts of the city, located on an almost vacant block. There were similar square, two-storied houses on each side of ours and two houses directly across from ours and from the house of Steve Psaris, our neighbor to the north. There was also one house directly behind ours. To the east were two blocks of fields and then Livernois, a wide, four-lane avenue famous for its profusion of used-car lots. To the west were two totally undeveloped blocks, still deeply wooded with maple, elm, and beech and thick underbrush. In my imagination this settlement of six families was a tiny America, an outpost of civilization between a vast open prairie and the mysterious darkness of a wilderness.

When I sneaked out of the house after dinner each night I headed directly for the security of the dense thickets and trees. Once into the woods, I would make my way to one of my favorite trees, most often a large copper beech whose low branches spread out almost horizontally, and lean back and survey the night sky. There was no industry in this part of the city, and so the stars were visible and on some nights spectacular. One night I began to speak both to and of them. Immediately I felt something enormously satisfying about this speaking, perhaps because nothing came back in the form of an argument. It was utterly unlike any speaking I'd either heard or made before. I liked the way my voice, which was just changing, would gather itself around or within certain sounds, the "r" of "rains," the long open "o" sound of "moon." I would say "rain" and "moon" in the same sentence and hear them echo each other, and a shiver of delight would pass through me. On cloudy, starless nights, when the air seemed dense and close, I'd hurl my new voice out at the sky by saying, "The clouds obscure the stars," one tiny delicious sentence, but for the most part I was not brief. Best were those nights after a hard rain. In the darkness the smell of the wet earth would fill my head almost to the bursting point. "The damp earth is giving birth," I would say, and then in sentence after sentence I'd go on to list all that was being born within and outside me, though in the dense night I could hardly discern where I ended and the rest of the world began.

I was no longer addressing the stars, for often they had deserted me. Was I addressing God? I'm sure I was not, for I had no belief in a God who could hear me even though I was learning Hebrew and reading the Bible and discussing its deeper meanings each week with my instructor, a chubby-handed little man who was preparing himself for the rabbinate. Quite simply, Eddie and I had worked it out together and come to a complete accord: there was no God or any chosen people. "What the fuck were we chosen for?" Eddie would shout out after one of our frequent losing battles with the taller Episcopalians, most of whom were driven to school in long Lincolns or Packards, while we made the mile-and-a-half trek on foot even in the worst weather. No, I believe I was already a blooming Platonist addressing the complement, all that I was not and yearned to become. When I was in the crow's nest of my copper beech the wet-earth smells rose around me and the wind quivered the hard leaves and carried my voice out to the edges of the night; I could almost believe someone was listening and that each of my words, freighted with feeling, truly mattered. I was certain I was becoming a man.

One spring day, returning from school through the great prairie east of our house, I came across a wild iris, a tiny purple thing growing on its own, just a single bloom with no sign of a neighbor, doing its solitary best to enlighten the afternoon. I ran home and returned with a bucket and shovel from the garage. I dug up the iris, making sure to take plenty of dirt and being careful not to sever the roots. In our backyard I dug up a few square feet of sod near the back fence and planted the wildflower. I watered it carefully, but even by dinnertime it looked as though it had had it, so pitifully did it sag. By morning it was a goner. On Saturday I combed the open fields and found two more wild irises. I dug a second hole and planted the two side by side, this time preparing the ground with a dark, evil-smelling fertilizer I'd bought at Cunningham's Drug Store. I watered one flower hardly at all for fear I might have drowned the first iris. By later afternoon it was clear they'd both died. I asked the advice of Sophie Psaris, Steve's wife, who seemed able to make anything grow. She assured me that not even she could transplant a wildflower and make it grow. As a girl in Salonika, she'd fallen in love with the blood-red poppies that stained the meadows each April, but though she'd tried to get them to take hold in her mother's garden, she'd always failed. "Try rosebushes," she said. "The flowers are beautiful and they grow easily." I decided there was something proper about the irises' stubborn refusal to grow inside our fenced yard, something dignified in their preferring death to captivity. Never again would I interfere.

A week later, with money earned from washing windows, I bought my first rosebush, a little thorny stick of a thing with its dirt-encrusted roots wrapped in burlap. "You want something that will grow like mad?" said Bert, the little wizened Englishman who worked in the garden section of Cunningham's. For sixty-nine cents he let me have a mock orange. In no time at all, he assured me, it would be taller than I, but, then, I was still less than five feet tall. "Why do you call it a mock orange?" I asked. "Because that's its name. You see, it doesn't give any oranges; you can't grow oranges this far north. It's not even a tree—it's a shrub—but the blossoms look and smell like real orange blossoms."

The instructions for planting the rose spoke of "sandy loam" and the need to place the roots six to nine inches deep into this "sandy loam." After my disasters with the irises, I was hesitant and so took a handful of our backyard dirt to show Sophie. "Is this sandy loam?" I asked. She took a pinch from my open palm between her thumb and forefinger and smelled it and then put a few grains on her tongue and spit them out. "Pheelip," she said in her heavily accented English, "this is just dirt, you know, dirt that comes from the ground." This didn't really answer my question, so with no little trepidation I took a second handful to Cunningham's to show Bert. Was this in fact sandy loam? He stared at me in silence for half a minute and then cocked his head to one side. Why was I asking? I explained how the instructions had spoken of a six- to nine-inch hole in "sandy loam." "Where'd you get this?" he said. I told him I'd dug it out of a hole in my backyard. "Yes, of course you did," he said, "it's dirt, it'll do just fine. Call it 'sandy loam' if you'd like." He assured me that if I just planted the thing in a hole and gave it some water it would grow. "It's a lot less fussy than we are," he added.

Somewhat heartened, I returned home and planted the mock orange in the already fertilized hole that had failed the iris and planted the rose beside the fence separating our lot from Steve Psaris's driveway. I liked the way my hands smelled afterward. I washed away the grosser signs of their filthiness, but I was careful to leave just enough dirt under my fingernails so that whenever I wanted to I could catch a whiff of the earth's curious pungency that suggested both tobacco and rust. Though the soil of our backyard was a dull gray-brown, the perfume was a foxy red.

The rose especially was such a sad little thing that in spite of Bert's encouragement I was certain it would not survive, but within a week tiny reddish twigs began to jut out from the woody gray stick. I would press my thumb against the new thorns just to feel their sharpness against my skin. Eddie liked to speak of something he called a "blood oath," a vow taken by two strong men and sealed by the mixing of their blood. At the time he was reading Dumas and Sabatini and often spoke also of taking fencing lessons, though we knew no one in Detroit who gave them. One day I considered puncturing my skin against the largest of the thorns, but I stopped short of this gesture. Sophie had assured me the buds would come as they had on their bushes. I knew from watching them they would transform themselves from hard green almond-shaped stones to the swelling red-tipped about-to-be-flowers.

One late-May morning, I glanced out of the back window of the breakfast nook to discover the mock orange in bloom. Caught up in the excitement of the beginning of the baseball season, I'd not been paying attention and was taken by surprise. There were suddenly more than a dozen tiny blossoms and a rich, deep perfume that reminded me of the perfume of my Aunt Belle, my mother's younger sister. After school I cut a small branch of three blossoms and placed it in a glass of water and set it in the middle of the dining-room table. To my surprise, that evening no one noticed it, and dinner passed with Eli, my older brother, discussing his plans for a camping trip in northern Canada. I listened in silence, and when the others had left the table I dropped the little branch down the front of my shirt.

The days were lengthening, and it was still light out when I sneaked out of the house after helping with the dishes. I made my way to the deepest center of the woods and climbed a young maple tree and gazed up into the deepening sky above. I must have dozed off for a few minutes, because quite suddenly the stars emerged in a blacker sky. Although I did not know their names—in fact, I did not even know they had names—I began to address them quietly, for I never spoke with "full-throated ease" until hidden by the cover of total darkness. A soft wind shook the leaves around me. From my own hands I caught the smell of earth and iron, which now I carried with me at all times. I reached down my shirt and extracted the mock-orange branch and breathed in the deep feminine odors while between thumb and forefinger I fretted the blossoms until they fell apart. I began then to address my own hands, which seemed somehow to have been magically transformed into earth. For the first time a part of me became my night words, for now the darkness was complete. "These hands have entered the ground from which they sprang," I said, and, tasting the words, I immediately liked them and repeated them, and then more words came that also seemed familiar and right. Then I looked on the work my hands had wrought, then I said in my heart, As it happened to the gardener, so it happened to me, for we all go into one place; we are all earth and return to earth. The dark was everywhere, and as my voice went out I was sure it reached the edges of creation. I was sure too my words must have smelled of sandy loam and orange blossoms. That was the first night of my life I entered poetry.

In the spring of 1952 in Detroit, I was working at Chevrolet Gear and Axle, the "abandoned factory" of a poem in my first book, *On the Edge*, and I hated the job more than any I'd had before or have had since, not only because it was so hard, the work so heavy and monotonous that after an hour or two I was sure each night that I would never last the shift, but also because it was dangerous. There in the forge room, where I worked until I was somehow promoted to a less demanding, equally boring job, the stock we handled so gingerly with tongs was still red-hot as we pulled it from the gigantic presses and hung it above us on conveyors that carried our handiwork out of sight. Others had mastered the art of handling the tongs loosely, the way a good tennis player handles his racquet as he approaches the net for a drop volley, applying just enough pressure not to let go and not enough to choke it. Out of fear I squeezed for all I was worth, and all the good advice, the coaching I received from my fellow workers, was of no use.

One night, just after we'd returned to our machines after the twenty-minute break, the guy I was working with—a squat, broad-shouldered young black man whose energy and good spirits I'd admired for weeks—tapped me on the shoulder and indicated with a gesture that I should step aside. Together we'd been manning a small punch press; he handed me the stock that came along a conveyor, I inserted it in the machine, had it punched, and then hung it on another conveyor. On this occasion he said nothing, though even if he had I wouldn't have heard him over "the oceanic roar of work." He withdrew a short-handled sledgehammer from inside his shirt and, gripping it with both hands, hammered furiously at the press's die. He then inserted a piece of stock in the machine, tripped the button that brought the press down, and leaped aside before the press could whip the metal out of his hands. The press froze. I went to summon the foreman, Lonnie, while my partner disposed of the hammer. Lonnie took one look at the machine and summoned two men senior to him, or so I assumed since they arrived dressed in business suits. For twenty minutes they searched the area. I finally figured out that they were looking for the instrument with which the press had been sabotaged. Then they separated us and grilled me. There was no question, they assured me, that the press bore the marks of violence. What had "the nigger" done? I answered that I'd seen nothing out of the ordinary, the machine just broke down, almost tore my hands apart. Oh, they looked at each other, I wanted it *that* way. Well, they could certainly accommodate me. Before the night was over, I was back on the "Big Press," handling those red-hot sections of steel, my hands stiffening and kinking inside the huge gauntlets. Within a few days I was once again dreaming of fire as my hands gnarled even in sleep. I lasted a few more weeks, and when it became obvious that the "Big Press" was mine forever, I quit.

Five years later, while living in Palo Alto, California, on a writing grant from Stanford University, I received an article clipped from a Detroit newspaper and mailed to me. It told of the closing of Chevrolet Gear and Axle; its functions had been moved to a new, highly automated plant near Pontiac. I had already tried at least a dozen times to capture the insane, nightmarish quality of my life at Chevy: that epic clanging of steel on steel, the smell of the dead rats we poisoned who crawled off into their secret places and gained a measure of revenge, the freezing winds at our backs as winter moved through the broken windows, the awesome heat in our faces, those dreamlike moments when the lights failed and we stood in darkness and the momentary silence of the stilled machines. In the springlike winter of 1957, sitting in the little poetry room of the Stanford library, which was mine alone each morning, half a country and a universe away from Chevy, I could recall almost without hatred that old sense of utter weariness that descended each night from my neck to my shoulders, and then down my arms to my wrists and hands, and how as the weeks had passed my body had changed, thickening as though the muscles and tendons had permanently swelled, so that I carried what I did with me at all times, even when I lifted a pencil to write my poems. It was not the thickening heaviness of myself I tried to capture in my abandoned-factory poem—I only managed a glimmer of that—for I was determined to say something about the importance of the awfulness I had shared in and observed around me, a worthy aim, certainly, but one that stopped me from writing the poetry of what I had most deeply and personally experienced.

Seven years later, in the spring of 1964, I was living in a large airy house in Fresno, California, a house of beautiful slow dawns. Each morning I would waken early, before six, and watch the light—yellow and pale green as it filtered through the leaves of the sycamore outside my bedroom—transform the darkness into fact, clear and precise, from the tiled floor to the high, sloping, unfinished wooden ceiling. It was a real California house. I would rise, toss on a bathrobe, and work at my poems for hours seated at the kitchen table, work until the kids rising for school broke my concentration. To be accurate, I would work unless the morning were spoiled by some uncontrollable event, like a squadron of jet fighters slamming suddenly over the low roofs of the neighborhood, for we lived less than a quarter mile from a National Guard airfield.

One morning in April of that year I awakened distressed by a dream, one that I cannot call a nightmare, for nothing violent or terribly unpleasant had occurred in it. I dreamed that I'd received a phone call from a man I'd known in Detroit, Eugene Watkins, a black man with whom I'd worked for some years in a grease shop there. Eugene was a tall, slender man, ten years older than I, and although he had his difficulties at home he rarely spoke of them. In fact he rarely spoke. What I remember most clearly about working beside him was that I never liked schlepping or loading or unloading in tandem with him because he had a finger missing on his left hand, and I had some deep-seated fear that whatever had caused that loss could easily recur, and I didn't want the recurrence to take some treasured part of myself. The dream was largely a phone conversation, one in which I could see Eugene calling from a phone booth beside U.S. 99 in Bakersfield, 120 miles south of where I lived. He'd called to tell me he was in California with his wife and daughter. They'd driven all the way from Detroit and had just arrived. They wanted to know what they should do and see while they were in the West. As I babbled on about the charms of Santa Monica, L.A.'s Miracle Mile, the fashionable restaurants neither they nor I could afford, the scenic drive up U.S. 1 to Big Sur, I knew that what Eugene was actually seeking was an invitation to visit me. I even mentioned the glories of Yosemite and Kings Canyon National Park—neither more than an hour from where I lived—and yet I never invited him. Finally he thanked me for all the information I'd given him, said goodbye, and quietly hung up. In the dream I saw him leave the phone booth and shamble, head down, back to the car, exactly as I would have in his place. I awakened furious with myself for my cold-

ness, my lack of generosity, my snobbery. Why, I asked
myself, had I behaved this way? Was it because Eugene
was black? Several black friends had visited my house.
Because he was working-class? I was living in a largely
working-class neighborhood. (Who else has an airfield
at the end of the block?) Did I think I was so hot with
my assistant professorship at a second-rate California
college, with my terrific salary that was probably no
more than Eugene earned? Was I trying to jettison my
past and join the rising tide of intellectuals, car salesmen, TV repairmen, and bank managers who would
make it to the top? What the hell was I becoming?

It finally occurred to me that I had not rejected Eugene, my past, the city of my birth, or anything. I had
had a dream, and that dream was a warning of what
might happen to me if I rejected what I'd been and who
I was. The kids were up and preparing for school, so I
climbed back in bed with my yellow legal pad and my
pen. I was in that magical state in which nothing could
hurt me or sidetrack me; I had achieved that extraordinary level of concentration we call inspiration. When I
closed my eyes and looked back into the past, I did not
see the blazing color of the forges of nightmare or the
torn faces of the workers. I didn't hear the deafening
ring of metal on metal, or catch under everything the
sweet stink of decay. Not on that morning. Instead I was
myself in the company of men and women of enormous
sensitivity, delicacy, consideration. I saw us touching
each other emotionally and physically, hands upon shoulders, across backs, faces pressed to faces. We spoke to
each other out of the deepest centers of our need, and we
listened. In those terrible places designed to rob us of our
bodies and our spirits, we sustained each other.

The first lines I wrote were for Eugene Watkins. I
imagined us together in the magical, rarefied world of
poetry, the world I knew we would never enter. Although
it's snowing there, when we leave the car to enter the

unearthly grove, no snow falls on our hair or on the tops of our shoes because "It's the life of poems; / the boughs expensive, our feet dry." But of course that was not the world I was returning to; I wanted to capture in my poetry the life Eugene and I had shared, so before the poem ("In a Grove Again") ends, the grove transforms itself into any roadside stop where two guys might pause to take a piss:

Meanwhile back in the car there are talismans:

A heater, the splashed entrails of newspapers,
A speedometer that glows and always reads 0.
We have not come here to die. We are workers
And have stopped to relieve ourselves, so we sigh.

I remained in bed much of that week. The poems were coming, and for reasons I couldn't explain, I felt my inspiration had something to do with the particular feel and odor of the bed. While there I wrote most of the Detroit poems that appear in my second book, *Not This Pig*. I believe that they were the first truly good poems I'd written about the city. They are by no means all sweetness and light. There was and still is much that I hate about Detroit, much that deserves to be hated, but I had somehow found a "balanced" way of writing about what I'd experienced; I'd tempered the violence I felt toward those who'd maimed and cheated me with a tenderness toward those who had touched and blessed me.

Class with No Class

In my mind's eye I see Zach Chase as a great patriarchal figure, a white-haired man of perhaps six feet, barrel-chested, commanding, as he sits at the head of a long glass-topped breakfast-nook table where dinner is always served unless special company is present, and I am not special company. Behind him leaded windows give onto the backyard and the four-car garage, the doors of which are raised, revealing three of the family's cars, all Cadillac sedans. The fourth, a smart little La Salle coupe, is not visible. Mr. Chase is talking loudly on the phone while the youngest of the three female servants clears the soup plates from the table as another brings on the meat dish. His sons whisper back and forth across from each other, the younger, Kenny, imploring his large sulking brother to please pass the crackers, which he will not do. Meanwhile Mrs. Chase—Maddie to her husband and friends but always Mrs. Chase to me—dressed in a flowered silky dress (probably genuine silk), her graying hair falling about her sculptured jaw, rambles on about the lateness of the arrival of spring to our town. I am as usual distracting myself by staring at the brooding seascape above Kenny's head, a curious painting to be hanging in such an airy, light-filled room. "A genuine Matt Meader," Zach Chase one evening assured me when he caught my stare.

"I don't wait five days to cash a check," says Mr. Chase into the receiver nestled lovingly beneath his chin. I want to put a large Cuban cigar into Zach's right hand, but in fact Mr. Chase does not smoke; he leaves that to his wife, who when she has the time employs a cigarette holder reminiscent of FDR's, perhaps her least favorite dead person, "a traitor to his class," as she described him to me when he bowed out near the end of this terrible war. "I have a check," Mr. Chase goes on, "I send someone to the bank so I can make money out of it. Otherwise it's not a check, it's only a slip of paper." Gently he removes the phone from its cradle under his chin; a voice can be heard speaking at the other end. He hangs up and smiles at those present. "Maddie, that was your brother. How can we do business together? Forty-six, he doesn't know a check." He shakes his head sadly.

Maddie smiles and remarks that the lamb will get cold unless it's passed around soon. Zach shrugs, checks his watch, and then slowly and deliberately loads his plate. He passes the platter to Leonard, who does not sulk to his father's face. What am I doing here at the distant end of this enormous table seated next to Mrs. Maddie Chase and suffering through a meal of canned cream-of-mushroom soup followed by overcooked lamb and curdling mashed potatoes? I am the tutor for the Detroit family Chase, whose chief duty it is to see that little Kenny, who can barely read at age fourteen, will somehow mysteriously pass from sixth grade, where he has languished for two years, into seventh grade, where he will go on paying attention to nothing except his wardrobe—which he spends hours discussing with me—and masturbation, which neither of us mentions. I am earning two dollars an hour, which for part-time labor is unheard of for a high-school kid, even such skilled labor as mine in the year 1945, but, then, I have taken on a task as difficult as cleaning out the Augean stables, and the tools with which to do it have not yet been invented. Little Kenny, though not retarded, is not swift, and he is totally indifferent to exiting sixth grade or to any sort of academic achievement. In fact he seems quite delighted with himself and his situation, and though small for his age and exceedingly rat-faced with his high narrow forehead and long tapering nose, he is utterly confident that he is attractive to girls. When we are seated side by side at the desk in his capacious room on the second floor of Maison Chase in an area of Detroit known as Sherwood Forest, he likes to assure me that clothes make the man, and although he is still so short and skinny he must buy his jackets and trousers in boy's sizes, he already owns three double-breasted midnight-blue suits, which he believes help lend him an air of maturity and confidence. When I push elementary arithmetic problems in his face, he sighs and for a few moments pretends he's actually considering them, but when he asks a question it almost always has to do with clothes. How do I think a very light, long-collared shirt will go with one of his midnight-blue suits, for example? And a black knit tie?

Mr. Chase has asked me to stay after coffee, for there are a few questions he would like to ask. Kenny smiles, Leonard sighs, Maddie goes on about her tulips and irises, none of which seem to be doing much of anything although this is mid-April in Michigan, and the bulbs are genuine pre-war, all the way from Holland. The young woman now serving the sagging mounds of vanilla ice cream—the only flavor Zach cares for—is black and about my age, and although she is in my high-school senior class we know each other barely at all, but, then, there are over a thousand students in my class. Her name is Gwen, and for this job she has been asked to wear a starched white dress that barely covers her knees. She moves with wonderful ease and grace as she holds her head very erect as though she were acting the part of a serving maid in a Noël Coward play. She smiles discreetly at me as she places the ice cream before me and turns to leave the room.

"Gwen," says Zach Chase, "tell me something."

"Yes, Mr. Chase." She stands speechless now, her body still and turned toward the door, her head facing Mr. Chase, who has bowed to his ice cream.

After dabbing his lips with a white linen napkin, Mr. Chase looks up and poses his question. "Do you think Phil is a good-looking boy?" I feel myself blush as I look away from Gwen. I have no idea why this question has been asked. I cannot tell if Gwen is as embarrassed as I, for she is deeply immersed in her English tea-maid role, but it is clear to me that Mr. Chase is eyeing her with frank lust.

"Why, of course," says Gwen carefully, "he's handsome. All the boys in this house are handsome," and without looking back she exits through the swinging door to the kitchen.

The room is silent for more than a minute, and it is a while before I realize that at the least Zach's question has called a halt to the babbling of his wife, who at last pushes her untouched ice cream away from her and in a loud and unusually commanding voice addresses her husband, "Zach, you are not thinking . . . ?" But before she can get any farther into the question it is clear from the shaking of his head that Mr. Isaac Chase has indeed not been thinking the unthinkable.

Then what was Zach Chase thinking? We will get to that soon enough. I've said almost nothing about that painting at which I often stare when forced to share a meal with the Chases, nor have I made it clear what an ordeal it is to eat with these people, especially seated— as I always am—next to Maddie Chase, who must certainly notice how stubby my fingernails are, how mercilessly I've bitten them down, who must notice the brown nicotine stains I can't seem to remove from two fingers on my right hand, and who no doubt gags at the odor of my unchanged socks. Mrs. Maddie Chase comes from a world I cannot imagine. Even now when I recall her I think of such expressions as "Philadelphia Main Line," whatever that could possibly mean, I think of women with no hair on their bodies, with bodies that scarcely exist below the throat, women who in their most difficult moments give off the sweet perfumes of newly washed babies. The tangible evidence of her four sons seems not to penetrate the deepest recesses of my imagination.

Back to the painting. Who could have chosen it? And then paid money for it, and then elevated the painter to some special level above ordinary mortals? Why does Zach Chase feel called upon to brag that he owns a genuine Matt Meader? Matt Meader was a Sunday painter who worked full-time for Harry Bennet, the man in charge of strikebreaking for Henry Ford. Bennet was the man who employed a squadron of toughs and goons many of whom were ex-felons paroled to him from Jackson Prison. Meader had done time before he went straight and worked as a labor spy and enforcer. I learned all this from my zaydee when in '42 he'd bought two genuine Matt Meaders on speculation from the artist himself. He paid fifty dollars for both. I'd thought then it had little to do with the aesthetic tastes of my grandfather; Meader had helped him locate a stash of new bearings stolen from the Ford River Rouge plant and stored in a garage behind a bar and grill on Trumbull Avenue near Briggs Stadium (later called Tiger Stadium). All the paintings were seascapes. The one in the Chase breakfast nook is particularly gloomy, depicting as it does a clipper ship tossed mercilessly by high winds under a gray sky. Where it does not break into froth the ocean is a deep green. No humans are observable either on deck or thrown into the sea. Most of the painting is water.

I'm not sure why the room was called the breakfast nook; they eat most of their meals there seated at a table that is at least twelve feet long, made of a huge glass oval top that rests in a gray matte iron frame. The chair I'm sitting on matches the table: it has a thick glass seat set in an elegant iron frame. I find it cold on my ass and uncomfortable. Although there are only five of us seated at the table there are ten chairs, and except for Mrs. Chase and me no two people are seated next to each other. This means that for the most part servants are expected to transport the platters and bowls from one human island to another, and of course the servants comply. Although I hate eating here, I too comply when I am asked to stay for dinner. Even then it was impossible to believe that the Chases believed I found it less than agonizing to dine with them, to suffer through every cheerless moment and then walk the three miles home in the dark. Then why did they ask me or command me to stay?

I doubt that America in 1945 was very different from America in 1992 as far as such as the Chases are concerned. I can't imagine what human experience would suggest to them that there was a need to change. In their own eyes they are upper-class, and they love it up there; they find it delicious, and one of the things that make it so delicious is having us down here but close at hand, where we can observe all the differences between our stations. Had I had the temerity to have informed Zach Chase that my mother removed the genuine Matt Meader from the living-room wall where my zaydee so proudly hung it that afternoon in '42, that, recognizing it as "fifth-rate," she wrapped it in newspaper and secreted it behind the table on which my enlarger stood in the blackest corner of my darkroom, Zach would have branded me a liar and a poltroon. How he came to such language having been born on the island of Manhattan to Lithuanian Jewish parents is another matter. "A secret Litvak with his nose in the air," is how my zaydee put it, "and his *schmeckle* in that *shiksa* queen when he's not with his whoors." My zaydee has a certain flair for figures of speech and direct expressions, but what my zaydee thinks or says is of no account to Zach Chase and his friends at the country club, where his sons are free to swim in a pool famous for being off limits to NIGGERS, JEWS, AND DOGS. To all of them, the gentiles and especially the few secret Jews, my zaydee is a kike, which is a Jew caught being Jewish, whatever in the world the world considers being Jewish.

I've learned all this even before the age of eighteen because I've had the good fortune to work for almost five years for people with more money than I, though, sadly enough, even in the year 1945, with the nation employed in war work, not everyone in America has more money than I. I've learned that if I didn't work for such people I probably wouldn't be paid; I've learned that from experience. Until very recently I've been too young to become a member of a trade union, so my bosses have found it easy to treat me any way they choose. A few— an alcoholic photographer, a paranoidal shopkeeper, and an illiterate scrap-metal dealer—came to rely on my services and so felt obliged to pretend to a modicum of respect. Another few have even demonstrated what I've taken to be genuine affection, but I have grown wary of affection; for good reasons I've come to associate it with not being paid. When the boss snaps at me I know where I am. Though he frequently snaps at his two younger sons, Zach Chase has never snapped at me, nor has he ever snapped at his wife. During the months I have been employed by the Chases I've come to believe in my zay-dee's insights into Zach's finances and that it was by means of Maddie's wealth that he founded his various enterprises. He never lets on he is in the least discouraged by his wife's behavior even when it seems utterly inappropriate to the situation at hand, though when she needs to be, Maddie Chase can be totally aware of her environment and can respond with the quickness and purpose of a shark.

Once everyone else has left the breakfast nook, Mr. Chase brings up the little matter he wants to discuss with me. He does not invite me to move closer to him, although I am seated at the opposite end of the table, nor does he speak in a hushed voice. It's obvious he doesn't care who in the next room hears what he has to say, for the only people in the next room—the kitchen—are the three servants, who are presently taking their evening meal and will soon be cleaning up. Two, Gwen and the cook, will exit by the back door before long. The third, Sadie, an elderly white woman from the upper peninsula, will put the finishing touches to the dishes that have been washed and dried by hand before retiring to her bedroom, just off the game room in the basement. There is a second servant's room above the garage, but the Chases do not employ a chauffeur, because both Maddie and Zach enjoy driving.

It is now I discover Mr. Chase had earlier sought a disinterested opinion on my looks because he has what might be called a proposition for me. Before dinner I had informed him that Kenny's academic performances have not improved one whit and that it is pointless for me to go on tutoring him. He brushed aside my remarks and indicated that this was no reason to terminate my services; he's pleased with the job I'm doing. Only a few hours later it is as though none of that was said. He looks up from his coffee cup and announces in a voice made husky by sincerity that it's important for Kenny

to be promoted out of sixth grade. A third year there
would be very bad for the boy's self-esteem. When I fail
to answer, he assures me there are a number of ways to
make sure Kenny advances. "A number of ways?" I say.
Suddenly he has my attention. "If we cannot change
Kenny's attitude toward the school perhaps we can
change the school's attitude toward Kenny." An interesting notion, I think, one that certainly would never
have occurred to me, and I nod my assent. Out of curiosity I ask how we would accomplish this, picking up
Zach's use of first-person plural.

Mr. Chase drains his coffee cup, runs his left hand,
tanned and ringless, through his head of fine white hair,
and looks me directly in the eyes. "We could approach
it a number of ways, a number of ways." He goes on to
discuss Kenny's home-room teacher, a Miss Foster, a
woman only a few years older than I, a not altogether
unattractive woman. He knows that Miss Foster and I
have had several conferences to discuss Kenny's various
problems. "What did you think of her?" he asks directly.

Outside the window behind Mr. Chase the late light
is dwindling or perhaps an early darkness is falling from
the air. I hear the door to the back porch open and then
close. The black cook and Gwen are no doubt beginning
their trek to Livernois Avenue and the long wait for the
evening bus that will take them to their neighborhood.
Their muffled voices fade. Mr. Chase and I sit facing
each other now in almost total darkness, and when I answer I cannot gauge his response. "I think she'd like to
be helpful," I say, "but with almost thirty students on
her hands there's only so much she can do."

"Get the light," he says. Quite suddenly we are facing
each other over the bare expanse of a slightly soiled white
tablecloth. "As I said, she's a young woman unattached,
only a few years older than you. I think you should get
to know her better, take her out. You can use Robert's
La Salle." Robert is his second-oldest son, now in the

army. The La Salle is a stylish light-green coupe I've
driven only on Chase family business. Zach goes on to
offer me free passes to any of the several movie houses
he owns and to assure me that if extra expenses are involved he'll take care of them. He hasn't the slightest
doubt that a young man as attractive as I can charm the
woman and if more is required he is prepared to make
an offer of an outright gift of cash. To Miss Foster, of
course.

There is something luxurious in the heavy sighs of the
wind as it makes its way through the darkened branches
of the elms and maples bordering the cultivated streets
of Sherwood Forest. The vast houses appear buttoned up
and secure; not one is closer than fifty feet from the
sidewalks. Many of the driveways I know well, having
shoveled snow from them during the many winters I've
lived in this area of Detroit. I've stood on many of the
back porches drinking hot chocolate and eating cookies
as part of my reward for a job well done. During all
these years I've known I was not part of this world, but
I'd never felt as alien as I do on this night. In one way
I'm pleased with what has taken place. I've refused Mr.
Chase's proposition. I merely excused myself from the
table, went to the front closet, where I collected my
schoolbooks and my cotton windbreaker, said good night
to Mrs. Chase, and left by the front door. I realize I will
have to look for part-time work elsewhere, but there is a
luxury in knowing money is not everything, for if it
were I would be nothing. Also I have made what feels
like a moral decision, though God knows it is an easier
one than most of those I will make or fail to make in the
years to come. Did I gloat over the irony that these rich
and self-satisfied people could not get their way about
something so simple and basic as advancing their son to
the seventh grade? I can't remember. I probably did.
Their two older sons entered the U.S. Army the same

year as my older brother, 1942, and though war has raged in North Africa, Europe, the islands of the Pacific, and at sea, neither of their sons has left the continental United States, whereas my brother has been with the 8th Army Air Force, stationed in England for two years. Mrs. Maddie Chase has told me quite openly that she feels the deepest gratitude to her husband, Zach, for arranging to have both boys working in military procurement in Maryland and she is surprised my family has not taken similar steps to safeguard the life of our boy. She has assured me that it took Zach only a few trips to the nation's capital, and it's been well worth it. Naturally she has never mentioned money; Maddie Chase never talks about money. On one occasion she offered to call my mother and advise her on what might be done to bring my brother back home from this dangerous war, but I discouraged her by saying my brother was happy where he was doing the best he could to stop Hitler. She merely sighed.

I should feel warm and righteous bathed in all these luxuries, but in truth I don't. The truth is I feel a little stupid, for it has occurred to me that I lack the least idea of how one person would go about bribing another person. This has never bothered me before, but it has suddenly struck me that I may be far too innocent to be alive in the city of Detroit. It is just possible that everyone else is on the take, and I am the one monumental idiot who fails to understand how even simple things function in a free country. For the life of me I cannot imagine how I would go about initiating a conversation that would conclude with my making an offer of money for something illegal and appalling.

I don't mean to suggest that at eighteen I am more moral or pure than the rest of the citizens of the world. I know I can lie. In fact for two years I have been lying like a maniac to girls my own age, lying about who I am, what I do, how I feel about them. I have made advances toward them, physical advances that I usually expected would not be welcomed, and I've done this because it pleased me to do so. For the most part these advances have been rejected quite frankly and emphatically, and though that has given me no pleasure I've accepted my rejections without ever resorting to physical or verbal abuse. In most cases I've bided my time and readvanced when the occasion seemed promising, though it usually wasn't. I've stolen things and felt no blame; in fact I've cursed my inability to shoplift and have envied my brother Eddie's deftness and daring, especially in book and record stores, where he has made amazing hauls. One summer, having discovered the racist policies of my employer—McKesson and Robbins Drug Warehouse—I spent each afternoon swiping such precious items as razor blades and film, made scarce by the war, and then selling the items to a local pharmacy. I did this with a sense of righteousness, though I was careful. One afternoon, having heard a rumor that our lunch boxes were to be searched, I put back the pilfered items and went legal for the remainder of my employment.

Waiting at the traffic light at Seven Mile Road and Livernois, I seriously contemplate the process of bribery. I ask myself, "How would one go about beginning a sentence that would conclude something like, 'and for this we are prepared to offer you four hundred dollars'?" Immediately I realize why Zach resorts to the pronoun "we," for it tends to suggest that some larger power is at work, perhaps the "we" of "We the people of the United States . . ." This misuse of language horrifies me in a way in which the misuse of my own hands has never affected me. I do not live under the banner of some philosophical or religious vision that tells me that my hands are any less me than my words or even the brain from which my words spring. In all honesty I believe my hands have never done anyone great harm, though there are occasions on which I wished they could have. Although I have quite suddenly shot up to almost five feet ten, most of my life I've been quite tiny and have lived at the pleasure of creatures who appear more powerful and careless than I. I am quickly adapting to my new growth. This horror at the misuse of language has a special power for me. For at least five years language has cast a spell over me I cannot entirely account for, and what I take to be my ability to use it has given me extraordinary delight. Tonight, crossing the great flat prairie of undeveloped blocks that lead finally to my house, I begin once again to speak the words that are mine only, composed by me to be spoken only to me and to the hints of spring rain in the air and to the stars above, which have emerged in thick clusters as the cool wind flattens the motherwort around me and the tall yellowing grasses and the wild flags.

Before I could take the first step to finding another part-time job, I received a call from Mrs. Chase. She was eager to have me fetch Kenny from school the following day, for the boy was very disturbed. About what she did not say. All was arranged. I would stop by the Chase home after my physics class, pick up one of the Chase cars, and collect young Kenny from school. Then Mrs. Chase and I would discuss the lad's future. Nothing was said about Zach's proposal of the previous week; for all I knew Mrs. Chase knew nothing about it.

The next afternoon, before I could even knock on the back door, Arna, a thick-shouldered black woman of forty or more, opened the door and handed me the keys to the La Salle. "She be out," she said, referring to Mrs. Chase. Arna was the cook and general captain of the kitchen; a good-natured powerful woman originally from New Orleans, she claimed to have cooked for a fraternity at Tulane. She took great pleasure in teasing me about my skinniness and was always urging sandwiches and cookies on me. She seemed unusually grim and circumspect, but before I could dismount the back porch she called me back. "Phil," she said, "come back here and have a smell." Once inside the kitchen, in which nothing was being prepared, I caught the scent of something unusual, a heavy depressing stink that suggested smoldering wet paper or charred fur. "You get that?" she said. I nodded. "Something went on here last night, I don't know what. You see if you can't find out."

Kenny was unusually dour when I picked him up in front of Hampton Elementary School, which was less than a mile from his house. His dress was surprisingly casual, no sports jacket and no tie. He did not want to go directly home; he wanted instead to go to Cunningham's Drug Store at the corner of Seven Mile Road and Livernois. He assured me his mother had instructed him to have a milkshake right after school, and he produced a dollar bill as though it were proof of her intentions. I drove him to Cunningham's and sat beside him at the counter as he ordered a double-chocolate shake. His mother's wishes apparently did not extend to me, so I merely watched him greedily consume the contents of the entire iced and gleaming canister which the soda-jerk had placed before him along with a small glass and a plate of cookies. The milkshake was so thick he couldn't make it with a straw and had to ask for a spoon. "That's better," he said when he was done, wiping his lips with a paper napkin and indicating that so fortified he was ready for the drive home. "Mother wants to talk to you about last night," he said in the car. He never called her "my mother" or "Maddie" or "Mom," but always referred to her simply as "Mother," as though she were everyone's mother or perhaps the only mother worthy of the title.

This time, with Kenny in tow, I entered through the front door, which seemed never to be locked, for there was always someone at home. The disgusting odor of burned fur was even stronger than it had been in the kitchen. "Let's wait here for Mother," he said, plopping down on a couch in the small parlor to the left of the entranceway, "I don't want to go upstairs, it stinks."

"What happened?" I said.

"We had a fire last night."

"A fire?"

"Yes, Mother and Father were out, and Len locked me in a closet and tried to burn the house down." Seeing my alarm, he modified his story. "Actually I think he just tried to scare me. He piled a lot of papers in front of the closet in his room and set fire to them. It spread. Sadie must have heard me screaming. She called the fire department." There hadn't been a lot of damage, he told me, though Len's room was a mess from the stuff the firemen had poured on the fire and sprayed around the rest of the room. Len had also set fire to his bed and some of the mattress had burned. "That's what smells so bad," he said. Len had been taken away. "By the police?" I asked. No, the police had never been called. Mr. Chase had called the family doctor, and after a conference he'd taken Len away.

Kenny was very cool about the whole thing. He was sure his brother hadn't meant him any harm. Things had just gotten out of hand. When I asked what things, he just said, "Oh, you know how strange Len is." In truth I had no idea how strange Len was, for I'd never had a conversation with him that lasted more than a few seconds. "You must have been scared or you wouldn't have been screaming," I said. No, it hadn't quite been that way, for Kenny had been making a lot of noise even before he'd been hustled into the closet; it was something he did often to make life uncomfortable for his brother. Leonard was so much bigger that he didn't dare confront him physically, so he got to him other ways. "You've got brothers," he said, "you know what I mean."

When Mrs. Chase returned home Kenny drifted off to "wash up." Maddie Chase seated herself at the opposite end of the couch and gestured for me to be seated.

Without looking at me, she fitted a cigarette into her FDR holder, lighted up, inhaled deeply, released the smoke, and at last spoke to me. "Mr. Chase and I would like to retain your services at least through the end of this school year. We believe it would be in Kenny's best interests to advance to seventh grade." I started to explain that I'd had no success whatever in getting Kenny to bear down on his studies, but Mrs. Chase went right on speaking as though she heard nothing. She reminded me that a considerable amount of energy had been expended for the past several months on Kenny's education, and she and Mr. Chase and Kenny for that matter had every right to expect results. They were now willing to allow me the use of the La Salle on weekends. I wasn't exactly sure what the La Salle had to do with Kenny's learning problems. "And now this!" she said, without indicating exactly what "this" was. I took it to be the disaster of the previous evening, which she was unwilling to name. She stubbed out the cigarette. "Philip, don't you fail us now. Don't you dare fail us." I was about to say something about trying my best when she looked directly at me and said quietly, "I hate that smell. It's disgusting." I was speechless. "I can't get the painters to come until tomorrow. I'm going to have the entire room redone," she went on. "The carpet is a total ruin."

I lasted less than two more weeks. I didn't formally quit. I just walked away from the job and never returned. Mrs. Chase phoned my house five nights running, and I never came to the phone. The last four times my mother lied for me and said I was working for Peerless Cleaners. On my final day I picked up Kenny from school, and he clambered into the back of the La Salle and stood behind me on one of the low tiny seats so that his face was all I could see in the rearview mirror. Once again he commanded me to take him to the soda fountain at Cunningham's. As I approached Seven Mile Road he said, "You know, my brother Robert got this car for a graduation present, but he went into the army, so he didn't have any chance to use it."

"Oh," I said.

"I don't think he'd want you using it on weekends."

"It wasn't my idea," I said.

"What if I were to tell him?" Kenny said. Before I could answer he commanded me to take a left turn at the next corner. When I asked where he wanted to go now, he simply repeated his command. I took a left. "Go to the end of this block and take another left, and then keep going until I tell you what to do." I took a second left. "I think I'll tell him you're using his car. It was almost new before you started using it."

"It wasn't my idea," I said.

"But you like using it, don't you?"

"Sure," I said, "it makes me feel important. I even like the smell of it, especially when it's raining outside."

"Take another left here and go to Seven Mile Road," he said. "You've never driven a car this good before. I think I'll get a brand-new Oldsmobile convertible when I'm your age. It'll be dark blue with a light-blue top. All I have to do is ask for it."

"Yeah," I said.

"My brother would hate it if he knew you were driving his car. I'm going to tell him." By now his face was almost next to mine as he leaned forward peering through the windshield as though scouting the road ahead to decide where our next turn would take us. "You think you're very smart because you're using this car and because you're going to graduate high school in June, don't you?"

I'd been wondering where all this was going.

"I'm much smarter than you."

"Oh?" I said.

"Yes, I was born rich."

I turned the car around very slowly and deliberately and jerked along in first gear, speeding up and slowing down. I could see Kenny's head snapping back and forth in the rearview mirror. "This is very good for a car," I said, "especially a brand-new car. It really cleans the pistons before they get a chance to get dirty." I went by Hampton Elementary waving at Kenny's classmates on their way home from school. By this time Kenny had hunched down in the back seat so no one could see him. I pulled into the large cement area in front of the Chase garage, turned off the ignition, and left through the back gate, heading down the alley for home.

Thus was I vanquished by the family Chase. This all took place in the actual America of my growing up, so I was never given the opportunity to leap into a turbulent river and rescue a helpless dog owned by a millionaire's beautiful daughter; besides, I wouldn't have risked my life to save a dog's, certainly not at age eighteen, when I thought I was living a dog's life. I'm sure everything worked out for the Chases; somehow Kenny got his doctorate in human mismanagement at the University of Lucre and Leonard was pronounced sane and responsible by a jury of his peers and now has a ranch in the suburbs of paradise and votes straight Republican and contributes to causes like the National Rifle Association and Right to Life. I know that the two older sons returned from their military duties and took up the family's practical affairs, Eugene gradually easing his father out of the construction business, which he moved to Las Vegas, while Robert took over the theaters and the real estate and moved out of Sherwood Forest before the Jews got in. I learned all this from Robert whom I met seven years later at a Red Sox–Tiger game at which Ted Williams mercifully did not hit a home run. Robert also had a proposition for me, but this one was strictly kosher: he wanted me to drive his car to New York City and back. He had a weekend's worth of dates with a woman he'd just met and was mad for. He didn't have the time to drive the car himself, but he wanted it there

to impress the woman. It was a green Olds 98 convertible. He offered me a hundred dollars and gasoline expenses, and I delivered the car to the door of the Plaza
after driving around for twenty minutes with the top
down to get rid of the smell of pot, which a musician
friend of mine had used to fumigate the back seat. The
friend, Pepper Adams, went on to become the greatest
baritone saxophonist in the world, but that September
he expected to be drafted into the U.S. Army, as did I,
so as to save Korea from Communism or democracy—
neither of us could get it straight—and Korea forty years
later might help put Detroit out of business. We lacked
foresight then and were planning on military careers.
Pepper and I both had wads of money, he from record-
ing with Benny Goodman and I from working twelve-
hour days to build a hunk of U.S. 24. We thought we'd
take one last fling in the Apple before we went off to
become heroes. I know I spent mine. Pepper told me he
almost bought a pair of alligator shoes at a shop on Fifth
Avenue—they were marked down 70 percent—and Thad
Jones, then a trumpeter with Goodman, got one pair and
urged a second on Pepper. Pepper said he vacillated but
finally decided he didn't care if his alligator went bare-
foot. The ride back was pretty quiet. Pepper stayed loose
and we drove through the night, switching off on the
driving every few hours. Ironically, dawn found us on
U.S. 24 between Toledo and Detroit, the excitement
gone, and the Ford River Rouge Plant up ahead.

When I returned the car to Robert Chase at his theater
at Nine Mile Road and Woodward Avenue I learned the
weekend hadn't gone as well as it might have. Arlene,
the woman he'd been enthralled with, was a graduate of
the University of Idealism who thought Anton Chekhov
was the greatest man who'd ever lived, and she dreamed
of writing the novel he might have written had he been
born in Newark in 1928. Robert thought *South Pacific*
was the greatest achievement of the human spirit, so their

deepest conversations never got off the ground. She was less than impressed by the Oldsmobile. "She never noticed it," he said. In fact she liked to "meet the city" and had walked him all over the place until his English brogues were killing his feet. She also liked the subway, felt it got her closer to "the breathing heart of the people," to whatever Dos Passos was after, whoever he was. "I think you and she would have made a couple, Phil," he said, totally appalled by the thought, "you could have talked about poetry and the rest of that shit."

Actually Robert was a good sort. At thirty he was beginning to lose his hair and he was taking the tragedy philosophically. He invited me into his office that morning to partake of a cup of coffee and a sweet roll. When it turned out there was only one roll left he broke it in half so that we might share it. I think the army had democratized him to a degree that would have horrified Zach Chase, who wouldn't split his last sweet roll with Gandhi. The office itself was a low-ceilinged, gray, windowless room, totally unexceptional save for the autographed photographs of famous Detroiters: Hall of Famers Charlie Gehringer and Hank Greenberg, Joe Louis in his prime, and a local industrialist who'd made a splash in speedboat racing on the Detroit River. When I looked closely at the signatures—the inscriptions were to Zach Chase—Robert said he thought they were fakes. A guy who ran a photo studio on Washington Boulevard, the city's swankiest shopping center, made them to order. He didn't do FDR anymore, but you could get Joe DiMaggio or Harry Truman. I was thinking about the long streetcar ride back to my apartment and the nap I needed now that the long night was beginning to catch up with me, when Robert said, "I don't get it, Phil."

"Get what?"

"I don't get what you see spending all those years in college so you can work on road construction. Same with Arlene. She has a master's degree from Chapel Hill, but she's doing dumbbell office work in New York to finance her writing. The stuff she wants to write never made any money, as far as I can tell. You're sure as hell not going to get rich on poetry, right?"

I shrugged and eased back into my chair. I thought I might try to explain how people got hooked on certain things like writing or playing music, but I was afraid I'd come off sounding superior; besides, I had no idea how much longer I could stay at it with no encouragement outside my small circle of family and friends. I was about to say, "Money's not everything," but I knew that was too easy to say for a single guy my age. I liked Robert, and I didn't want to put him down, so I answered with a question. "What would you say if I told you that when I was fourteen an old bearded man who looked like a rabbi came to me and said American poetry needed me?"

"Who was he?" Robert said.

"Walt Whitman."

"I'd say you were either lying or out of your mind."

"You'd be right," I said. When the phone rang I rose to leave, but Robert gestured for me to stay. It was strictly business, something to do with corner lots that weren't selling. The way Robert cupped the phone under his chin and leaned back in his leather desk chair reminded me of his father's air of delight in the telephone. Instead of lowering his voice and speaking quietly and confidentially, slightly overwhelmed by his own sincerity, as Zach always had, Robert raised his an octave, as though he were absolutely gleeful to be discussing business matters. I studied him behind his enormous, glass-topped desk with its two separate phones, its silver pen-and-pencil set; here he was, not yet thirty, clothed in suit and tie, ready for a week of dealing, already leading his father's life. I thought then I could see his future "mapped and marred by all the wars ahead," but I could not see my own. In fact I had no idea where I would be in a month or what I might be doing. Clearly I preferred my own life to his, for even homely Wayne University had a school of business I wouldn't have been caught dead going near. When he hung up he handed me an envelope. "Don't forget your money," he said. We rose and shook hands. "Take care of yourself," he said.

"I have to," I said, "I'm all I've got."

On the Woodward streetcar all the way to Clairmount, where I transferred, that final line I'd blurted out confounded me. Was it true? I asked myself, and if so what did it say about me or anyone? Waiting for the crosstown bus at Clairmount, across from the all-night pharmacy, I watched the young kids on their break from Northern High School. In what way, I asked myself, had I come any farther than they? What had a college education given me that these carefree kids lacked? I see now I was asking the wrong question. The significant question was: what had a college education taken away from me that these kids still possessed? And the answer was nothing. The rest of that day fades into sleep and smoke; I know I got back to my apartment, I know I took up my life again, I know I went back to looking for work and waiting for the draft to find me.

"I'm all I've got" is not a line that belongs to the history of wisdom or eloquence. I was not proud I'd said it and I was even less proud that it was probably true. But it occurs to me there are worse descriptions of one's human estate, and it does separate that twenty-three-year-old from a great many other young people I've come to know. An example: In 1985 a former student of mine in a modern-poetry course at a flossy expensive Eastern school told me that he was glad he had done so daring a thing as to take my course the previous year. We were standing on the tennis courts his family had endowed and which now bore their surname. He would be graduating within a week. As the number-one singles player on his university's team, he had just won his final match of the year and may have been feeling a bit expansive and overly generous toward himself and me. Seeing the look of befuddlement on my face, he went on to explain that his plan was to gain his M.B.A. from Harvard, and a bad grade in my course, even a C, might have derailed him. I remarked that I'd never thought of myself as daring. And he nodded without getting my point, so I went on to explain that when I'd grown up a young man was thought of as daring when he went on foot in search of the source of the Nile or exchanged all his worldly goods for the life of a desert visionary. This tall, handsome, athletic young man whom I knew to be intelligent and supremely sensitive stared at me as though I'd lost my mind. When I added that it was difficult for me to think of anything that took place in the safety of an academic setting as daring, he merely laughed. I got his point, and he got mine.

I observed the same thing in my own family, for both my brothers are creative and brilliant men, and they are neither of them timid about much of anything. They are in fact bold men. Yet by the time each was twenty-three years old they had let the expectations of the middle class into which we were born, and the particular expectations of our family, the business my grandfather and father had founded in order to support their families, determine the course of the rest of their lives. For my twin brother this has clearly been less than satisfying. Forty-two years later he is still in the same business, still harboring the same artistic ambitions he had all those years ago, still a painter of great promise and now one of considerable accomplishment. At age fourteen my twin and I vowed we would never participate in the corporate business of this country, a business that appalled us by the brutality of its exploitation of the people we most loved. For me the answer was quite simple to formulate: I became working-class. My mother, a remarkably witty woman, used to joke that I'd botched my social experiment. "Philip set out to prove there is social mobility in America," she used to say, "so he got born smack-dab in the middle of the middle class, grew up in the lower middle class, and then as an adult joined the working class. He got it backward." Once I discovered poetry and fiction I came to believe that if I were to work with my hands I would leave my mind and imagination free for my writing, and this proved to be true for a number of years, until the work began to take its toll on me, to submerge me in exhaustion and bitterness.

Disgusted with factory work in my mid-twenties, I decided I would live by my wits. I remember hearing a friend use that phrase, "live by my wits," and thinking there was a certain nobility in it. A classmate from my college days had opened an advertising agency in downtown Detroit and, knowing I could write, he offered me a well-paying job, which I worked at for one long day. I spent almost eight hours inventing silly lies about dry-cleaning establishments, dancing academies, and savings banks. At five that afternoon I left, knowing I would never return. It had nothing to do with machismo. In his extraordinary book *Weekend in Dinlock* Clancy Sigal depicts the life of a Welsh coal miner who also happens to be a serious painter of genius. The young miner cannot come to terms with a life that does not bring him into direct contact with the coal face, for to him and everyone else in Dinlock that is a man's work and to do less is to be less than a man. That miner had very little in common with me, for when I was twenty-five my favorite job had been with Railway Express, where for some three months I'd been assigned a delivery route that had so few stops I was able to spend four hours every afternoon in the downtown branch of the Detroit Public Library, where at my leisure I read through their collection of Tolstoy, Balzac, Dostoyevsky, and Stendhal. After I quit my writing job I went out the next day and took a job driving for an outfit that repaired electric motors. It was not the boon I'd hoped for, but at least it got me out every afternoon in whatever fresh air Detroit had.

I am pleased I did not fulfill the expectations of my class and that even years after the events recounted above my worldly goods did not fill one suitcase. My years in the working class were merely a means of supporting my real work, which in my case was not my father's but my own. My life in the working class was intolerable only when I considered the future and what would become of me if nothing were to come of my writing. In one sense I was never working-class, for I owned the means of production, since what I hoped to produce were poems and fictions. In spite of my finances I believe I was then freer than anyone else in this chronicle. In order to marry and plunder a beautiful and wealthy woman I did not have to deny I was a Jew; for the sake of my self-esteem I did not have to reign like a chancellor over my family and my servants; in order to maintain my empire I did not have to fuel it with years of stifling work; in order to insure my legacy I did not have to drive my sons into the hopelessness of imitating my life. Of course it meant years of living badly, without security or certainty, what I have called elsewhere "living in the wind," but it also meant I could take my time, I could take what Sterling Brown called my "blessed time," because after all, along with myself, it was the only thing I had.

The Key

I can still recall a college course I took in James Joyce. The distinguished Dr. Prescott raised his delicate voice above a whisper to assure us that the underlying theme of *Ulysses* was the Search for the Father. The class nodded its assent. I nodded my assent. The professor continued; it was the identical journey of Telemachus, of Hamlet. The class nodded. I thought for a moment and shook my head no. The class stared at me in wonder. Dr. Prescott's face clouded with sadness. We are seated around a long, scarred wooden table in the seminar room on the second floor of Old Main. Dr. Prescott's hands are clasped in rabbinical fashion above the open pages of the Modern Library edition. We, the students, have just lifted our eyes from the holy text itself, which in the tenth week of the semester is marred and mangled by our undecipherable notes. Employing the Socratic method he first encountered and then mastered at the University of Wisconsin during "those thrilling years between the wars," the professor is about to call on me.

It's 3:50 p.m. on a warm April day about halfway through the present century, and it is quiet or relatively so at this great urban university, because the traffic light at Warren and Cass is red. Foolishly, I do not cast my gaze downward to page 417 and its incomprehensible paragraph; thus the beams of my eyes intertwine with those of the gentle professor. "Mr. Phillips," he says, for although he knows the text with incredible precision he has yet to master the names of his students, "would you care to speak?" The light changes from red to green. Racing their engines, the cars, the city buses, the huge Kenworths and Internationals hauling precious cargoes of new Plymouths and Dodges, drag for the light at Second and Warren, and beyond that the light at Third and Warren, and beyond that Livernois, Dearborn, Down River, Flat Rock, Toledo, the wide world. Dr. Prescott's question and my unformulated answer vanish forever in the roar of 1952.

It was only later in life that I learned that the goal of this father pursuit was the slaughter of the old man. The source again was academia, two young instructors I knew who aspired to the publication of literary scholarship. They lived in my town, and before I knew better I fell into the habit of spending one Friday night a month with them. Invariably the evening would culminate in the reading of an unpublished article, even though I would try to steer the conversation toward sports or jazz or great movies. But one of them had a far greater need to be heard than I, and so we, his audience of two, would sit at opposite ends of a long couch, each with an empty beer can in hand, while he pranced before us dramatizing some sprightly little piece for *Notes and Queries*. He too was a Joyce scholar, but unlike Dr. Prescott seemed to have unraveled thousands of tiny mysteries without having understood the book at all. The final paper of his I endured was entitled "Joyce, Freud, and the Need to

Kill the Father." I survived by trying to imagine what his students whispered to each other while he lectured them to death. When the performance was over he asked my honest opinion. Naïvely, I gave it. I said it was all nonsense. I'd lived thirty-six years and never once felt the need to kill the father. The two young scholars gave me a look that has become familiar over the years, one that means simply, You're not in our league. It was good knowing that, knowing that at last I was free to go bowling one more Friday a month.

I have three sons, with whom I have spent more than half my life. I have slept beside them, my mouth open, the porches of my ears exposed, my snores no doubt wracking their dreams. I have said no to them so many times that there are countless requests they would never make of me. I have disappointed them so many times, failed to bring back even modest gifts from my long trips, and forced them to travel with me when all they wanted was to doze in their familiar rooms, listen to their radios, or play with their buddies. And in all these years I have never felt the least danger in their presence.

However, in the last fifteen years I've become aware of a certain type of young man who would love to kill me. Him I have encountered many times, and I always recognize him by the heavy stench of muskrat he gives off when his carnivorous face leans into mine and he tells me how much more I mean to him than his own father. Usually he has gotten drunk earlier in the evening, perhaps just to say this, and then he staggers away into whatever party he has ruined for me. Before I can find my coat and get out the door, he's back, sweat soaking through his black shirt, his speech gone flabby, trying to set up a meeting for the next day, a lunch together, some fulsome occasion during which we can plan his career. When I refuse, he'll get my phone number and sooner or later will call me in the middle of the night— now completely sober—to tell me I've betrayed him, him and all the other decent young men who once believed in me. Then he'll write letters without a return address detailing my failings and laboriously listing the other men my age who have not sold out, kissed ass, bowed to lick the hem of power. At least he used to do that—now I outwit him; he can't phone me in the middle of the night because I have no phone, and I never open letters saturated with sweaty musk.

I learned a great deal in my early years. I think this was largely because I loved school, especially on rainy days. When the sky darkened and the rain began to smear the windows, I felt there was no place in the world warmer and friendlier than my fourth-grade classroom at Roosevelt Elementary School. I would look around at the blank faces of my classmates and think how lucky I was to be one of them. My teacher, Mr. Dubrow, was in his first year as a professional, and during the early weeks I could feel his anxiety like a palpable thing. He was the only teacher I ever had who looked up at the clock more than his students; at times he seemed utterly stunned to discover how little it had moved in what must have felt like an eternity. As the year wore on, little by little I could feel him relax and even take a liking to us. I was his favorite because I got a hundred on every exam, even if I had to cheat, and this seemed to confirm his belief in himself as a teacher. He loaned me all sorts of books to read, beginning with the short stories and tales of Nathaniel Hawthorne and concluding with his old history textbooks from college, which were far more enjoyable. At the end of the year he put one hand on my head, opened his great wet brown eyes as wide as possible, and told me never to stop learning. I promised him I would not.

I'm afraid I broke that promise before I left school. I attended the worst high school in the world. At another high school I might have learned all there was to know about inertia or how bodies in motion tended to stay in

motion or why boys and men continued to search for
their fathers, but at Wilbur Wright Technical High I
learned to keep nothing of value in my locker, to forge
my mother's signature, and never to eat in the cafeteria.
It was such a sorry place that even the teachers took to
playing hooky or showing up late. During my entire
senior year my Spanish teacher arrived at our eight
o'clock class on time only twice. Usually someone would
be posted to watch for her. "Here she comes," the sentry
would shout, and the class would rush to the windows at
the back of the room to see her alight from a Yellow Cab,
which would then continue down the avenue bearing her
boyfriend to whatever life awaited him. We would take
our seats, bow our heads to our books, and await her
entry. She would arrive slightly breathless with her heavy
rabbit coat hanging open and little beads of sweat forming above her upper lip and on her forehead. Always hat-
less and scarfless, she usually wore a white nylon blouse
that plunged enough to reveal her prominent sternum and
the tight skin that glowed a rich orange. When she
turned to hang her coat on the back of the door, the boys
gesticulated wildly, rising out of their seats to shape her
rear end, which was certainly neat and tight, or thrust
their arms upward in what passed for a symbol of the
entry into heaven or the out-and-out charge through the
valley of paradise. She always gave us enough time to
regain our seats and our composure before turning to
greet us. "*Buenos días.*"

I felt a special affection for Miss Correos because, in spite
of her dark eyes, black hair, and shortness, she made me
think of what my mother must have been like when she
was young. Of course my mother would not have been
caught dead in a rabbit coat. I can hear her now, speaking of Marie Hollander, her chief rival at the office.
"Stupid bitch had the nerve to stand there in a Persian
lamb and tell me she and Lou are going to Miami for two

weeks. Says she has reservations on the sleeper." Mother flicks ashes on the carpet, shuffles the cards in a furious blast, and deals herself another hand of solitaire. "She's coming back from bedding down with her latest stud, her girdle's on crooked, her lipstick's all over her forehead. And she has the nerve to stand there in the lobby dressed in that Persian lamb giving me that crap. I told her, if I were you I wouldn't go to Toledo with Lou. I didn't say anything about the stupid coat; I figured enough is enough." Marie Hollander was the person at the office slated to take over if Mom should stumble or fail to show up after a "long weekend at the lake," a phrase that served to account for any absence from work. "She wants my job! You should see the way she shakes her ass when she takes her little dictation pad into Carlisle's office. She can show more crotch just getting into a chair than I own."

How much my mother wanted a mink or an ermine I'll never know. She wasn't the type to dwell on what life hadn't given her, but it's not hard to imagine her modeling one of those great puffy Danish ermines, standing in front of the mirrored door to the hall closet, sucking in her cheeks to get a more Nordic look, and whipping her long ash-blond hair from side to side. Her own silver-fox jacket she never modeled. She'd go to the closet one minute before the buzzer announced her waiting date at the downstairs entrance of the building, throw the jacket over her shoulder, shake her head as though she were rejecting cod-liver oil, sigh, and check her purse for cigarettes. From behind she always looked a little uncertain in high heels, as she tottered back and forth. I don't think it was an affectation; I doubt she ever knew how exciting it made her, as though each step were an adventure. "Come on, jerk," she'd say. "Come on, Mama's waiting!" And the buzzer would sound. "Don't wait up for me," she'd holler, and I'd hear her clacking down the hall to the elevator. What she actually meant was, *I don't want to see you around when we get back*. It meant there was a strong possibility that it would be *we*, and I was to be out of the way. "How do you explain an illegitimate son to the tenth-rate mind of a General Motors exec?" was the way she put it to me.

Of course I knew how I was explained to the entire world. I was the son of her older sister, Trish, who had died of TB in Santa Fe, New Mexico. My father had gone broke in the Great Depression and disappeared into the moveable handout that was then America. "Sure, you had an Aunt Trish," my Uncle Clem would tell me, "but she died at fourteen, so of course she didn't have no husband. Who ran away was me. I just had to get out, you know, join the circus, see the world, all of that crap I done." We'd be painting someone's living room, and Clem would talk steadily to me. He had a very philosophical cast to his nature and almost perfect technique as a house painter. The brush moved delicately and yet swiftly, and the paint came out smooth and straight. "Your mother wants to talk about Trish; this way she gets to. She can say, 'I want you to meet my nephew Philip, the genius son of my sister, Trish, who had all the brains.' Course it wasn't true, it's your mother got all the brains, then I come next, so you can imagine how swift your Aunt Trish was. You're just lucky she wasn't your mother or you'd be dumber than me. Oh, your mother is a deep one, but don't think she ain't got strong feelings. She still has to talk about Trish. I don't. I could spend a whole lifetime and never talk about Trish or anyone else. Some people got to talk about their life, some don't. I'm one that don't. Your Aunt Trish alive today, she'd be . . . let's see . . ." He'd stop painting, put down the brush, and start counting on his fingers, shutting both his good eye and his blind eye and bobbing his head ringed with light curly hair, one bob for each year as the smoke snaked up from the cigarette dangling from his mouth. "She'd be thirty-two. That's all, just thirty-two. You're wondering how she could be your mother's older sister. She was the youngest. Just twelve when she and your grandpa left for Santa Fe." Of course I knew all this already, since Uncle Clem came around to Trish every couple weeks. I often wondered what he talked about on weekdays, when I wasn't around to listen. No doubt the same things he talked about when I was there—his family, his growing up, his short career as a bootlegger, how he went on the bum when he was sixteen and stayed away until the war brought him home in the uniform of an Army Air Force technical sergeant, expert on radio. How he'd lost the sight in his left eye after a fight in a jail in Wyoming. "I had to protect my virtue, Phil, some things are worth fighting for." One thing I was sure he never talked about was his marriage or his own three kids he hadn't seen since their mother vanished from his little cottage near Fort Benning, Georgia.

How does a man without a father inaugurate the search for the father? Was I searching for the lost son or the father I never had when I fled New York this past May? For years I loved the city, loved it so much I worked for pittances just to live there, and no matter how far it drove me into debt I felt it was worth it. This year the winter dragged on into April; everyone I knew seemed to be walking around in his own inner snowstorm. The night after my last class at NYU, I trudged wearily toward Seventh Avenue without a trace of that joy I usually felt when a job was done. Waiting for my train in the Sheridan Square subway station, I looked up from a copy of the *Post* into the eyes of a man no more than twenty feet away whose face was made of wood. Stunned, I looked back at the paper and tried to control my breathing. I peeked. That neither the expression nor the features changed did not surprise me; living in New York I was used to that. The way the fluorescent light reflected off the unnatural, creamy-white forehead told me it had to be painted. I couldn't stop looking at him, and every time I did I was sure he was staring directly back at me, a sort of hideous, three-dimensional Mona Lisa. Then it occurred to me that this was not a person but a life-sized dummy dressed in a white shirt, black bow tie, and an enormous blue overcoat that spilled over his lap and onto the dirty concrete floor. Nowadays who would dress like that, even in New York City? When the Broadway Local, my train, pulled into the station and stopped, he rose stiffly from the bench, cast a last look at me, and entered the train. I waited in the empty station for the next one.

That night, before dawn, I wakened in my dinky, over-priced apartment fifteen floors above Morningside Drive and 119th Street. To the north I could see that even the Chicken Shack at 125th had closed. To the west I could see the early traffic coming in over the George Washington Bridge. Once just the thought of that sight could fill me with such rotund, romantic feelings I would have to fight back the tears. Unable to sleep, I called TWA and booked passage on the first flight I could get to Milan.

Unlike so many of his cronies, Uncle Clem never made the move to California. When his wife, Rae, and the three girls came back from their wanderings, he bought a dusty little frame house on Evergreen Street, painted it a brilliant white, and settled in for the long haul. I'd always pictured Aunt Rae as a Southern belle, a tall, snooty woman in white with a hat the wind would have carried off if she hadn't plastered it down with one hand. Actually, she was a squat, broad-shouldered woman, a hairdresser from Asbury Park who snapped her gum violently while plying her craft on a cut-rate basis in her kitchen a few mornings a week.

The daughters seemed happy enough to give up the road, and Clem was deliciously proud of his refound family. When the oldest daughter, Car—short for Car-

men—began to have suitors, as Clem called them, he
loved to stage formal dinners at the long oak table he'd
rescued from somewhere and refinished. He'd sit up at
the men's end, often with me on his right hand and the
new boyfriend on his left. (They never seemed to last
more than a week or two.) "Philip," he'd say in his most
theatrical voice, "what could anyone see in a face like
that?" Meaning, of course, Car's face. She sat stiffly at
the foot of the table trying not to blush. Although she
had beautiful, thick black hair, there wasn't much to see
in her face, which seemed always to be posed for an invisible photographer. Car was just as clearly not his
daughter by blood as the two younger ones, Mae and
Kay, with their tight blond curls and sharply hooked
noses, were. As the evening wore on and Clem got into
his second six-pack, his remarks grew more and more
tasteless. "I looked in your Pontiac out there," he'd say
to the evening's young man, hideously uncomfortable in
jacket, shirt, and tie, "and you ain't got Hydramatic
Drive. How you expect to court my daughter with that
gearshift thing in the way?" The young man would grow
gloomily silent. "You're gonna have to do better than
that if you're gonna get Car in your car." Car seemed to
enjoy the attention, and her chin would rise higher and
higher above the table loaded with platters of congealing
mashed potatoes and boiled meats. Aunt Rae would make
no bones about the fact that she was not cut out for do-
mestic service. By the time we'd get to coffee and Clem's
cigar, she would have long since stalked off to her bedroom, usually in tears.

I learned how profound her unhappiness was one day
when I was driving for Railway Express and had just
made a delivery down the block from their house. I saw
Mae and Kay on their way home from school, and they
invited me in for lunch. It was strange sitting at the big
table with Aunt Rae in Clem's place, me in my usual
spot, and the three girls across from me all deeply in-

volved in conversation about the projected joys of the weekend. Rae seemed delighted to see me, but no sooner had I opened my bag of sandwiches than she burst into tears. I was sure I'd violated some canon of etiquette and closed the bag. "No, no," said Aunt Rae through her tears, "go ahead and eat." I noticed the girls paid no attention whatever to her weeping; they just kept spreading thick slices of Wonder Bread with butter, peanut butter, and apple butter and washing them down with glasses of milk.

"I ruined my life," said Aunt Rae. (She pronounced it "rooned.") "I should never of come back to him. I didn't know how happy I was out west." I didn't even know she'd been out west; the Oldsmobile she referred to as hers still had Georgia license plates. "We were making do. We were poor but clean, but the girls were missing so much school. I just didn't know what to do." This time when I put my sandwiches back and closed the bag she didn't seem to notice. "Now I know I did the wrong thing." Once more her face contorted, and the tears poured forth, streaming down her face and onto her empty plate. Car asked if there was any more milk and, still weeping, Rae went to the kitchen and returned with another frosted bottle.

From the closed cab of my truck I thought I could hear her wailing through her tears, "I rooned my life," as she and the girls waved goodbye to me from the tiny porch.

I was about to write, *Life is such a crazy puzzle*, but I resisted for fear of sounding like an idiot. Now the less cautious me insists: *Say it! You believe it!* And so I put it down because I do believe it. Perhaps within a few more pages the sense of all this will become clear.

Unlike her brother, my mother did make the move to California. She took early retirement from General Motors and let Marie Hollander have her job. "Phil, it'll kill her. Without me to fight with she'll have nothing to live for." Mom was tired of working for other people, and wasn't Los Angeles the golden land of opportunity? (She never said anything that stupid, but she must have been thinking it. For all I know it was true back in 1956.) She was tired of her apartment, the heavy burgundy drapes, the dark armoire streaked with stale polish, the green velvet bedspread with its mysterious golden "Q" in the center. ("I got it for less than half-price because there aren't any 'Q's around here," she explained.) She was tired of the Norge refrigerator that hummed off-key half the night, the electric oven that burned the three birthday cakes she tried to bake for me, the orange shag rug that smelled like a burlesque theater ever since I broke a bottle of Vitalis on it and tried to hide the stench with deodorant. She was tired of the silver Ford coupe she parked five days a week behind the GM building and the sarcastic remarks from her co-workers. She gave away the silver fox to the old Finnish woman who did the heavy cleaning and laundry once a week. Wiry Mrs. Pekela stood in front of the hall mirror in white sneakers and high blue socks with my mother's only silk skirt trailing out from under the jacket. "Lofly, lofly," she mumbled, turning round and round.

"Here's your Aunt Trish and your grandpa the week they arrived in New Mexico," Mother said as she sorted through a carton of old letters, postcards, snapshots, theater bills, and the like. Aunt Trish was a skinny kid in a dark dress with a white lace collar. She stood as straight as a nun, her hands clasping a shiny purse. Grandpa stood next to her in a tan three-piece gabardine suit, one hand resting on her head, the other holding a cigarette. He had on those two-toned shoes fraternity boys wear in bad movies. Just behind them was a huge saguaro cactus. "Hotel Romolo, Tucson" was stamped on the back of the photo.

Mother handed me a postcard of the *Île de France*, the

luxury liner she'd taken to Europe in 1927, and a tiny alabaster ashtray she'd swiped from her cabin. "I went second-class," she reflected. "Thought I'd meet the hoi polloi. Instead I met a couple chiropractors and a tree surgeon." She handed me a postcard that was unmailed and in mint condition. "You want to keep that," she said. I couldn't tell if it was a question or a statement of fact. The man in the picture was dressed in a greenish-gray uniform, white shirt, and black tie. His bulbous, almond-shaped eyes gazed longingly into the camera. The trim moustache and faint goatee were tinted a hideous strawberry. The large, jaundiced head was entirely bald. It was Gabriele D'Annunzio.

"Why?" I said. She didn't answer. Instead she handed me a flat steel key that said "Mosler" on one side and bore a seven-digit number incised on the other. I asked her what it opened. "Beats the hell out of me," she said.

Uncle Clem claimed he'd never had much of a childhood. Grandpa had needed help in his bootlegging operation and Clem was his only son, so there was no choice but for Clem to grow up fast. By the time he was fourteen, he was making gin. The specialty of the house was a cherry brandy Grandpa called "vishnac." He got fantastic prices for it and claimed it was superior to Cordon Bleu. Uncle Clem still had a huge crock of it, as thick as maple syrup and almost as sweet. One evening shortly after Aunt Rae made the trip east to visit her sister, a trip from which she would never return, I visited Uncle Clem. In the basement he poured me a brimming jelly glass of vishnac. I gradually forced it down.

He was assembling a model of a World War I biplane from a kit he'd bought at Woolworth's. It was the kind constructed of paper stretched over a skeleton of glued-together pieces of balsa wood and then coated again and again with lacquer until it glowed like Chinese jewelry. With only one thick lens in his reading glasses, he worked meticulously under a bare overhead bulb. "Wanted to sell me two lenses for one eye. I said, 'Doc,' though he was no doctor, even in his white coat with a pocket full of pens, 'you ain't got a lens can make my right eye see.' Claimed I'd look better with two lenses. I says, 'Look at me, Doc, do I look like I care how I look?' " Actually Uncle Clem always looked sporty no matter how he dressed; even in the basement in his underwear shirt, flowered boxer shorts, and heavy work boots, he possessed an undefinable stylishness which the thick tufts of curly red hair on his back and shoulders didn't destroy. "This here's a Spad," he said. "Do you know what a Spad is?" Clem was working on it as slowly as possible so he wouldn't finish it until just before Christmas. That way it would be new when he gave it to himself as a gift. "Kind of a surprise," he said, smiling.

I showed him the flat steel key and asked him what he thought it would fit. Scarcely looking at it, he flipped it in his palm and handed it back. "Don't you know?" "No." Even though he'd never had occasion to have one himself, he knew it was the key to a safety-deposit box. "Someone's got another one; they always give you two. And then they keep a third they don't tell you about so they can count your money." He told me there was no way of knowing which box in which bank it fit from the key alone. "Besides," he added, "you don't want to look too hard. You never know what you're gonna find."

Less than an hour northeast of Milan, Bergamo was a wonderful relief from the din and stink of traffic. I felt as though I were a world away from Manhattan, and I was. Each morning my wife and I would take a city bus and a funicular up to Bergamo Alta, the medieval town that sat on a high hill overlooking the yellow plains of Lombardy which faded into a distant haze of dust and smog. I enjoyed entering the dark little *duomo* in the company of squadrons of Italian school kids whose teachers breathlessly pointed out the treasures before them, which the children then photographed no matter how dark it was. I was even touched by their faith in their little plastic cameras. Each afternoon I sat for hours over a cheese sandwich and a bottle of mineral water writing notes in my journal and postcards to distant friends. The gray clouds that sagged over the little piazza never dropped more than an invisible, silent rain. By three the upper town was closed and asleep, and my wife and I would walk the five miles back to the hotel. She would name the trees, flowers, shrubs, and birds I pointed out, and though she never asked, I would name and date the more exotic cars and motorcycles along the way. After a nap, I would awaken in the evening ready for another walk and then dinner. I'm not sure what I was recovering from.

On our last day in Bergamo, I went into the little tourist office on the piazza to gather whatever I could find as mementos of a calm time. It was almost noon, and the woman was closing up shop. Surveying a colorful brochure which suggested another place entirely, I noticed a photograph of a two-seater biplane of World War I vintage; it was suspended from the vaulted ceiling of the Museum of the Risorgimento: "Close up—The aeroplane in which Antonio Locatelli, a three-gold-medal hero, flew to Vienna with Gabriele D'Annunzio."

"This is here?" I almost shouted at the woman. "Here?" she said, as though I meant the very room we were standing in. "Here in Bergamo?" I said. Yes, it was here in Bergamo, but the *museo* was closed. "Because of the hour?" She looked even more puzzled. "Because it is noon, lunchtime?" I added. No, it was closed for repairs. It would open soon, very soon, as soon as the repairs were completed. Perhaps even before the new year. She plucked her keys from her purse and swept me out the door.

"Look what's here," I said, thrusting the brochure in

front of my wife, who was waiting at our usual table. "So?" she said. She'd been looking at the works of Raphael, Pisanello, and Beato Angelico that morning. "This is here, in the *Museo* of the Risorgimento!" She knew and she knew it was closed. "Let's go before one," I said. "Maybe I can talk them into letting me in." She was clearly ready for a little lunch, but she gathered her guidebooks and trailed silently after me. The young man who answered the side door of the old armory that had been converted into the museum spoke very little English but knew enough to tell me the place was closed for repairs. I told him I *had* to see the airplane. He assured me it no longer flew and even when it did it was very uncertain, very dangerous. "No, I need only to touch it." My wife translated. The young man took off his sunglasses and rubbed his eyes. I took out a ten-thousand-lire bill. He looked interested. He and my wife spoke again. It would take another ten thousand for two people to touch it, she explained to me. She told him she had no desire to see or touch it; he was clearly disappointed. She returned to the café to wait for me, and I entered the shaded doorway.

I won't bore you with the details of my journey up the unlit stairway to the *piano superiore* and the room of Antonio Locatelli. Oh, yes, the plane was there, in a little alcove, with the dim light of a side window seeping down on it. It was not so tiny I couldn't visualize two men hunched down behind the little Plexiglas shields on the long flight from Treviso to Vienna. It was not so long ago I couldn't imagine the two poets—for Locatelli was *scrittore bergamasco* as well as *aviatore*—entering the modern world, flying into their own poetry, the first epics of speed and destruction. It was not hung so high I couldn't trail my hand along the glowing fuselage and lower wing, which were surprisingly uneven and rough. What I cannot depict with any clarity is the response of the bearded young man—at the time it seemed like a mixture of shock and personal affront—to the great belly laughs that burst from me.

My first full day home from Italy felt particularly luxurious. On such occasions I usually sit speechless in my favorite chair, stunned by the affection I feel for my books waiting patiently on their shelves, the old photographs that watch me from their frames. One of the pleasures of the first day back is the huge stack of mail which has sat so many months it no longer cries for an answer. One letter in particular caught my eye. The return address was radio station WFMT on Wacker Drive in Chicago, and the envelope falsely claimed it was from Studs Terkel, so I opened it with excitement. The letter ended as follows:

> I grew up with a Father who was a shoe salesman and a Mother who was a scientist. I did not know right from wrong. I was taught early to honor my Father for the wrong reasons. I did not begin to honor my Mother properly until the past few months. I was born wounded and grew up angry and hard. I am finally free of my Father's ghost, and I am standing in my own vivid and powerful light.
>
> At our meeting I presumed to speak intimately to you; I was not entirely sober. You may remember; I hope you don't. Either way I would like to renew our friendship and to send you the manuscript of my first book of poems (which I lack the expertise to publish), much of the inspiration of which you gave me. My past offensiveness, I now realize, was due to the unhealed wounds caused by my Father. That phase has entirely passed. I have learned proper respect for others and complete forgiveness of self. I humbly make this request in the

spirit of the honor and courage which animates our writing.

Respectfully, yours, Rick Rainer

When I bowed to the page I caught the acrid odor of muskrat beneath the truly disgusting aroma of lavender. It was time to visit my mother in L.A.

My mother claims she doesn't know the exact date of her birth. She celebrates it on Bastille Day, and this past July 14 she was eighty. She didn't want a party, she loathes false sentiments and claims such occasions sponsor them. She asked for the usual—a dinner out at a place of her choosing and a gift neither extravagant nor readily available in Los Angeles. I held my breath as she unwrapped the little leather-bound volume of the lyrics of D'Annunzio I'd brought from Italy. "Did you read this?" she asked. "You know I don't know Italian," I said. She leafed carefully through the pages until she found what she was looking for. "Here goes," she said, winking at me over the top of her reading glasses.

> *E la mia forza supina*
> *si stampa nell'arena,*
> *diffondesi nel mare. . . .*

"Can you follow that with your Spanish?" she asked. I told her I got some of the words, but couldn't truly get the meaning.

"Well, you're missing a lot. This is poetry, rhyme, meter, the whole nine yards."

I asked her to translate it.

"I'm a little rusty, but I'll do my best." She paused a moment, took a deep breath, made a false start, straightened her glasses, and then intoned in a voice she never used in ordinary conversation. " 'My supine strength is pressed down into the sand, the beach, it spreads into the sea.' " She looked up and smiled. "So far so good. I'll give you a little more. 'My vein is the river, my forehead the mountain, and my pubis [pubis?] is the forest.' And more of the same. Very modest fellow, and the verse comes out as easily as hamburger out of a meat grinder or toothpaste out of the tube, except it never ends. What do you think?" I said nothing. "Actually," she said, "it's a lot worse than it sounds; it loses a lot in the original. But the binding is fine." She held the book up by the covers and sighted along the spine. "Perfectly sewn, genuine calf. Like serving Mogen David in Waterford crystal."

She was sorry it wasn't chillier and that she didn't have the old silver fox. "Furs drive Californians nuts; you're not supposed to kill anything that doesn't have a bank account." The restaurant she'd chosen for the occasion was both modest and Polish, the Warszawa in Santa Monica. It was a pleasant surprise. Seated by a tall, elegant, moustachioed waiter, Mother ordered for both of us, a cold beet borsch to begin with and an inexpensive Zinfandel. "Good fruit taste," she said, "finishes very well." She gave me the wink that told me she was still my mom. "Would Madame like something a bit more elegant and festive?" asked the waiter in a heavy Slavic accent. "No, Mac," she said, "just a clean ashtray. And I'm not a madame."

She lighted her cigarette, took an enormous drag, and slowly surveyed the restaurant, which was largely hidden in candlelight. "Place this dark, they're usually hiding something." She sniffed the butter in its little wooden tub. Over pierogi she asked me if I thought this was what Milosz, one of her favorite poets, had grown up on. I confessed that I couldn't imagine Milosz as a child or an adolescent, as anything but a grown-up. She nodded. "I wonder if he could have been like those snotty, vicious anti-Semites that threw stones at us on our way to school.

They always looked so splendid in their student jackets and pressed shorts." "Where was this?" I asked, putting down my fork. "In Lithuania, where I went to school." "You went to school in Lithuania? I knew you were born in the old country, but I thought you grew up here." She smiled. "Philip, I'm not talking about growing up, I'm talking about going to school."

We skipped dessert. Mom felt she could do without the calories, and she didn't want to miss the fights which were on the tube that night. Since moving to California she'd become a true prizefighting maven. On the Santa Monica freeway she drove like Alain Prost, sliding her BMW from lane to lane in order to maintain a steady seventy-five miles per hour. "This cable TV has changed my life," she said as she tapped the accelerator and down-shifted for the Robertson exit. "We get the best from Atlantic City, Las Vegas, Madison Square, the Forum, you name it."

Perhaps you're thinking by now that I don't know where all this is going, that I'm just plucking these details randomly out of my years to create a crazy-quilt design, and the only key I have bears the name "Mosler" on one side and a seven-digit number on the other. (Actually I mislaid that key years ago, so there is no key at all.) Perhaps the pattern is obvious, no key is required, the underlying theme is the overlaying theme, the search for the father goes on and on until he's found or until he comes home from his wanderings, and then you don't kill him, you hug him.

The last time I heard about Clem—he's too diffident to phone me and he won't write because he's afraid I'll correct his spelling and grammar—was when I saw Car in Scranton this spring. Her name is now Carmen Elorde. She married Flash Elorde, now a tiny, middle-aged high-school coach who—in his steel-framed glasses—looks like a small-town pharmacist. He's such a sweet, soft-spoken man with such a gentle manner it's hard to believe that for seven years he was a leading contender for the bantamweight title. Car now outweighs me, chain-smokes, and has dyed blond hair. When I asked how her father was doing, she answered in her rough, gravelly voice that he was great, he'd given up house painting, gone to advanced electrical school, and now repaired TV sets in the basement, the same one where he'd assembled his model airplane. Of course Car meant Clem, for he was her father as far as she was concerned. Aunt Rae's wandering, I learned, was over. I didn't ask where she's buried, but I imagine her restless spirit inhabiting one of those resort towns on the way to Atlantic City, Asbury Park, or Ocean Grove. I'm sure if I stood now in the gray light of dusk with autumn coming on, I could feel her soul descending like mist on the black waves battering the boardwalks.

You see, this is turning into an autumnal tale. Maybe you're feeling a little cheated, but in fact autumn is coming on. I feel it these days as a wet chill jeweling the grass I cross each morning. I feel it when I open the paper and read the pennant standings, the Tigers having slipped to twenty games below five hundred. I see it reflected in the bright faces of my students, who sit respectfully, almost docilely through my poetry classes, as though I were some sort of grand old man, a sage, who could explain the meaning of the simplest lines. "Just keep reading the stuff, and you'll get it, or you won't," I say, and that holds them for a while. In truth, I am getting autumnal, what with my hair thinning and my waist beginning to bulge. One day I should go back to spend the last day of summer and the first day of autumn at one of those wonderful, run-down Canadian amusement parks out of my growing up. You could stand to one side and see the merry-go-round come to a stop and know it wouldn't start again until another summer had come round. Fun time was over; work time was beginning. I owe it to myself to return to the Ontario side of Lake Huron and stand in the damp silence embracing my mortality for all I'm worth, knowing for certain—at least for a day—that all true stories are autumnal.

In fact I know I won't go back, any more than I'll go back to the seminar room on the second floor of Old Main to hear once again the good Dr. Prescott lecture on James Joyce. Chances are that the professor has joined the final bibliography of the air, and there's no one to hear the traffic break in on his serious, hushed voice. Who could ever forget the final day of class in his *Ulysses* seminar? After folding his small, delicate hands on the closed book, he removed his glasses so that he seemed in his near-sightedness to be looking at all of us and none of us. "Are there any last questions?" he said. We were twelve totally befuddled students who knew at least that it was too late to begin asking. No one said a word. Dr. Prescott began his summation, the magical key by means of which we could open every impossible, Byzantine text. "As you may know, Joyce was a writer who asked his reader to give him a lifetime," he said. "I am that reader, and I can tell you it was a wasted life."

Once we'd returned to my mother's apartment from the Polish restaurant, I, of course, asked her, "Why all those years ago did you give me that picture of Gabriele D'Annunzio and hint that it was terribly important?" We were sitting facing each other and having our post-prandial coffees and brandies. The hum of the Santa Monica freeway was only a faint monotone in the background. The fights weren't on for another half hour or so; it was a good time to ask.

"Philip," she said, "what are you asking me?" She kicked off her shoes, and I sensed that she was getting ready for a real talk, a descent into the past or a takeoff into the future.

"Did you ever know Gabriele D'Annunzio?"

"Not in the way you mean, no, I never 'knew' him. I read him in the original when my Italian was good. I read enough to know he was a writer of some originality and talent who became his own impresario and, in the process, a fool. Besides, the women were lined up for blocks to get to know him, and what was he going to see in me when he could have the immortal Duse?"

"No false modesty, Mom. In 1927 you must have been something."

She nodded slowly, as though she were recapturing her own image as a woman of twenty. "Catch you, Philip," she said. "In 1987 I'm still a bargain."

"But why all the mystery with the picture and the key?"

Sadly to say, at first she did not remember the key to which I had attached so much importance. When I jogged her memory, she finally recalled who had given it to her. "Remember Max the liar?" she said. "He claimed to have stashed money all over the place, and that was the key to one of the stashes. Which one he didn't tell me."

"Why did he give it to you?"

"Probably to impress me," she said. "Some men think money is exciting to a woman, and if they hand you a thing like that it's like saying, 'Sweetie, see how I trust you, I'm putting my nuts in your purse.' That was just one reason I said goodbye to Max the liar. I hate to say it, Philip, but a lot of men are hopeless. I'm sure you've noticed it."

"But the picture of D'Annunzio, presented with a hushed aura? Why that?"

"Figure it out," she said. "I don't want to insult your intelligence." She put on her bifocals and looked at me steadily after checking her watch for a moment. They were running films of the first Ali-Norton fight that night, and Norton was a particular favorite of hers. "You really want to ask me another question, don't you? You want to know who your father was?"

I could tell by the way she was looking at me that she expected a serious answer. Here I was, a man in his sixtieth year, and I had to ask myself the old Dr. Prescott question: *Was I searching for the father?* I knew without the least doubt that if I simply asked, *Who was my father?* she would answer me without the least temporizing. As it was, in my ignorance, he could have been anyone old enough but not too old in 1927: Jack Dempsey, the Prince of Wales (who had yet to give himself body and soul to Wally Simpson), Henry Ford, Herbert Hoover, Thomas Mann, Picasso, Charlie Chaplin, Hart Crane, Babe Ruth, Walt Disney, Bertolt Brecht, Benny Goodman, Moishe Oysher, Gabriele D'Annunzio, Joe Blow. The list was finite but enormous, and by a simple question I could reduce it to one. You don't need a key that says "Mosler" on one side and opens a long-forgotten door to know what I did.

The Poet in New York in Detroit

In the winter of 1953 I was working at Chevrolet Gear and Axle, a factory in Detroit long ago dismantled and gone to dust. I worked the night shift, from midnight to eight in the morning, then returned by bus to my apartment, slept for a time, and rose to try to write poetry, for I believed even then that if I could transform my experience into poetry I would give it the value and dignity it did not begin to possess on its own. I thought too that if I could write about it I could come to understand it; I believed that if I could understand my life—or at least the part my work played in it—I could embrace it with some degree of joy, an element conspicuously missing from my life. No, I was not a young Werther seeking some outlet for my romantic longings for the world. I was a humiliated wage slave employed by a vast corporation I loathed. The job I worked at each night was difficult, boring, and stupefying, for there in the forge room the noise was oceanic and the heat in our faces ferocious. And the work was dangerous; one older man

I worked with lost both hands to a defective drop forge, and within a few hours—after a cursory inspection—the machine was back in operation being tended by another man equally liable to give his body for General Motors. A friend had given me a copy of Goethe's saga. I'd read it and merely laughed. If you had the time to survey the mountains and the sky, what was the problem? Oh, yes, you had to embrace the world in all its splendor, you had to reach with aching arms to hold the ungraspable, the sublime. I nicknamed the book *Stormy Werther* and threw it away. I too had aching arms, a thickened back, swollen wrists, and a heart full of emotions I couldn't deal with, fury and rage at a world that seemed already to have defeated me.

Since I worked only eight hours a day and slept only five or six each morning, I had plenty of time to attack my poems. My inspiration at that time was Keats, but though he knew a world at least as difficult as mine it scarcely entered his poetry clothed in the terms in which he encountered it. It was there barely disguised in the third stanza of the "Ode to a Nightingale," which I would recite over and over to myself:

Fade far away, dissolve, and quite forget
    What thou among the leaves hast never known,
The weariness, the fever, and the fret
    Here, where men sit and hear each other groan;
Where palsy shakes a few, sad, last grey hairs,
      Where youth grows pale, and spectre-thin, and dies;
        Where but to think is to be full of sorrow
        And leaden-eyed despairs,
    Where Beauty cannot keep her lustrous eyes,
      Or new Love pine at them beyond to-morrow.

Unquestionably his life had been far harder than mine, and yet he had made immortal poetry out of it. He had struggled against poverty, trying his best to support two younger brothers and a sister; I had only myself and my impossible first wife. He—as a student surgeon—had walked among the sick and dying, at twenty-three he had nursed an eighteen-year-old brother to his death, and even with the first unmistakable signs of TB in his own body— the disease that had killed his brother—he had gone on transforming his life into poetry. I had my health, my strength, and a whole undiscovered continent to write about, and yet I sat at the kitchen table each afternoon failing to complete a single poem that satisfied me, one that could capture the rage I felt at a world that reduced men to what I had become. Of course he had the advantage of being a genius, and another advantage too: he had inherited a tradition that by age twenty-three he knew intimately, one that showed him how to achieve Beauty. He also knew something that I wouldn't learn for years: that Beauty mattered, that it could transform our experience into something worthy, that like love it could redeem our lives. I wanted fire and I wanted gunfire, I wanted to burn down Chevrolet and waste the government of the United States of America.

On weekends I would often go to the Detroit Institute of Arts to try to enter another world, if only for an afternoon. There I found what at first I thought might be the model for the poetry I hoped to write, Diego Rivera's famous frescoes, especially those panels which depict the making of an automobile at Ford's River Rouge empire. I knew no other great art that dealt with my working life. Dos Passos's *U.S.A.* contained a mediocre chapter concerned with assembly-line workers in Detroit as well as a brilliant portrait of Henry Ford, one a worker could love. I thought Céline, in his fury, might show me the way in *Journey to the End of the Night*, but, reading the book, I discovered he clearly was not familiar with industrial labor. It was Rivera, the sworn enemy of my enemies, or no one.

From a distance the frescoes were a miracle of design

that left me breathless. As the weeks passed I began to
discover why his images were not helping me with my
poetry. As I drew closer I found the bodies beautiful,
their gestures like those of dancers as they moved in con-
cert, and although their faces were often averted, turned
away from the eye of the beholder as though shamed by
peonage, those I could see were calm, dignified, and
concentrated upon their tasks. The bodies tended to be
elongated, the limbs long and slender, turning on their
narrow waists as they lifted in unison. And the tones,
dominated by warm earth colors, were wrong, far
brighter and more vivid than those of the actual world
I knew. When I closed my eyes I saw it all in black and
white, black men and white men and white fire. And the
actual bodies I knew were otherwise, so heavily muscled
they seemed earthbound like Blake's Newton, perhaps
made of earth, certainly thickened with earth and the
metals of the earth. The habitual gaze of those of us
who worked at Chevy was downward too, as though whatever stood above us was stunning and victorious and not
to be gazed at for fear it could kill, this strange God of
the underworld, for surely we were in the underworld.
I wondered seriously if Rivera had seen a different world,
if the Ford plant at River Rouge, then the world's largest
industrial complex, could be that different from Chevy.

Some months later, employed as a driver for a company
that repaired electric motors, I entered Ford Rouge—
because of Ford's notorious anti-Semitism I refused to
seek a job there—to pick up a burned-out motor on the
assembly line, and found the same world I knew at
Chevy, black and white and gray. I heard the same deafening roar, and saw the same men, stunted and isolated
by their labors. Rivera's great design, his beautiful dance,
was nonsense; automobiles were produced by a colossal
accident that shattered men and women. It was what I'd
known it was: a world that must be raged against with
all the eloquence and fury a poet could muster. And then,

by one of those magical strokes of luck that come to the
poet in need, I read,

> I denounce everyone
> who ignores the other half,
> the half that can't be redeemed,
> who lift their mountains of cement
> where the hearts beat
> inside forgotten little animals
> and where all of us will fall
> in the last feast of pneumatic drills.
> I spit in all your faces.

I had known García Lorca only as the author of the
"gypsy poems," a writer of lovely, exotic poems that meant
little to me. But now one Saturday afternoon became a
miracle as I stood in the stacks of the Wayne University
library, my hands trembling, and read my life in his
words. How had this strange young Andalusian, later
murdered by his countrymen, come to understand my
life, how had he mastered the language of my rage? This
poet of grace and "deep song" had somehow caught my
emotions in a way I never had, and suddenly he opened
a door for me to a way of speaking about my life. I accepted his gift. That's what they give us, the humble
workers in the fields of poetry, these amazingly inspired
geniuses, gifts that change our lives. I later read that
upon first entering New York he had cried, "I don't understand, I don't understand," as I had cried in the face
of Detroit. Months later, taken by a friend to view Wall
Street at midnight in moonlight, he had cried, "I do
understand." What I knew even on the first afternoon in
the library was that, before understanding had come,
poetry had come.

I dove into the *Poet in New York* and everything I
could find about its author. "Gongorism," "surrealism,"
"obscurity": the critics' terms were useless to me. What

I was reading made perfect sense to me and at the same time no sense at all. I had discovered the poet could live in the tiny eye at the center of chaos and write. I had at last discovered the true meaning of what my earlier hero, Keats, had called Negative Capability, "when man is capable of being in uncertainties, Mysteries, doubts without any irritable reaching after fact and reason."

What an extraordinary gift to receive in my twenty-fifth year. I would like to be able to say that immediately my own poems flowed from his model and his inspiration, but that was not so. He was a genius, I was a humble and dedicated worker. My one great mentor, John Berryman, had already taught me that certain poets were too much themselves to allow you to imitate them with impunity; he had said that when warning me away from that other great poet of New York, Hart Crane, and toward the influence of Hardy and Frost. What Lorca gave me as no other poet had was a validation of my own emotions, which meant a validation of what I was trying and failing to write. As Wilfred Owen's poetry eight years before had taught me that I was a worthy human being even though I hated and feared the possibility of killing or being killed in war, García Lorca's *Poet in New York* taught me I was a worthy human being although I was filled with hatred for the life I was living, for what capitalist, industrialized America had reduced me to. I saw also in this great book that, if I were able to remain true to my own personal vision of this America, sooner or later my poetry would come—certainly not a poetry as amazing as his, but nonetheless a poetry no one else could write.

Never in poetry written in English had I found such a direct confrontation of one image with another or heard such violence held in abeyance and enclosed in so perfect a musical form. What in my work had been chaotic rant was in his a stately threnody circling around a center of riot. Here was the first clue to what my poetry would

have to become if I were to capture my experience. Had
I not read

> A wooden wind from the south, slanting through the
>   black mire,
> spits on the broken boats and drives tacks into
>   shoulders.
> A south wind that carries
> tusks, sunflowers, alphabets,
> and a battery with drowned wasps

I could not have written

> Out of burlap sacks, out of bearing butter,
> Out of black bean and wet slate bread,
> Out of the acids of rage, the candor of tar,
> Out of creosote, gasoline, drive shafts, wooden dollies,
> They Lion grow.

I had to work another thirteen years before I was able
to begin to realize his gift to me, which is not really very
long when you consider the life of a poem that means
something. This is not to suggest that my poems mean
anything to anyone else or will outlive me. I do know my
poems are themselves, and tributes both to the people I
shared my life with way back then and to this amazing
visitor to our shores, whose voice for me rings as truly
today as it did that Saturday almost forty years ago when
I first read

> No, no: I denounce it all.
> I denounce the conspiracy
> of these deserted offices
> that radiate no agony,
> that erase the forest's plans,
> and I offer myself as food for the cows wrung dry
> when their bellowing fills the valley
> where the Hudson gets drunk on oil.

Living in Machado

The village of Castelldefels is less than twelve miles
south of Barcelona. I took my family to live there after
my wife and I discovered it possessed an Anglo-American
school that was first-class and inexpensive and that it
cost far less to live there than in Barcelona. A woman at
the American consulate had given me elaborate and very
exact instructions as to how to locate a particular Dutch
realtor who could rent me a *torres* (the term used in Catalunya to denote a detached house) for far less than such
space would cost in Barcelona, where, I was assured, I
would have to bribe several people before I could get
anything at a reasonable price; apartments stayed in the
same family for generations, and no one would rent anything remotely affordable before cleaning out an American, since all of us were rich.

The Dutch realtor, who described himself as an agent
(not a secret agent or a commercial agent or even a real-
estate agent—merely an agent), turned out to be a wonderfully civilized and witty man as well as an honest

one; he spoke every known language with a made-in-Hollywood accent and a vocabulary that suggested he'd learned by reading nineteenth-century fiction. (To make the point that French food was better tasting and more reliable than Spanish he would say, "The Spanish kitchen is not so fine, I think, as the French, you think?") His name was Hans Breen, and within a few days he had my family of five installed in a spacious and crude dwelling directly across the way from his own, which was an identical twin to ours but fixed up to resemble a habitation, whereas ours was barren enough to suggest a cavalry barracks. Once my kids were properly enrolled in school, my goods from America collected at the main post office in Barcelona, and extra blankets and two butane heaters loaned for the coming cold weather, Sr. Breen felt it was responsible for him to take off on his annual vacation, which this time was to include Rome, Florence, Paris, and two weeks in his native country visiting old friends in the publishing business, which had once been his own business after a hitch in the former Dutch East Indies. He waved goodbye gaily at us from the front seat of his tiny Renault, which he drove with an élan and abandon suggesting that underneath his proper exterior he was actually a Brazilian baby millionaire sowing his wild oats.

The departure of Breen meant that our only link with the Spanish language was broken. I decided it was my duty to rectify this problem, and I set about spending two hours a day after lunch studying Spanish by means of a textbook given to me by a colleague at Fresno State. Why the book began with a study of the subjunctive I had no idea. I began searching for occasions on which I might employ it; I would say, "If that were a loaf of bread how much would it cost?" or "If this were a *bodega* what sort of wines would you be likely to offer for sale?" My wife suggested, slyly, that there had to be a better way of learning the language and the sooner I hit upon it the better. I had already noticed that my oldest son could, when we went to our favorite local restaurant, employ the simple present tense in ordering a four-course meal and wine for his parents, a liter of white for Mama, a liter of red for Papa, and he could be polite and effortless about it and win smiles from the dour waiter, who preferred to watch "Voyage to the Bottom of the Sea" undisturbed by the requests of customers. Mark had the meal under way, the bread on the table, the simple green salad oiled and soured, while I was still formulating my opening remarks: "If you had a paella today, would it be possible for the five of us to receive it this evening?"

This was late summer of 1965, the first time I'd been out of the country since my bachelor days and the only time I'd traveled any distance with the responsibility of a family of five. I was on a sabbatical leave from Fresno State, which gave me the munificent sum of half my annual salary of ninety-eight hundred dollars for the year. I had picked up another thousand by teaching summer school for the first time in my life and still another by teaching two summer poetry workshops. A friend and patron had also added some thousands to this, but we had spent almost a third of our total in getting to Spain by means of a long trip through Europe in a VW Square-back sedan we'd purchased in Wolfsburg, where it was manufactured. Although our rent was less than sixty-five dollars a month including utilities, and food was cheap and good, and wine was next to nothing, I was worried about money. I wasn't sure how I might earn some, but no matter what I did I'd have to learn Spanish. The few Americans I'd met at the Institute for North American Studies in Barcelona all spoke wonderful Spanish and struck me as unaccountably cheerful, as though they would rather be living here than in any other city in the world, while I longed—secretly—for Detroit, New York, even Fresno. I was homesick for the first time since I'd moved to Fresno in '58. I wrote a great many letters to friends back in the States and received almost nothing in return. These were loyal friends, but most of them were employed and lacked the time to sit down immediately and respond in spite of whatever note of urgency they might pick up in my letters. In fact I was doing my best to disguise my need. I wanted this first foreign family venture to appear to be a success. I had pushed it hard in spite of the advice of many people who'd insisted I couldn't afford it.

In Spain postage stamps are sold at the post office and also in tobacco stores, all of which are controlled (or were under the Franco government) by a national monopoly. Often these little tobacco shops also sell stationery items, notebooks, airmail envelopes, pads of writing paper, pens of all kinds, ink in bottles and cartridges, pencils. The lines at the post office are usually formidable and the senior clerks behave like vice admirals of a defeated armada, so most people take their personal letters to these little tobacco shops. Exiting the nicer of the two in the center of Castelldefels, I noticed a small sign next to the Pelikan fountain pen I had been admiring. It read in English, "Spanish Lessons Given," though "lessons" was misspelled "lesons," which did not inspire confidence. I went back in the shop and in my Spanish asked the young, dark-haired woman if I might inquire about the lessons. (It was perhaps the first occasion on which the subjunctive seemed appropriate.) She stared at me uncomprehendingly, so I reached inside the display case and plucked out the little handmade sign. "Oh," she said in English, "you want my brudder. After one," she said, pointing at her wrist, "he is here."

Thus it was that afternoon I met Sr. Juan Rusiñol, a tall, long-faced Catalan gentleman, who indeed offered private Spanish lessons at his own *torres*, which was less than a mile from mine, for a hundred pesetas an hour, or $1.67 U.S. Since I was spending almost a hundred dollars a month on my children's education, I thought it reasonable to spend a few dollars on my own. We arranged for an initial lesson on the following afternoon, commencing at 4:00 p.m., when his stint at the store was completed.

It's impossible to explain by what magical process I believed the Spanish of Sr. Rusiñol would become my own. Somehow I did not envision hard work, hours of memorizing, and the writing of lessons, and so I arrived at his *torres* the following day in a state of considerable excitement, akin to the excitement one feels when one is about to encounter the psychiatrist who will rid one of all his or her phobias by means of the right word or the right pill. Seated in his little upstairs study that looked out on a dismal display of brown-stained trees, and equipped with pencil and notepad on which to inscribe the phrases I needed to memorize, I felt my hopes begin to sag. It was not until later in the hour, when the sun had dropped behind the western hills and the evening came on with a suddenness I was unused to, that things began to brighten. Sr. Rusiñol asked what I was by profession. I answered with as much simplicity and dignity as I could muster, "*Yo soy poeta.*"

Thus there began what was probably the first course ever offered in the village of Castelldefels on the subject of modern American poetry, taught by one young American poet to one not-quite-so-young Catalan poet, for the moment after I had uttered one of my first declarative sentences in simple present tense in Spanish, "*Yo soy poeta,*" Sr. Rusiñol switched adroitly to English and responded, "I too am a poet." "*En español?*" I asked. "No," he said, "in my native language, Catalan," at which point he opened the door to his study and called to his nephew, who had been studying in the next room. A tall, slender boy of perhaps ten years appeared at the door; he seemed in no way abashed by the presence of a stranger. In Spanish Sr. Rusiñol asked the lad how the school day had gone. The boy's response was incomprehensible to me. They exchanged a few more brief remarks and the boy went back to his room. "Could you understand what he was saying?" asked Sr. Rusiñol. I confessed I hadn't caught a word. To my relief I discovered he had not been speaking Spanish; all day he worked at school in Spanish, and the moment he returned home he reverted to his own language, which was Catalan. "You wonder why this country is insane?" he asked. (Actually I had never wondered, for Spain under Franco made just as much sense as California under Reagan.) "We go to school in one language and think in another, a language it is no longer legal to publish in, to debate in, to speak at a gathering of more than five people."

Before I could formulate a Spanish sentence in which I could pose a question regarding the nature of Sr. Rusiñol's poetry, he asked me in English whose poetry I thought larger, that of T. S. Eliot or that of Walt Whitman. As I struggled for the vocabulary to express my sense of the immensity of Whitman, Sr. Rusiñol switched the focus of our discourse one more time in his favor. "If you are more comfortable speaking your own language, please do so, as I comprehend it." That my desire to speak one of his other languages had brought me to this room in the first place seemed suddenly unimportant in comparison with the overwhelming urge for the two poets to reach an accord in this village that seemed at best indifferent to poetry. The rest of our time seemed to rush by as I spoke on my differing loyalties to these two great American poets. Almost two hours passed before my mentor rose to let me know our session had come to an end. Before I left he handed me a dog-eared copy of a lesson book entitled *Spanish Made Simple* and instructed me to master the first three lessons before our next meeting. As we shook hands, Sr. Rusiñol told his first and only lie in my presence. "Your accent is very good," he said.

Barcelona in 1965 was a raw, sprawling industrial town which on most days brooded under an enormous cloud of gray smog so heavy that for months I thought it was about to rain. Spain's burgeoning automobile and motorcycle industries were located in the western and northern suburbs of the great city, which spread out for ten miles or so in each direction save the east, where the sea stopped it abruptly. Barcelona's great modern architect, Gaudí, had not yet been discovered by the non-Catalan public, and thus most of his buildings were encrusted with industrial filth and several were misplaced on the maps the state tourist agency handed out. Actually tourists were rare, although tourism was the nation's greatest supplier of foreign capital. The millions of Northern European visitors came mainly for sun and sea; in summer they drowsed along the beaches of the Costa Brava north of Barcelona, and in autumn and winter they headed directly toward the warmer coasts of Andalusia. One had little doubt one lived in a police state: heavily armed cops were everywhere, almost always in pairs. (The story was these "twins" spied on each other and thus were unbribable.)

Still, something anarchic from the city's past clung to the place. Although Antoni Gaudí was a religious mystic and his art was meant to pay homage to the Catholic God of his upbringing, the buildings themselves were wild and totally unpredictable, made up as they were of beams shaped like bones, rooms without corners, windows suggesting the eyes of sea creatures, metal railings that undulated like the waves of the ocean, and from the niches of his great unfinished cathedral, La Sagrada Familia, peeped the stone eyes of snails and turtles. The project was approaching its hundredth anniversary and the citizens spoke of it as soon reaching completion, although the whole roofless jumble lacked more towers than it possessed, and only a dozen or so stonecutters were on the job. Even the cardboard scale model in the tiny museum next door was unfinished, though I was assured the drawings for it—in Gaudí's own hand—were extant. In the older quarters of the town near the port there were Renaissance palaces of great beauty cheek by jowl with the tenements of the workers. In the ancient, narrow streets the noise was unimaginable as the two-stroke *motos* tore past. The people themselves seemed to have forgotten how to talk outdoors, and conversations were conducted in a series of outbursts and harsh shouts. The anger of this repressed working class—once so thoroughly politicized and unionized—burst out constantly in unrehearsed moments of street theater. Anything approaching significant political action was outlawed, and the various police forces included a special political police nicknamed the *gris* because of their heavy gray serge uniforms. State cops were everywhere toting their tommy guns and taking notes on the least departure from the ordinary: a foreign license plate, a late party, a new houseguest, an especially aggressive dog. Up and down the streets they went at all hours with their little notebooks, writing in what I imagined a terribly efficient script. My neighbors ignored them and went about their lives with noise and abandon. A mile from our *torres* a camp full of Gypsies lived in a small clearing under a railroad viaduct. I would see the men in town in their wide-brimmed Cordovan hats strutting like peacocks. Everyone assured me their plans called for theft and I must never leave my house unguarded for long. As far as I could tell, the police pretended they did not exist, and their women begged shamelessly, screwing their heads to one side as though they were simple or deformed. I walked a wide circle around them.

My second lesson with Sr. Rusiñol began in Spanish. I had pored over the first five lessons in *Spanish Made Simple* and was prepared to discuss the objects in a typical Spanish living room (although as yet I hadn't seen one) or enumerate the various members of a family, but my maestro asked me to describe the landscape of New England and contrast it with that of the Great West. Before I could see what was coming, he requested my opinion on the part those landscapes had played in the work of Ralph Waldo Emerson and Robinson Jeffers, whose reputation was clearly larger in Catalunya than it was in Fresno. I explained as best I could that other poets had replaced Emerson and Jeffers, though the former was still an extraordinarily influential essayist and moral thinker. "Americans no longer read Robinson Jeffers?" he asked in English. "Then whom do they read?" I made mention of Wallace Stevens and William Carlos Williams, and in my faltering Spanish described them as the two great mountain peaks under which the rest of us wrote. Neither name meant anything to him, and he seemed utterly puzzled and more than a little saddened at the passing of Jeffers, who he assured me had made an indelible impression on him. I assured him that Jeffers had made an indelible impression on me as well, but the young were looking for something less spectacular, less orgiastic, less operatic. Of course I was speaking in English now. "Less operatic?" he said. "Do you mean less like Mozart or less like Wagner?" We were communicating. "Less like Wagner," I said. "Would you also say they want a poet who is less Spanish?" For some reason he thought of Jeffers as Spanish in character. Here I confessed my puzzlement, for though certain Hispanic poets were well known in the United States, García Lorca and Neruda, we knew almost nothing about the rest of their poetry and absolutely nothing about the nature of Spanish life.

After a brief silence during which he seemed to be considering my remarks, I asked if we might continue in Spanish. He bowed his head in a courtly manner and asked me to count to a hundred, to name the days of the week, the months of the year, the various trees outside his window, the colors of the sea and sky, the parts of the body, the features of the face, the reasons for living.

How Sr. Rusiñol located a copy of the old New Directions *Selected Poems of William Carlos Williams* edited by Randall Jarrell I have no idea. The stationery store offered a selection of new and used paperbacks for sale, but I'd never spotted a book of poems among them. Most of the books covered the range from English editions of James Bond thrillers all the way to English editions of John le Carré. At the next lesson my teacher informed me, in Spanish, that he had read the entire volume and was puzzled as to why it was regarded as poetry. I leafed through the familiar pages, wishing I'd brought a copy from home, and then remarked without thinking that perhaps there were certain poets who didn't translate well. I had heard that the French, for example, hadn't the least idea why Wordsworth was regarded as a major poet. Sr. Rusiñol remarked quietly, so quietly, in fact, that I immediately realized my tactlessness, that he had read the poems in the original. "Yes, of course," I said, "but perhaps one has to be an American to 'hear' Williams. I'm told the English find nothing in his poems." This was a spur-of-the-moment invention; I had no idea how the English responded to Williams aside from the fact that Denise Levertov, Thom Gunn, and Charles Tomlinson had all responded to him as ardently as anyone.

By this time we were conducting whatever lesson was going on in English. I offered to read him one of the poems to demonstrate its musicality, and he indicated with a nod of his head that I should proceed. I chose one of my early favorites, "Dedication for a Plot of Ground," which for me possesses an enormous rhythmic drive. I looked up after what I'd thought was an impressive and passionate rendering to find Sr. Rusiñol looking thoroughly befuddled. "I do not hear poetry," he said, and so I began to quote Frost's remark about poetry being what gets lost in translation, but this time, hearing my error, I veered off into an irrelevant paragraph about the greatness of Frost, whom the English also could not hear, knowing perfectly well that the English poet Edward Thomas was one of the first important writers to properly measure the true greatness of Frost.

Sr. Rusiñol took the book from my hands and, holding it tenderly, leafed through the introduction and stopped at an early poem, which I could see he was rereading to himself. He looked up with a wry smile on his face and said, "Tell me, in your own language please, why Mark Anthony is in heaven."

I started to talk about Williams's belief that our failure could be traced to the failure of our first European ancestors to submit to our hemisphere; they had fled the Old World in order to find a new world to locate their minds and imaginations, but instead of abandoning the garbage they brought with them, they imposed its order on America. He interrupted me. "Is this the Catholic heaven Mr. Williams is referring to? Does he put an adulterer into heaven as an insult to the Catholic church?"

"I don't think in this poem," I said, "he really cares about the Catholic heaven. Of course, being a pagan, Mark Anthony couldn't go to the Catholic heaven, and Williams was not a Catholic anyway. He means heaven to be a place of final reward for living as one should, for committing oneself totally to the passions that he, Williams, had committed himself to. It's Williams's own version of heaven." At last I was warming to the task.

Sr. Rusiñol looked once again at the book he so gently held in both hands and this time read aloud.

> . . . how many times
> from grass and trees and clouds
> enters my north room
> touching the walls with
> grass and clouds and trees.
> Anthony,
> trees and grass and clouds.

For a long moment he sat in silence, and then he looked up at me and asked, "Did I read that properly?"

"Yes, of course."

"Do you hear poetry in what I read?"

"Yes, to me that whole poem is very beautiful."

"Perhaps," he said, "your Williams is like our good Machado, for in our Machado there is something that only we Spaniards can hear, some nuance that crosses no border. The French also do not acknowledge him, though, like Americans, they have regard for our Lorca and even Juan Ramón. For us the good Machado is the pinnacle, the apex, the Alp that looks down on all the rest of our great modern poets."

What American "high culture" there was in Barcelona collected around the Institute for North American Studies on the Via Augusta, in one of the posher neighborhoods, some miles up the great sloping hillside on which the city is built. In 1965 there weren't enough cars in Barcelona to make parking a problem, so quite often I'd stop off at the *instituto* to check out books, for they had been kind enough to grant me the use of their library. I, in turn, had given them a poetry reading, for which the director, Dr. Frauenfelder, rewarded me with the largest bottle of Johnnie Walker I had ever seen.

One day, spotting me poking around the library, Frauenfelder asked me to come upstairs to his office and meet someone who shared my passion for poetry. It was thus I met Hardie St. Martin, who had only recently embarked on his monumental anthology, *Roots and Wings*, a collection of modern Spanish poetry translated into English largely by American poets. He had already enlisted the cooperation of Kinnell, Merwin, Haines, Stafford, Wright, and Bly. He asked me if I were interested in contributing, and I assured him I was, although as yet my Spanish was almost nonexistent. It didn't matter, he remarked, Bly couldn't order a glass of water in Spanish, but he had a genius for translating the poetry.

Sitting in Frauenfelder's cramped office, I was immediately drawn to this little man in a gray-striped suit and red tie. Hardie sat bolt upright, his delicate hands together in his lap, and laughed frequently. His speech, which was produced almost entirely in the front of his mouth, was at first difficult to grasp, for he did not so much speak as chant. He had wonderfully white, gleaming teeth, which one saw a great deal of because his mouth was never closed. He took so much pleasure in all he said that I found I took pleasure from it myself. The names of Spanish poets peppered his conversation, all pronounced in a manner unfamiliar to me. I took his accent to be authoritative, for José Hierro was to him Pepe Hierro and sometimes merely Pepe, and Francisco Brines was Paco, and there was a great salad of others whom he hoped to include in his project, poets whose names were utterly new to me, Gloria Fuertes, Gil de Biedma, Claudio Rodriguez, all of whom he seemed to know on a first-name basis.

In a few hours he was off by train to Madrid, which he assured me was a far more exciting and international city than Barcelona, for the citizens stayed up until the small hours of the morning talking poetry and philosophy and drinking brandy, whereas the dour Catalans were

asleep before midnight so as to be prepared for the following day's commercial labors. Why he had chosen to
live here and not in Madrid went unexplained. With his
olive skin, close-cropped curly graying hair, and odd
oval-shaped skull, Hardie looked like the embodiment of
all things Mayan. (I later learned he was born in British
Honduras, the child of a Venezuelan mother and a father
from the States.) When he switched into Spanish, which
he did every few minutes, I found him incomprehensible,
for he failed to end one word or begin another; it was one
seamless stream of watery sounds upon which the em-
phasis fell everywhere and nowhere. Still, his delight in
and immense knowledge of poetry were exciting for me.

Our second meeting was at our *torres*. Hardie arrived
unannounced and unexpected one Sunday afternoon with
two Spanish friends, only one of whom spoke any English at all. Antonio, a big horse-faced man, sat in a chair
nursing a glass of red wine as he prepared himself for
his voyage into English. He had one of the harshest
voices I'd ever heard, and he used it to drop his pearl:
"Kirk Douglas," he said. I'm afraid I was less impressed
than I should have been. He gathered his breath and
took a second chance: "Burt Lancaster." But since he
didn't pronounce his "t"s it came out "Boor Lancasser."
He was by trade a construction worker in Barcelona, an
Andalusian originally, who like so many of his *landsleit*
had come up to Barcelona when only a teenager to find
work and, finding it, had settled in. The other fellow was
a small, morose man who frowned a great deal, refused
to sit, and downed glass after glass of red wine without
thanking his hosts. They were killing time while they
waited to meet a third friend, José Maria, in a bar. In
spite of the din Antonio created, Hardie did his best to
keep the attention on things poetic. He had the day before received some translations of Machado from Bly;
they were remarkable, and he wanted to share them with
me as soon as possible. He recounted a tale of Bly's ad-

ventures in England, and how without effort Robert had
appalled the Brits with his pronouncements on the ulti-
mate nature of poetry. It was clear that Hardie was under
the sway of this great romantic figure who was Bly or
some creation of Hardie's he called Bly. At one moment,
out of the corner of my eye I caught the morose fellow
fondling himself as he stared at my wife. Hardie caught
my glance and quickly looked over his shoulder. The
man laughed in Hardie's face and shouted something unintelligible. Hardie leaped to his feet and confronted him.
The man shouted back, and then Hardie slapped him
across the face. Antonio rose from his chair and ordered
the man out. A few minutes later Hardie and Antonio
left to keep their appointment.

Spanish Made Simple is a book designed to aid the commercial traveler who wanders into the uncharted regions
of Mexico without a native guide. It teaches one how to
ask for the prices of *sarapes* and *rebozos* and even *retratos*,
it helps one order a meal or locate a bus stop or call for a
taxi. Mastered, it would also allow one to spend a cordial
evening in the company of a Mexican *comerciante* and
his *esposa* and *niños*. It is remarkably mum on the subject of prosody and seems to have no opinions whatever
on the entire dramatic unfolding of poetry in Spanish
from Góngora to Blas de Otero. Thus I was severely
handicapped during my hours with Sr. Rusiñol, for he
kept veering away from the language of daily intercourse
to speak of Miguel Hernandez, Juan Ramón, and his
favorite, the good Machado. It was actually some weeks
before I discovered that Juan Ramón, whom I pretended
to have read, for he had assured me that everyone had
read him, and Juan Ramón Jiménez were one and the
same person. Once, when I had the temerity to ask if he
admired the shorter lyrics of Jiménez, he stared at me in
puzzlement. I repeated the name and when he remained
silent wrote it carefully on my notebook, which I turned

so he might read the name I was sure he knew. "Do you mean Juan Ramón Jiménez?" he said in English. Of course I did. Ah, Spaniards did not refer to him as Jiménez but, rather, by his "real" name, Juan Ramón. I was slightly puzzled, and he saw it immediately and assured me this was a fact.

"Why do you not say 'Federico García' instead of García Lorca or simply Lorca?" I asked.

"Aha," he said, "because half the country is García and only Lorca is Lorca." Yes, of course, it all made perfect sense.

In Spanish I asked why when he referred to Antonio Machado he always said "*el buen Machado*" (the good Machado) and not simply Machado? Because, he explained, they had two Machados, both poets, brothers in fact, one Manuel, or Manolo, as he was often called, and the great Antonio. Did they call Antonio the good Machado because he was the superior poet? Only partly, Sr. Rusiñol assured me. Manolo had been something of a dandy, a fop, a popular figure in the Madrid of his day, who lived the high life, wrote some distinguished poems, and devoted most of his energies to enjoying himself. He was what Spaniards referred to as a "*señorito*": a young man or formerly young man who wallowed in his pleasures and privileges. "Let me show you one of his poems," he said. He rose and peered nearsightedly at his bookshelves until he located a slender paperback that was falling apart. "There's no point in purchasing him in a finer edition," he said, for the frail book he held was exactly what Manolo deserved. The poem, "Felipe IV," focuses mostly on the king's wardrobe, which is dark and tasteful and contrasts with his pale complexion and frail, blue-veined hand. It reads like a portrait of a portrait by Velázquez.

"Very elegant," I said. "It's a sonnet, isn't it."

"Yes, 'elegant' is one word you might use."

"And another?" I said.

" 'Decadent' would do even better. Notice that the king has put aside the scepter in favor of a '*guante de ante*,' a suede glove, which was more likely part of the costume of Sr. Machado. I've seen him painted with a book in hand but never a suede glove."

"Is this typical of his work?" I asked.

Sad to say, it was, and though the subject left Sr. Rusiñol cold, he admired the craft of the poem, which was as studied as Sr. Machado's style of dress. "That was the point: to be preoccupied with style during an era of social upheaval. From this it was only a small step to a portrait of Charles V, and then another smaller step to the Generalísimo." It was clear he was referring to Franco, for Manuel—who outlived Antonio by eight years—had done well under the dictatorship.

"And Antonio," I asked, "what were his affiliations?" I grew bolder: "What were his politics?"

Sr. Rusiñol took a deep breath and measured me carefully. "Antonio Machado, our greatest poet of this century, was naturally a man of the people. He put his whole soul into the struggle for *libertad*." Did he mean that the good Machado took the side of the Republic during the Spanish Civil War? "I mean exactly that," he said, staring me down, "and when our side lost he gave up his life." I had not failed to hear that crucial "our," which Sr. Rusiñol had so fearlessly uttered in the presence of a man he had no good reason to trust, although we were brothers in poetry.

The Rusiñols had crossed the border from Catalunya into France in 1939, just before the fall of the last Republican forces. At that time Juan was only a boy of fourteen, but he remembered the events with remarkable clarity. Once on the French side of the frontier, they had been interned with other Republicans in what one could only properly call a concentration camp, where they lived until the onset of World War II, which was only six months in coming. Once the so-called "fake war" was over and the Nazis grew serious about taking France, many of the refugees saw what was coming and escaped. Some returned to Spain, some joined the *maquis*, and others merely survived the best they could. But the most indelible event that etched itself on the tablets of the memory of Juan was the death of the great Spanish poet Antonio Machado, who had crossed the border in their company. "It was as though Spain itself were dying," he said.

"Did you know who he was?" I said.

"Everyone knew who he was. And, of course, my father told me how great a poet he was and that he had written poems in defense of the Republic."

"Was your father also a poet? Or a literary man?"

No, his father had been and still was an auto mechanic. He seldom worked with his hands anymore, for now he owned the large repair shop on the road to Gavá, but back in '39 he was employed as a mechanic in the Republican Army. But he was a Spaniard and a Catalan, so he knew the literature. "To this day I think he regrets he was not one of those who offered to fulfill the poet's last wish."

"What was that?" I said.

"He asked to be buried in Spanish earth. He did not ask to be buried in Spain itself, for even at the end he was the same considerate, gentle man. To have taken him back to Spain for burial could have cost the lives of those who returned him and God knows what the fascists might have done with his body. He merely said '*la tierra de España*,' the earth of Spain. Those were his words. My father was there and heard them. Over the years he's repeated those words to me many times."

"How did they do that?"

"They simply crossed the frontier at night and dug sacks of the true soil of Spain and returned. When he was buried they packed around the coffin this earth from Spain." He, Sr. Juan Rusiñol, only a boy of fourteen, was there at the end; he would remember that day for the rest of his life. I asked if it had been a rainy Thursday. No, it had not been a day out of a poem. "Perhaps," he said, "Vallejo did die as he predicted, on a day of downpours in Paris, but Machado was buried on a beautiful day in early spring. That was the irony, the day was very beautiful, a day he would have loved. It might have been a Thursday; I do not recall everything. I was not yet a poet, so I did not truly know how much I was losing."

Once again Sr. Rusiñol rose and went to his bookcase. This time he returned with a book bound in boards, the spine covered with what appeared to be cracking red-dyed leather going white. He held it up for me to read the title, *Nuevas Canciones*, and above the title, also in gilt letters and in very small print, the author's name, Machado. Along the length of the spine were five star-shaped golden blossoms each framed by a golden vine. He moved his chair around the table and sat next to me and opened the book, leafing patiently past the title page, yellowing with age and stiffening, to the dedication page, which read "*A la memoria de D. Cristobol Torres.*" Underneath the dedication, at a forty-five-degree angle in black ink gone brown, was the one name clearly though inelegantly inscribed, "Machado," the poet's own signature.

He stopped leafing through the pages when he reached a poem that began, "*Hacia Madrid, una noche, / va el tren por Guadarrama.*" He read in a slow, somber voice but a voice that was his own, without melodrama or incantation. When he'd finished he asked, without looking directly at me, if I'd understood the poem. I said I'd followed some of it. A train is traveling at night toward Madrid; it travels under something in the sky. "A rainbow," he said, "a rainbow made of water and moonlight." I confessed I'd lost the next few lines. He recited from memory, "*Oh luna de abril, serena, / que empuja las nubes blancas!*" "Oh, moon of April, serene / that pushes the white clouds!" He nodded his approval, and began to recite again, looking down at the book or pretending to do so. A mother holds a little boy in her lap, and the child in his sleep sees the green countryside pass by with its sun-brightened little trees and golden butterflies. "Yes, even at night, in his dreams," said Sr. Rusiñol, "the child sees the daylight world bursting with promise, for what he sees is his own world coming into being, and that world has all time to grow in. And the mother?" Once again he recited, " *'Ceño sombrío / entre un ayer y una mañana, / ve unas ascuas mortecinas / y una hornilla con arañas.'* And the mother's face is fixed in time," he went on, "for the life of the child is her burden as well, perhaps, as her joy. She sees the fire dying, she sees in her mind, the fire dying in the oven invaded now by spiders." He recited the last line slowly, ending, " *'y una hornilla con arañas.'* " He smiled. "Before there were in your house ants who did not know you, there were spiders in the oven, but García Lorca would have been the first to admit his debt to Machado."

"The tragic passenger who talks only to himself, is he Machado?" I asked.

"No," said Sr. Rusiñol, "though others have read the line that way. Antonio Machado would never enter his own poem as the tragic passenger. No, that man is simply the tragic passenger of the poem, he who must travel the way of life alone."

"But wasn't his life spent largely in solitude? Didn't his young wife die very early?"

Yes, that was true, that was no doubt how he learned intimately how tragic life could be, but never would he refer to himself as the "tragic passenger." "You see," he said, "he enters in his own person in the following lines," and he held the book up closer to me so that I might verify his claim. And he read, *"Yo pienso en campos de nieve /*

y pinos de otras montañas.' This is Machado speaking, for he has his dreams of winter landscapes, of fields of snow, and the high pine trees of other mountains."

"And then God enters," I said.

"Yes," he said, "Machado often invites Him into his poems, for there is room for everything in his writing. In this case a God by whose light all of us see and who in turn sees all of us, and he asks this God of his a single question. Do you know what the question is?"

"He asks if he will ever see His face."

"Yes," he said, "he asks if that day will ever come, for He sees all of us, our hearts and souls, at all times, but will we ever see even His face?" Sr. Rusiñol closed the book slowly and pressed his thumbs down on the back cover. He was sorry he could not lend me this book, for it was a gift, but he would gladly loan me a paperback edition, an *antología*, a selection of the poet's best work. He would be pleased to help me read these poems, for this way I might come to better understand both the Spanish language and the Spanish people.

Quite abruptly Hardie moved to Castelldefels. He gave up his rent-controlled apartment in Barcelona. He claimed he was sick of the noise of the streets and the overpowering stink of diesel exhaust. A lawyer friend—a man he'd met the week before in a bar—had arranged it. He had no confidence in my "Herr Breen." We sat in the living room of his brand-new *torres* enjoying a glass of sherry. Antonio was glued to the television on which *Real Madrid* was as usual trashing the Barcelona soccer team. A small fire of damp oak smoldered on the hearth; this was something Hardie had never before enjoyed, and he took great pride in the elegance of his newfound home. True, so far the plumbing had proved a disaster. When I asked how much rent he was paying, he avoided answering. Instead he assured me that, save for the month's rent to his agent, the lawyer friend, there were no hidden costs like those he was sure my Herr Breen would spring on me before I departed.

I changed the subject to the anthology. Could I work on some translations of Machado? Why, he asked, did I want Machado? I told him of my conversations with Sr. Rusiñol, the Catalan poet. "Every gentleman in Catalunya is a poet, including your Sr. Rusiñol," of whom he had never heard. "No, I'm sorry," he said, "I've assigned Machado to Bly." Bly had a particular affinity to the difficult Machado. It was not simply that both men led a solitary rural life, it was also their constant striving for simplicity and wisdom.

"But Bly is married and has kids," I said. "He's surrounded with friends and cronies, he is outgoing, boisterous, a shrewd literary entrepreneur, an influential editor. He has a bountiful nature, but he's essentially theatrical, exactly what Machado was not."

Hardie casually waved me away. I was taking the whole thing too personally. His attention had strayed to the contest between *Real Madrid* and Barcelona. "Look, *Los Niños*," his nickname for *Real Madrid*, "are going to score." The Madrid crowd was also standing and shouting as one, the players were dancing about and hugging each other. Each year it was the same. The two cities revealed their natures on the fields of sport. The speed and élan of Madrid triumphed over the stolid persistence of joyless Barcelona.

"I think you would do well with Unamuno," said Hardie, closing down the literary discussion.

While experimenting with his breathing, my son Mark passed out, hit his chin on the arm of a wooden chair, and received a nasty cut, which in spite of home bandaging was still oozing blood the next morning. I asked Sra. Fuertes, who lived across the street, the name of a reliable doctor, and she sent me to a Dr. Esteban Ruiz with offices just off the town's main square. The doctor saw patients at 10:00 a.m., and his office was a daunting sight, not perhaps as daunting as St. Vincent's emergency room at one-thirty in the morning, but bad enough to leave a sane person quaking. The huge waiting room was crowded to overflowing with a variety of people, bandaged and otherwise, many of whom appeared to be unconscious in the heavy haze of cigarette smoke. I was struck by the fact that most of the men had been injured in some way about the head: eyes, ears, foreheads, entire skulls were hidden in great swaths of graying cotton. I was immediately seized by several elderly women in black and ushered to the front of the room, where a woman in ordinary street clothes sat behind a simple deal table with a large notebook. The women urged me forward and asked me to explain the purpose of my visit. I told the attendant, a rather elegantly turned out woman in her thirties, the nature of my son's injury and indicated with my fingers that stitches might be required. *Sí, sí!*, the doctor would determine the nature of the remedy. She took my name. The elderly women then led me to an empty chair, awakened the man seated in the adjoining chair, and asked him to move so that the *extranjero* and his *joven* could be seated side by side.

Across from us sat another father and son. The father had buried his face in his hands, and the son—a boy of no more than eight years—was whispering into his ear. When the father looked up I recognized him immediately, for he was one of the younger officers from the local Guardia Civil barracks a few blocks from my house. He had removed his jacket and wore wide leather crossed belts across his shoulders and a wide black belt at his waist from which his holstered automatic pistol hung. He nodded gravely at me and once again hung his head, breathing deeply like one who has just finished a difficult race, his chest heaving under the gray-green shirt. The boy whispered again in his ear, but the man merely shook his head no, and went on gasping for breath. Expecting a long wait, I had brought a copy of Orwell's *Homage to Catalonia*, which I'd wrapped in butcher paper to hide the title. I questioned the wisdom of reading it.

The next time the officer sat up the boy took a pack of cigarettes from his father's pocket, selected one, and pushed it toward his father's mouth; the man accepted it without comment and leaned to the flaring match his son produced. The officer rose and began to pace back and forth the length of the room. At last he stopped and leaned into an illuminated wall of glass bricks; the day was a brilliant one, the sky of Catalunya a deep blue, the light lacking the golden dust for which it is famous. He was a short, sturdily built fellow so wide across the shoulders his shirt seemed about to burst its seams. He leaned his head into the glass bricks and then drew it back; a moment later he let his head fall with a sharp report. Before he could withdraw it and repeat the act, his son was on his feet. The boy was tall for his age, dressed in a white shirt which, though he wore no tie, he had buttoned at the throat. He was very slender and wore gray shorts that seemed too small for him. For a moment the noise in the room, largely made up of coughs and groans, subsided. The boy began to stroke his father's hand until at last he caught his attention, and then he led him slowly back to his seat, where he sat beside him, comforting him with little pats on his back as he whispered in his ear.

Suddenly I was aware that my name had been called; the door which bore the name of Dr. Esteban Ruiz had opened and a nurse—or at least a woman in a nurse's starched white uniform—had called out my name. Several of the women in black indicated with gestures that I should arise with my son and go forward. Before we could reach the door the young officer was there ahead of us, his son behind him pulling back on one hand. "My wife," he said, "where is my wife?"

"In a moment," the nurse said, "in only a small moment. Please, be patient."

Dr. Esteban Ruiz looked amazingly like my friend the poet Peter Everwine, though he was shorter and his moustache a bit fuller and darker. He was seated behind his desk in a small room lined with glassed-in bookshelves which looked as though they hadn't been invaded in years. He had been reading the sports section of *La Vanguardia*, one of Barcelona's worst and most widely read newspapers, which he shoved to one side as he rose to greet me. Alas, Dr. Ruiz did not speak English. In Spanish he asked what the problem was.

Mark immediately took over the conversation. "Here," he said in Spanish, "I've wounded my chin."

Dr. Ruiz removed the Band-Aid and stared lovingly at the wound. "It pains you?" he asked. He was assured by father and son that the cut no longer caused pain. "Then what is the problem?" We explained: The wound continued to bleed. Would stitches be required? The good doctor mused. He had no affection for stitches. Not in such a case. First they must be put in, which required great care; then they must be removed, which required a second visit. And there was the likelihood of a scar, not a large scar, but not a welcome sight on the chin of so handsome and blond a young man. No, he had a better solution. He rummaged in his top desk drawer until at last he located a great round piece of adhesive tape. He peeled away the plastic backing, studied my son's chin for some seconds, and then abruptly slapped on the tape. Mark staggered back. The doctor apologized, and then carefully tamped down the edges of the tape. "Perfect," he said. "You will be sure to remove it in a week, and you will still be very handsome."

"And so blond," I added.

I paid the woman at the desk. She also shook my hand and expressed her pleasure in serving the father and his handsome, blond son. She was none other than Señora Ruiz, the wife of the doctor. I could see the Guardia officer and his son nowhere. The old women in black pointed me toward the door, nodding their approval.

When I told Hardie of the extraordinary civility of the women in the doctor's waiting room, he stared at me in disbelief for several seconds and then laughed. He turned to Antonio and related my tale. Antonio shrugged and muttered a few, indecipherable words which Hardie translated. "Those old women have nothing to do but hang around all day waiting for someone to die."

"What did the doctor charge you?" Hardie asked. I told him how tiny the fee had been, five hundred pesetas.

"Five hundred pesetas is not a tiny fee. It's eight dollars. You were paying for half the patients that morning, that's why they ushered you up to the front. Once the doctor got your eight dollars he could treat the others without regret for what they had to give him. We don't have socialized medicine here, this isn't Europe." The injured workers were covered by a form of compensation that paid $1.50 for an office visit. The rest bring eggs or maybe a slab of ham *serrano* or maybe a few sausages. Had I noticed a certain pungency in the air? Now he was howling with laughter at the spectacle of this street-wise American city boy being suckered by a bunch of village widows. I knew he was right and said nothing about the young officer and his son.

At the dining-room table he presented me with my first translation assignment: a poem by Unamuno which deals with a blackened sculpture of the dead Christ in the Church of the Cross at Palencia. Although the language is slightly elevated and the poem more rhetorical than most American poetry of the 1960s, I found it presented a stunningly intimate portrait of the poet's feelings toward this God-man or man-God whose deity the poem struggles not to accept. I was surprised by how much I liked the poem. "What do you think of the poem?" I asked Hardie.

"It doesn't matter what I think of the poem. It is Unamuno. It is an important poem by one of the key figures of the Generation of '98, one of the keys to an understanding of what took place in this country's poetry. You must hear this calm, clear, unembroidered voice, the voice of a serious man speaking to serious men."

"To you this is a calm, clear voice?"

He took a deep breath and explained I was not reading American poetry or even English poetry. If I knew what was being written before the Generation of '98 I would come to understand what a revolution these poets had fostered.

"As significant a revolution as the one Wordsworth fostered a century before, when he turned English poetry toward the language of ordinary people?"

"Far, far more significant," he said, smiling, for it had produced poetry of much greater importance.

With its serious adult voice addressed to any and all adults, with its hope to create faithfully and in every detail the homely scene, with its naked passion for its subject and its nostalgia for a lost faith, how wonderfully and hopelessly out of fashion this poem seems.

> *From* THE DEAD CHRIST LYING IN THE
> CHURCH OF SANTA CLARA
> *(Church of the Cross)* IN PALENCIA
>
> This Spanish Christ that hasn't lived,
> black as the dung-ripened fields,
> lies like an immense plain,
> horizontal, packed down,
> without soul, without hope,

with closed eyes, his face to the sky
that hoards its rain and scorches our bread.
And with his black feet, hooked like an eagle's,
he seems to want still to imprison the earth.

Or perhaps God, penitent,
dressed in this miserable rag,
wanted to taste the death of this world,
in order to flush his conscience of guilt
for having made man, and with man
evil and pain.

Popular superstition imagines that his nails
and hair bring in
from this life the callused, the shelled,
dry superstitions,
whatever he scratches up, whatever he binds around
his harvested head.

This motherly piety of the poor daughters
of Santa Clara has skirted
with cloth of white silk and gold
the repulsive privates,
although this pouch of bones and pus
is neither male nor female;
this Spanish Christ without sex
lies far beyond that difference
that is the tragic knot of history,
for this Christ is ground of my ground.

Is there a poetry magazine in America that would accept such a direct poem, with its unapologetic appeal to our deepest beliefs?

One night, feeling a bit downcast in the terrible weather of the end of autumn in Catalunya, I stopped for a drink at a small bar on the road to Sitges, a lovely little fishing village down the coast from Barcelona. At the rear of the bar was a large square window through which I could see the waves crashing against the rocks below the terrifying coast road. "Bad day," said the bartender, a paunchy middle-aged fellow who wore a white apron tied around his middle like a cummerbund. He poured himself a Tio Pepe and drank to my health and then poured me a second brandy on the house. Above the window hung two crossed pitchforks, a display I often found in bars and inns throughout Spain; the tines were twisted and knotted like arthritic fingers. The rain was whipping in from the low dark clouds scudding over the hills to the west of us. All that afternoon I had been sure it would snow, though my neighbors assured me it was out of the question. It was too early in the year, said one; another claimed it snowed only once every ten years and this decade had already had its snowfall. As I tramped along the highway or padded, head down, along the shore, I was sure I caught glimpses of snowflakes falling through the air. I had been walking for hours every day. I would spend much of the mornings in bed, the warmest place in the house, trying to urge a frozen poem into being, and then after a small lunch of bread and *chorizo* I would go for a long walk to escape the smell of butane or the smoke from the fireplace. Usually in the late afternoon my youngest son, Teddy, would accompany me on the long walks along the shore, but today he was taking part in a game of soccer in the large field behind our house. Although my sons were not proficient at the game, they had to be included, because Teddy owned the single ball in our neighborhood that could be substituted for an actual soccer ball, which no one owned. With Teddy by my side the walks were far more rewarding, for we would question each other about the events of our day, how the year was going, and usually wind up casting about in our memories for our fondest images of home. Lacking his company, I had sought relief in this tiny roadside bar.

The door swung open and a blast of cold damp air invaded the place. Two Guardias hung their ponchos and leather tricorn hats on hooks by the door. The younger of the two also hung his tommy gun there while the other slung his rifle over his shoulder. "One bad day," he said to me, and drew a stool up next to mine. Before seating himself, he saluted me, and then laughed and extended a wet hand, which I shook. "Tomas Garcia," he said, "at your service." I presented my name, and he looked at me quizzically. "You are not a Catalan?" he said. I told him he was right. "How odd," he said, "you look exactly like a Catalan." He went on to explain that a week before he had come in out of the cold and introduced himself to a man at the bar, and the man, shorter than I and perhaps a bit older, had presented him with his calling card, which he extracted from his wallet. It read *C. Blanco, Catalan Fisherman*. "What a country, eh, we all have calling cards."

I told him I lacked a calling card and asked if he had one. "No," he said, "no one seems to doubt the nature of my employment." His comrade laughed and added that it was difficult to figure out what they were doing on a miserable night like this. "What do you think we are doing?" he asked me.

I would have preferred not to have been drawn into this conversation, but it was too late for that. "I think you've been getting wet," I said.

"You are very observant," said the first and more cheerful Guardia. "Our mission is to make sure the enemies of Spain do not deliver great bales of hashish to this shore. There are hundreds of vessels out there in the dark just waiting for us to come into this bar and get drunk so they can unload their cargoes of drugs. Were you aware of this?" I told him I was not. "Then you do not read the newspapers; they are full of warnings. Every day they publish a new warning against the fleets of our enemies." He unshouldered his rifle and handed it to me. It was actually a tiny, bolt-action carbine; it weighed no more than a .22 and looked about as effective. He had inserted a cork into the end of the barrel, no doubt to shield it from the salt air. "This is what they have given me to defend the sacred shores of Spain from the Communist fleet. I haven't a chance. The string on the cork is broken; one shot and I'm through."

"I cannot say if it is a good translation," said Sr. Rusiñol. He knew the poem so well he couldn't really imagine it other than it was. It was a poem his father had shown him when he was still in his teens, when he was struggling with his own religious doubts. Indeed his father had given him an *antología* of the poems of Unamuno.

I asked if Unamuno was one of his father's heroes. He was silent for a while, and then he said, "Unamuno is like a great monument for us all: philosopher, novelist, poet, savant, educator. He was the director of our greatest university as well as our greatest literary figure. As Machado is for us the soul of Spain, he is the conscience."

"Do you like his poetry?" I said.

"Always you ask this question, 'Do I like . . . ?' Who am I, Juan Rusiñol, to like or dislike this giant?" The only significant question would be, he explained, "what Unamuno would think of the writings of Juan Rusiñol."

"Do you read him for pleasure?" I asked.

"Pleasure? Do you read Walt Whitman for pleasure?"

I told him that of course I did, that when I read "Song of Myself" there were times I could barely contain my joy. I had to get up and put the book down and dance about the room or sing, even though I had no singing voice.

"You are lucky, very lucky," he said. "We parade

solemnly around our Unamuno with hushed voices, we
do not dare dance and sing in his presence. Like this poem,
he was august, far larger than life. He lived in the same
room with God, all his life he spoke with God as one
might speak to a brother whose love you were unsure of.
He was like a God himself, and then he died with such
courage and grandeur to remind us what a man can be,
to remind us that man is created in the image of God or
God is created in the image of man." I had never seen
Sr. Rusiñol so passionate. He went to the window and
pointed down at the dismal yard where the pines and the
few shoddy, leafless trees bowed to the sea winds. "You
know he was a Basque, Miguel de Unamuno, but at the
end he defended us too, the Catalans. Although he was
not of the left, he defended those of the left; he defended
everything alive in Spain that stood for life. It is impossible to believe today," and he gestured out the window
at the yard below, "that this poor earth of Spain could
again give us a man like Unamuno."

"How did he die?" I asked.

"You do not know? Then I will tell you." And so the
whole sad story unfolded: how, as rector of the University
of Salamanca, Unamuno was forced to take part in a
celebration of Nationalist Spain which turned out to be
a celebration of death. He had sat on the podium with
Franco's wife and listened to an insane speech by the
fascist General Millán Astray, who had spoken of the one
half of Spain as a cancer which must be removed by a
surgical process. He had whipped up the audience—
largely Falangists—to a frenzy, and soon they along with
the general began the fascist chant of *"Viva la muerte!"*
(long live death). When the audience finally calmed,
Unamuno rose.

Sr. Rusiñol went to his desk and rummaged about in
one of the side drawers until he located a small magazine
that resembled a comic book in its flimsy structure. "I
would like you to hear his words, for they are famous to

us." He read them slowly in Spanish. At the end, without looking back, he began to translate and paraphrase what he had read. At times it was a lie to remain silent, Unamuno had said, and so he would speak. As a philosopher he had dealt in paradoxes all his life, but this meaningless, necrophilous cry "Long live death!" repelled him. "General Millán Astray is a cripple," he said. This was true, for he'd lost an arm and an eye in combat as head of the Foreign Legion. "And if he has his way, the general will create many more cripples. The general would like to create a new Spain in his own crippled image." At this point the general could not contain himself and screamed, "Death to the intellectuals! Long live death!" A machine gun was pointed at the head of Unamuno, but it did not silence him. Sr. Rusiñol bowed again to the text and translated with precision. Unamuno spoke:

> This is the temple of the intellect, and I am its high priest. It is you who profane its sacred precincts. You will win, because you have more than enough brute force. But you will not convince. For to persuade you would need what you lack: reason and right in your struggle. I consider it futile to exhort you to think of Spain.

Amazingly enough, when Sr. Rusiñol finished he was dry-eyed. He looked at me directly and remarked that it was General Franco's wife who probably saved the poet from being murdered on the spot, though it hardly mattered, for six weeks later he died of a broken heart. "I understand your Walt Whitman died an old man, in bed. Whereas our García Lorca died against a wall, still in his youth. We love our poets."

I decided the best thing I could do was select a short poem by Machado and do my best to translate it. If I waited for permission from someone, even from myself, it would never come. I chose one that began, "*La casa tan querida*," because I could translate the first two lines without consulting a dictionary. Also it did not rhyme, and the lines seemed of no fixed length, so most of the usual formal considerations were irrelevant. The syntax of the first stanza—which was a single, very complex sentence—gave me fits. I wanted not to have to resort to breaking it into two or even three sentences. Hours passed, and I felt I was simply moving words around and not getting any closer to a version of the poem I'd be happy with, but a curious thing was happening during these hours: I was falling in love with the taste of the Spanish on my tongue.

I went for a long walk down by the sea and began quoting passages from the poem. To my great surprise I had memorized all of it, though I no longer recalled how I'd translated most of it. The poem concerns a man who goes back to view a house that was very dear to him because once a certain woman lived there. The place is now an uninhabited wreck, and the wreck reveals its worm-eaten skeleton. The short second stanza goes:

> *La luna está vertiendo*
> *su clara luz en sueños que platea*
> *en las ventanas. Mal vestido y triste,*
> *voy caminando por la calle vieja.*

We discover it's night. The moon "is shedding / its clear light of dreams / that silver the windows." Why would the windows still remain in a junked house? Perhaps the speaker is remembering it as it was even though he places the experience in the present. Perhaps he is demonstrating how the past takes pre-eminence over everything. I repeated the final sentence over and over, for I was describing myself, alone, bundled in thick, coarse sweaters against the sea winds, feeling each of my thirty-seven years twice over. "Shabby and sad / I

make it down the old street." The experience was utterly
not mine, for there was no woman of romance anywhere
in the world whose loss I still regretted, but there was in
me a yearning for a place of the past, a house to which I
could return and be taken in, a place that had once mattered and still mattered. No such place existed. I had had
the American experience of finding the old house replaced
by a parking lot, and this was 1965—two years before
what in Detroit would come to be known as the Great
Rebellion—and much of the neighborhood of my growing up was still unburned. It would take another twenty-
five years to show me how fully Machado's poem dealt
with a life I could never live, for by the time I truly became that shabby old man the places of my growing up
had been obliterated. The American experience is to return and discover one cannot even find the way, for the
streets abruptly end, replaced by freeways, the houses
have been removed for urban renewal that never takes
place, and nothing remains, not even a junked skeleton
"silvered by moonlight." When I want to find an image
of my Detroit I go to the poetry of World War II—for
instance, to this passage from Miroslav Holub's "Five
Minutes After the Air Raid:

> In Pilsen,
> Twenty-six Station Road,
> she climbed to the Third Floor
> up stairs which were all that was left
> of the whole house
> she opened her door
> full on the sky
> stood gaping over the edge.

Once again I shared my translation with Sr. Rusiñol.
He pored over it for several minutes, and then looked up
at me. "You are pleased with this first sentence?" I had
to admit I was not. It sounded graceless and awkward.

I was certain I was doing a great disservice to the original. No doubt I was right, he murmured, but still it was a noble effort, this effort to create one sentence out of so complex a sentence. He was sure I had understood the original and got the meaning right, but he could not help me, for his English was not up to the task. "May I ask you a somewhat personal question?" he said. "Did you get any pleasure from reading this over and over, as you must have?" and he smiled broadly.

I told him it had given me a profound and curious pleasure I could not explain and one that I was unprepared for, and suddenly I found myself reciting the second stanza, as I had done so many times to myself. When I had finished, Sr. Rusiñol nodded his approval and said, "You have crossed the border into Spain."

I struggled another day with my little Machado poem and finally decided to share it with Hardie. He took it immediately to the dining-room table, which served as his office, got down his Machado from a shelf, and compared the translation and the original for a full ten minutes. "Bly likes this poem too," he said. "He translated it, but I doubt I'll use it in the anthology. He did a better job than you."

"I don't believe it," I said.

From another shelf he removed a large envelope, went through it swiftly, his reading glasses slipping off his nose, and finally withdrew the Bly translation and handed it to me. After reading it carefully, I said, "You're wrong, Hardie, it stinks." Hardie was clearly taken aback. I was not trying to question his taste where Spanish poetry was concerned; no one knew it better than he. I felt my ear for English was adequate for the judgment. "Look," I said, "how he cheats. He creates a parenthetical sentence where there isn't one, and it sounds awkward as hell. This man deep in a meditation on the past blurts out in Bly's version, 'she lived there.' Doesn't that strike you as a violation of the whole poem? And '*maltrabado*' doesn't mean 'badly lasting.' Look how graceless the second stanza is in his version and how lovely it is in mine. I admit we both louse up the first stanza; it's untranslatable."

"Nothing is untranslatable," he said, "but you're right, neither of you do well with the first stanza."

"And the second?" I said.

He laid the two side by side and studied the original again. I knew this was serious business for him; his commitment to Spanish poetry was his life. Finally he raised his head and put his reading glasses back in his breast pocket. "They're different. Robert's is Robert's, an effort at rendering the original as exactly as possible. Yours takes a few more chances. What I'm curious about is why the two of you were attracted to this poem. There's nothing remarkable about it."

Somehow I didn't dare say that I'd known all the words in the first two lines and so decided impulsively and on such thin evidence that this was the right poem for me, nor did I want to admit how many hours I'd spent poring over the dictionary, and how much I was still in doubt about my rendering of the first stanza. Instead I said something about the universality of the theme, that we all imagined going back to a place of first love, a place of beginnings, and how, going back, we did not find the place or found it utterly different from the place stored in memory.

"It's a familiar poem about lost love," he said.

"It's far more than that," I said, "far more. Each of us harbors a dream of a place that retains some magic for us. We believe that if we could return to that place and time and begin again our lives would somehow be different, fuller, and so we return. It's almost a quest. Machado's portrait of it is so moving and surprising; the place is at once nothing, a wreck, a pile of junk, and yet at the same time the false vision remains as true as what's before his eyes. We may go away totally denied and defeated, but our capacity for belief remains, even the evidence of our actual sight fails to kill it: '*La luna está vertiendo*. . . . The moon is shedding / its clear light of dreams / that silver the windows.' The capacity to dream is limitless."

Hardie shook his head and clasped his small, delicate hands before him on the table. From the other room Antonio could be heard howling with laughter over some incident from "I Love Lucy," a local favorite. "I hate to say this, Phil, but you're beginning to sound like a Spaniard."

I translated one more poem by Machado, "Amanecer de otoño" ("Autumn Begins"), but this time showed it to no one. When our sons' Christmas break came we went south to the great cities of Andalusia. On the way there we passed through the small town of Lorca, the first of the so-called "white towns" we'd seen. At noon we parked in the center of the town and walked around buying bread, cheese, salami, and wine. I knew it was not the home of García Lorca, but nonetheless I felt it was a place of poetry. Going west from Alicante on the way to Granada, we passed close to the birthplace of Miguel Hernandez; back then he was only a name to me, though before the next year ended I discovered his amazing poems and failed to translate them with grace or accuracy and so joined all his other translators. We found the Alhambra on a clear, cold afternoon, the courtyard of stone dogs, the great floating vista from the battlements. In Sevilla we stayed at the worst hotel in the world, all five of us for $1.60, and when I awakened in the middle of the night I found peasants sleeping in the hallways, each on his mattress of newspapers. One small fellow, fully dressed, looked up at me, and half his face was smeared with black ink. I would never lose that image of public lies become personal affronts. There was a little

balcony outside my room, and from it I looked down into
the rail yards. All night the switch engines chuffed in the
darkness. This was a comforting image, for I had worked
in the rail yards behind the Michigan Central Terminal
a few blocks from Tiger Stadium.

The next day, in Córdoba, I was walking in the bright-
ness of noon with Teddy, and we were speaking Spanish
for the practice of it. A man, dressed in suit and tie and
also with a small boy, approached me and asked if I were
Catalan. He was quite sure my accent was Catalan. I
said I was, and we shook hands and exchanged a few
words, for this was New Year's Day, and the whole city
was in a festive mood. To be in Córdoba with the sun
shining on New Year's Day, I thought, what else does
one need to know one is blessed. Teddy asked me why
I had lied to the man and said I was Catalan. I told him
that I hadn't wanted to shame the man in front of his son
and tell him he was eight thousand miles off target. I
reminded him what a man on the Gran Via in Barcelona
had said to me, a perfect stranger who had interrupted
a similar conversation to tell me not to speak Spanish to
my son because I'd only ruin his perfect accent. "Look
how considerate this man was even if he didn't know
what he was talking about," and we laughed at the recol-
lection of the earlier event.

I thought that perhaps Sr. Rusiñol had not been lying
and my accent wasn't bad and that people actually took
me for a Catalan. People were always coming up to me
on the streets in Barcelona and speaking to me in Catalan,
and when I answered them in Spanish as best I could, they
would apologize. When I told this to Sr. Rusiñol, he had
said again that I looked Catalan, and now that my clothes
were from Spain it was natural for people to assume I
was one of them. I had asked what he meant when he'd
said I look Catalan. "We are all part Jewish," he'd said.
"From your family name I assume you are Jewish, of the

tribe of Levi." I nodded. "You look like one of us, fairly tall, slender, with the long face, the long slender fingers," and he'd held up his hands. "You could be my brother."

On the way back from Córdoba it began to storm. The narrow, two-lane road toward Madrid was awash and slippery. Again and again I could feel the VW give a moment, begin to slide, and then take hold. To the west the gray disk of the sun kept breaking through the clouds, and I hoped for some relief that never came. It was a Sunday, before noon, with no truck traffic on the road. Here and there we passed a solitary man on a bicycle or walking under a yellow plastic poncho. At a crossroads west of Jaén, two Guardias in leather helmets had parked their motorcycles on the shoulder. One stepped into my lane and held out a palm, and I stopped. He peered in the driver's-side window, which I rolled down. His aviator sunglasses were dotted with raindrops; rain dripped off his helmet and ran down his face.

"You are Hollanders?" he said.

"No," I said, "North Americans."

"Where are you going?"

"Jaén," I said.

He pointed toward the east and stepped back. I could hear the creaking of his heavy, wet jacket. "The road is clear, you may go," and with an impatient wave he commanded me forward.

A few miles later an old black Citroën, what my boys called a gangster car, had stopped in my lane facing me. I slowed almost to a stop. Two men were peering under the hood. One straightened up, placed his hands at the small of his back, and stretched as though in pain. Before diving in again to his labors, he turned and gave us a broad smile from under his black fedora.

"Jaén is where Machado lived much of his adult life," I said to my wife. "I'd like to stop there." From the back seat Teddy asked if we were going to find the hillside where he'd been shot. No, I told him, Machado had not been shot. He had simply lived here and taught high-school French, lived alone after his young wife died. "He was a humble man," I said. "He just taught and wrote. I doubt his students or neighbors knew he was a great poet."

"If you don't ask someone where the hillside is, you're never going to find it. You should ask that Guardia; they know everything."

"I can't ask the Guardia. They were probably the ones who shot him. And that was Lorca back in Granada."

"All we do is drive up and down country roads in the rain," Teddy said to no one in particular, "looking for a good hillside to shoot someone. Up and down the roads. And we don't ask anyone."

In Bailén, due north of Jaén, the rain was coming down in such great sheets I could barely see to drive. I pulled over and parked. We sat while the roof drummed on and on. A thick-bodied woman in black wearing a gray apron splashed by as best she could in her felt carpet slippers. We made a clumsy dash for the doorway of a bar. Inside the place seemed to be swimming in its own mild drizzle. At the far end three men sat playing a game with tiles; a naked bulb hung over their heads casting a faint greenish light.

"Can I be of service?" said a bartender who suddenly appeared from nowhere. I shook out my raincoat and hung it from a peg on the wall. I cleaned my glasses, and the place came to order. We asked for ham-and-cheese sandwiches and orange sodas for John and Teddy. Fran had a coffee, and Mark and I had red wine. "This is Sunday weather," said the bartender. "For several hundred years it has rained every Sunday."

We did not turn south toward Jaén. The bartender assured us the rain was heavier there on Sundays, and the cathedral, though very old and sacred, was shabby. "Part of the roof is missing, and on Sundays everyone gets soaked. It is the capital," he said, "so it has many court-houses and a *plaza de toros*." By now I was not sure if Machado lived in the province of Jaén or the town. I had the impression he'd lived in a small village, one he could walk to the edge of on spring afternoons when his classes were over. It may even have been here in Bailén, which ended so abruptly that we were instantly in the country driving between plowed fields that turned their brilliant red earth toward the grim sky.

La Mancha was more of the same, though the earth turned brown and then farther north a dull gray. The white cities vanished, replaced by unwalled towns the color of mud that seemed to hold their breath against the weather. Just south of Valdepeñas a solitary hunter with an air rifle slung across his shoulder waved at us from a field of stubble. "Wouldn't it be great to see Toledo under this sky?" I said. "It's pure El Greco." From the back seat Teddy said, "Pop, you wouldn't do that to us." Discouraged by the rain, I turned east and headed for the coast.

In a seaside village just north of Valencia, Fran and I took a long walk after dinner in the clear balmy air. It had been a brilliant afternoon when we'd arrived, the promenades thick with families out for their Sunday strolls, and all five of us had joined them, glad to be un-cooped from the car. Catalans would tell you that this was part of their world, but the people had a southern gaiety that the Barcelonese usually lacked. Returning to the hotel, we found Teddy asleep in our bed. We un-furled the huge road map of Spain and retraced that day's course east from Córdoba, north to La Mancha, and then east again over the mountains to Valencia. "We can make it home tomorrow easily," I said.

From the bed Teddy mumbled, without opening his eyes, "That's our vacation. We get in the car and drive, drive, drive, and then stop and take pictures of the church, and get back in and drive, drive, drive."

"You left out the part about getting wet," I said.

"I left out the part about getting wet," he said.

Sr. Rusiñol had never seen the great jewels of the south, Granada, Sevilla, and Córdoba. The *extranjeros* saw much more of Spain than most Spaniards, who rarely traveled in their own country. The farthest he had ever been from home had been a few visits back to what he called "French Catalunya" to see relatives and friends of the family who had chosen not to return to Spain or whose political activity before or during the civil war made it impossible. (The Franco government did not declare a general amnesty until 1969, thirty years after the surrender of the Republic.) I described the magnificence of the Alhambra. I described the ancient quarter that climbed the great hill with its narrow streets with their channels of running water that added a strange and constant music to the place. He had read much about the beauty of the city and of Sevilla, with its stunning antiquities. I neglected to tell him how we had passed the famous Ghiralda without stopping, believing it so ordinary it could not be the place. Nor did I mention our hours in the Jewish quarter, huddled in doorways in a vain attempt to stay dry. I spoke instead of the great sadness of the railroad station, of the solitary soldier who sat there alone in the late afternoon waiting for the train for home, a train I was sure would never come. Outside the light was falling; it would soon be New Year's Eve, and, sitting there alone in the great station, he became for me a symbol of my own distance from the life I knew. I spoke of the mean little hotel we'd stayed at, and how, standing on the balcony outside my room, I'd made the mistake of looking in the window of the room next door and there saw a soldier in bed with a woman. Her garments were scattered across the floor; his rifle leaned against the door. In a moment this had registered on my memory, and I was certain it would remain forever. I had turned away and tried to imagine the care with which he had slowly and precisely dressed the chair and placed his boots at the foot of it.

And Córdoba, what had I thought of her? he wanted to know. I spoke of the great mosque now converted into a Catholic house of worship: how on the outside it had seemed like nothing, a sort of dun-colored warehouse, but when we entered, it had exploded in a maze of brilliant marble arches, and how on that Sunday, the first Sunday of the new year, the chorus of children's voices had floated ethereally from the baroque Catholic corner, and how my wife and I had merely stood for half an hour in awed silence.

Then I spoke of the ride home and how we had stopped so near the former home of Machado. "No," he said, "Machado lived neither in Jaén nor Bailén but in Baeza, a village east of the city of Jaén though in the province of Jaén." It was, he had read, a very ancient mountain village, and probably nothing like the ugly mercantile, rain-swept Bailén. "You can feel the beauty and dignity of Baeza in his poems," but it was of course "cold Soria" which had at first been the most inspiring landscape of his life. It was there he had lived with his young bride before she died, and it was from Soria he had fled to save his sanity. I asked if I'd been near Soria. "No, Soria is in the north, in Castile, on the banks of the Duero. That is the landscape of his greatest poems." He began to recite from memory, "*Yo voy soñando caminos / de la tarde*," until he completed this famous poem. "Even after he had left he still dreamed of walking those roads in the afternoon. Always I see him walking 'among the golden hills, the green pine trees, the dusty live-oaks,' and asking where the road leads. In my mind I hear the wind stirring in the trees along the river. We know the beauty and sadness of the Duero from his poems." He took my notebook and drew a rough outline of the Iberian

Peninsula; then he marked a city, and said, "It is in that cold land that Soria sleeps."

"Sleeps?" I said.

Yes, it slept, for that is how Machado presented it. He knew that region only through the poems of Machado. In one poem even the stones seemed to be dreaming. "What happened to you on the balcony of the hotel in Sevilla: that is what took place in the soul of Machado." He had suddenly switched to English. The light was failing outside, though the days were growing longer. Sitting across from me, his back to the window, Sr. Rusiñol was only a dark presence whose features I could no longer make out, but the voice went on. "Anyone who writes poetry knows that experience you spoke of, and no one knew it better than Machado. At the end of his great poem 'Fields of Soria' he writes of that world, 'You have settled in my soul,' and then he asks, 'or were you there from the start?' At such moments it is impossible to believe that who you are and what you behold are not one and the same. Do you know what I mean?"

Yes, of course I knew what he meant, but I had been surprised on that balcony because I did not expect the experience in so foreign a place.

"Nothing is foreign," he said, and offered no explanation.

He flicked on a small light over his desk, which I suddenly noticed was devoid of its usual clutter of books and papers. By my watch I saw it was past five, and so I rose to end our lesson, but Sr. Rusiñol gestured for me to be seated again. He bowed his head and spoke quietly. "I must tell you that I am going away, and so for a while these lessons must come to an end. I have enjoyed them very much. I will miss our discussions of your poets and ours, but in truth I do not think you require any more lessons. You speak Spanish now with great facility." I'm sure even in the dim light he could see my surprise.

"It is not critical, this going away, it is merely a duty I must perform. We will meet again." And now he rose, and as I rose he hugged me in the traditional Spanish *abrazo*. I reminded him that I still had his copy of *Spanish Made Simple*. "Please keep it as a memento of these hours," he said, and he saw me downstairs and out into the soft evening air. I never saw him again.

The Castelldefels I knew is gone. Barcelona came out to meet it, and it's now a suburb of over forty thousand souls, many of them housed in raw cement high-rises. It has joined the modern world and possesses its own traffic jams, drug merchants, and topless bars. The train still comes in every two hours from the Plaça Catalunya, but even on a Sunday morning in June it's not crowded with picnickers, maybe because the beach is oil-smeared and the truck traffic has fouled the air. The little tobacco store that sold stationery and pens is no longer there, or if it is I couldn't find it, though I did find my *torres* and learned from the new Dutch agent I could rent one like it for fifteen hundred dollars a month, American. Hans Breen retired, and after all his years of wandering went back to Holland to settle down. Hardie's old *torres* was occupied by a young family. The elder Rusiñol's garage has become a new car agency and flogs VWs manufactured in Spain. At the bakery I learned the Rusiñols were long gone, and no one I talked to remembered the poet.

Perhaps that is why, when my old friend José Elgorriaga asked me to help him translate Machado, I agreed to do so. I knew it could not be done, I argued against the venture, I insisted my style as a poet was all wrong, but my friend only agreed. Everything I said was true, but he needed the help of a poet, and I was the poet he had. He handed me a sheaf of photocopies of his favorite poems that almost disappeared in the spiderwebs of his notes and with them yellow-lined sheets with trots in

English. And then he sat me down and read me the poems in his beautiful Castilian Spanish, occasionally rising in the dusty center of his tiny campus office to declaim a passage that moved his soul with its beauty. I had not witnessed such love of Spanish poetry since the departure of my Catalan friend.

Have you ever been moved in the soul? I know that is a ridiculous question, but I ask it because much of my life I didn't know such a thing was possible. I grew up with no concept of the soul, and when the conversation turns to the nature of the soul I will remain at sea forever. As a young Jew I prayed, but never for my immortal soul, and as an older Jew I never prayed at all. (In a recent poem entitled "Soul," I recount a true tale in which a Mrs. Morton made my brother Eddie and me go down on our knees and recite for company the prayer that should we die before we wake God would take our souls. We found the spectacle so appalling that no threat of punishment could ever induce us to repeat it. We were saved when my mother caught Mrs. Morton stealing her jewelry, and she was sent "packing—with no references— into the larger Christian world.") As solitary observer and memorializer of the Castilian landscape, Antonio Machado is often moved in the soul. He tells us again and again without the least reserve, he tells us with such simplicity and clarity we come to believe him absolutely, and in doing so we come to understand our own deepest experiences and to believe entirely in their authenticity. It is hard to imagine a more useful poetry.

In Machado's poems nothing hurries, for the world has been as it is for centuries, though of course it constantly changes so that it can return to what it was. "Mounted on small brown donkeys," he writes, "the travelers are lost from sight / where the roads drop below / the rolling hills, though now they rise / in the distance of afternoon, tiny painted figures / that stain the blazing canvas of dusk." We could be in ancient Chinese poetry or traveling with Yeats's figures carved in lapis lazuli. When "the wind stirs in the river poplars" you know that once again this autumn the dry leaves will deliver their ageless "chant to the water's song." Yesterday the branches "bent to the weight of nightingales" and tomorrow "the scented winds of spring / will hum through your branches." All time is one time in the soul of Antonio Machado, and there is a time for everything. The world whirling in its endless dance of time does so with a poise and dignity our lives lack—or lack until we read Machado, until we pour ourselves into his poetry and he in turn pours his vision into us. The inner landscape of his heart is a "city in ruins," his Soria, and viewing it each day, the "heart deepens with sadness," a sadness—as he says—"like love." He looks out over this world—I suppose his contemporary in English poetry might say he "gazes" out over this world—and he sees it as it is and at the same time as it has been for centuries, for to him nothing has changed except that it all lives in time and so is never the same. The whole history of Castile is the history of Machado, an empire gone to ruins, and the moment which is his life, the lasting moment he lives and relives, becomes the place itself. Think of being the very world you behold, of having been that world since time began, think of the present moment stretching back to no beginning and forward to no ending, and you too might say, "Fields of Soria / where the stones seem to be dreaming, / you go with me!"

Think of being a world of country trails, meadows, outcroppings of rock, fields of brambles, thorns, thistles, briars, burdocks, bees and their honeycombs, jackdaws, sheep. Think of the roads closed in snow, the high frigid winter plains of Castile rife with the memories of a Spanish empire long lost, the towns with their collapsing churches, stone fountains, belfries, the houses with their rusty gates and barred windows. From his Andalusian days the water wheel turns like a clock, the nightingale sings in the dark, water runs in troughs to the music of time. Where there is a tool it is an ax, where there is food it is dark bread, where there is perfume it is the lemon tree in blossom, where there is a weapon it is the crossbow, where there is music there is a lyre. Logs smolder on the hearth, an old man wrapped in wool shudders by the fire, his woman sews, and the lost son never returns.

And they go on waiting, for the lesson of this great maestro—he taught far more than high-school French—is patience, the greatest lesson the poet can learn, for without it he or she is subject to every corrupting influence. Impatience is our nightmare. As Kafka wrote, "There are two main human sins from which all the others derive: impatience and indolence. It was because of impatience that they were expelled from Paradise; it is because of indolence they do not return. Yet perhaps there is only one major sin: impatience. Because of impatience they were expelled, because of impatience they do not return." As one reads and rereads the poems of Machado it becomes impossible to believe even a single poem was rushed into being or hurried toward some form of completion. Consider this: I am writing about one of my contemporaries.

I delight to imagine Machado at his evening walk. The world comes to him whether he is on the cold roads of Soria or in a mountain town of Andalusia. A river comes into view curved like a crossbow, the boughs of the plane trees bend to the weight of bees, the wind stirs in the long grasses at the edges of sight where a few travelers appear over the green mounds of the distant hills; they speak back and forth in a language as soft as water overflowing cisterns; the rocks empurpled in the dusk dream in eternity. The air deepens and stills in the fields; time stops. Something like a vision rises in the golden dust of sunset, a vision of a world sweet enough to welcome the human heart freed from vanity and greed. I delight to imagine Antonio Machado alive in a world of others as good as he, a world as glorious as the simple language he found to create it.

Poems by Antonio Machado

TRANSLATED BY JOSÉ ELGORRIAGA
AND PHILIP LEVINE

FIELDS OF SORIA

I

Dry and cold, the land that is Soria.
Through its hillsides and savage peaks,
through tiny mountain meadows and burned hills
green spring passes
scattering among the perfumed herbs
and wild grasses the white, frail margaritas.
The earth does not come back, the fields sleep.
As April begins snow still whitens
the shoulders of Mount Moncayo;
muffled, the traveler passes, his face
half hidden in a scarf, and the shepherds
pass wound in their trailing capes.

II

The plowed fields
like remnants of dark burlap,

the crabbed orchard, the beehives, the patches
of deep green to which the sheep bow
between leaden, rocky hills, they sow
a first dream of a bright Arcadia.
In the distance, on the stiff branches
of the roadside poplars appear
sticky new leaves—a sea-green mist—
and in the gaps of valley and ravine
bloom the wild blackberry bushes
and violets bursting in their fragrance.

III

Mounted on small brown donkeys
the travelers are lost from sight
where the roads drop below
the rolling hills, though now they rise
in the distance of afternoon, tiny painted figures
that stain the blazing canvas of dusk.
Climb a hill and from the peaks
where eagles nest, survey the fields,
they are sunflowers of blood and steel,
leaden flatlands, silver knolls,
embraced by whole hillsides of violets
crested with peaks of blushing snow.

IV

Against a backdrop of sky the outlines of farmers.
Autumn begins with two slow oxen
plowing a hillside;
between their black lowered heads
and under the heavy yoke swings
a basket of wicker and broom;
it's a child's cradle.
Behind the oxen plod another pair,
a man bent towards the earth,

a woman pitching seeds
into the carved furrows.
Under a bloodied cloud of fire
in the running green and gold of sunset,
the lengthening shadows swell.

v

Snow. Open to the land the inn
reveals logs smoldering on the hearth
and a boiling pot bubbling over.
A north wind cuts across the crusted earth
scattering the silent snow
in white whirlwinds.
As over a grave the snow
mounds on tilled lands and trails.
An old man, huddled by the fire,
shudders and coughs; from a clump of wool
his old woman spins a thread, and a little girl
sews a green ribbon on her scarlet cloak.
The son of the old couple, a mule driver,
made his way over the white earth
until one night the trail disappeared
and he buried himself in the mountain snow.
Now a space sits empty by the fire,
and on the forehead of the old man a frown
has carved its dark stroke
like one an ax would leave in wood.
The woman beholds the land as though she heard
steps over the snow. Nobody comes.
Nobody is on the nearby road,
nobody in the fields that surround the inn.
The little girl believes that in the green meadows
she will run with other little girls
in the blue-and-golden days to come
when the white daisies bloom.

VI

Cold Soria, *pure pinnacle*
that crowns Estremadura,
with its turreted castle looming
in ruins over the Duero,
its walls eaten by the years,
its houses stained with soot!
Dead city of lords and masters
who fought or hunted,
of shielded entranceways
that declare a hundred noble families,
city of starved greyhounds,
scrawny, sudden dogs
who breed in packs and plunder
the filthy alleyways
and howl in the dead of night
under the crows' cawing!
Cold Soria! From the Hall of Justice
the bell tolls one hour past midnight.
Soria, Castile's city,
so perfect in moonlight.

VII

Silver hills,
gray knolls, purple outcroppings
of rock through which the Duero
arches its crossbow
around Soria, dark live oaks,
untamed acres of stone, bare peaks,
white trails and river poplars,
afternoons of Soria, mystical and armed city,
today my heart deepens with sadness
for you, a sadness like love. Fields of Soria,
where the stones seem to be dreaming,
you go with me! Silver hills, gray knolls,
purple outcroppings of rock.

VIII

Once more I came back to see the poplars
golden beside the Duero along the road
between San Polo and San Saturio
beyond the ancient walls
of Soria, armed outpost Castile
raised against Aragon.
When the wind stirs in the river poplars
the high voices of dry leaves
chant to the water's song;
on their trunks are carved
the names of lovers
and the years there too are carved.
Poplars of lovers, yesterday your branches
bent to the weight of nightingales;
tomorrow the scented winds of spring
will hum through your branches;
poplars of lovers, beside
the running waters that pass into dreams,
poplars by the banks of the Duero,
you are with me, my heart takes you with me.

IX

Yes, you are part of me, fields of Soria,
calm afternoons, violet hills,
stands of poplars along the riverbanks, green dreams
of the gray soil and the burned land,
biting sadness
of this city in ruins.
You have settled in my soul,
or were you, perhaps, there from the start?
People of the high Numancian plains,
you who keep the faith like the old believers,
may the Spanish sun crown you
with joy, light, and all things good!

AUTUMN BEGINS

A long road between
gray outcroppings of rock
and a few sparse meadows
where black bulls graze. Thickets of wild berries and
brambles.

Drops of dew
still dampen the earth,
and a row of gilded poplars
bends along the river's curve.
Behind the violet mountains
the first light of dawn breaks.
His rifle shouldered, a hunter,
among his quick hounds, plods down the road.

THE HOUSE SO DEAR

The house so dear
where she once lived,
now on a heap of junk
or leveled ruins, reveals
its black and worm-eaten
untended skeleton of wood.

The moon is shedding
its clear light of dreams
that silver the windows. Shabby and sad,
I make it down the old street.

I GO ON DREAMING

I go on dreaming the roads
at dusk. The golden hills,
the green pine trees,
the dusty live oaks!
Where does the road lead?
I go on singing my way
along the trails. . . .
—Twilight darkens the air.
"In my heart I felt
the thorn of a passion;
on a day I drew it out, and since
then my heart no longer feels."
For a moment the whole countryside
deepens into a meditation,
silent and somber. The wind stirs
the poplars along the river.
The evening fills with shadows.
The winding road—
a faint whiteness now—
fades and disappears.
My lament repeats its song:
"Sharp, golden thorn,
if only I could feel you
nailed through my heart."

IN THE CENTER OF THE SQUARE

In the center of the square, on the rough stone
the water spurts. Nearby, in the orchard, the tall,
bare skeleton of a cypress lifts the stain
of its dead branches over an ivied wall.

In the wide square the afternoon falls
on the sleeping foreheads of houses. The windows gleam
with the dying echoes of the sun, their balconies seem
haunted by the shapes of vague skulls.

In the deserted square an endless calm in which the soul
drawn like a soul in pain takes its ritual stroll.
Water gushes into the marble basin. In all that
    darkening air
the water's song is all there is to hear.

The Shadow of the Big Madrone

My first night in California I spent in a motel in Squaw Valley; it was late summer of 1957, and the place was being developed for the coming winter Olympics, but in August it was all but deserted. I was alone, having left my wife and two sons in Boulder with my mother-in-law while I came ahead to find a place to live. I'd come down with some sort of flu the day before and had stopped just before sunset west of Salt Lake City. I'd been seeing things on the road all day, things that weren't there, flying cats and dark birds who disappeared in the shadows; these creatures were beginning to spook me, but it wasn't until I'd stopped for an ice-cream cone that I realized I hadn't eaten all day and had no appetite. Very strange. The guy who made the cone for me said the usual, "Hot enough for you?" and as I nodded it struck me that I wasn't sweating at all, but everyone else at the roadside stand seemed stricken by the heat. My forehead was burning, so I drove on to the first motel and stopped. All I had with me were a few aspirins and some antihistamine pills, which I took. Before dark I was asleep. When I wakened some hours later I was so drenched with sweat I had to move to the other bed. At 5:00 a.m. I wakened again and got on the road ahead of the truckers and crossed the Great Salt Flats before the day's heat came on. At a filling station in eastern Nevada I asked the man at the pumps what the speed limit was. I watched his eyes behind sunglasses move across the hood of my teal-green '54 Ford two-door. "I don't think you got to worry," he said. Before dark I'd climbed my third mountain range in as many days. Never before had I seen such dramatic landscapes. In Michigan anything taller than a Cadillac is considered a hill.

Taking a small radio into my Squaw Valley motel room, I still felt lightheaded and slightly high on nothing. I didn't know if it was due to the altitude or the previous day's fever. I lay out on one of the beds and listened to the most amazing radio program I'd ever heard, on a station called KPFA in Berkeley, which was hours west of me. The program consisted of one man with an extraordinarily affected and ponderous professorial voice reminiscing on the famous people he'd known personally. His articularity and the range of his associations dazzled me: Gertrude Stein, Jung, Robinson Jeffers, Isaac Bashevis Singer, Luis Companys, Tu Fu. When the program ended I discovered it had been Kenneth Rexroth. A true poet on the radio! What a rich world I'd stumbled into. I was so excited I had trouble sleeping that night and once again rose and dressed in the dark. By noon I'd crossed the Bay Bridge into San Francisco singing "I Cover the Waterfront" in my glorious baritone that fortunately no one heard. Ahead of schedule, I stopped at a diner for coffee and directions and was amazed by the graciousness of the counterman, who drew me a map all the way to Los Altos, on the peninsula south of the city. There I would find the home of Yvor Winters, who had generously offered to put me up until I found a place to live.

That spring I'd received a short terse letter from Winters informing me that he'd chosen me to receive a Stanford Writing Fellowship. This was a great relief for my wife and me; our second son had come down with a childhood form of asthma and we were advised to seek a more gentle climate than that offered by the Midwest. For two years I'd been teaching technical writing in the Engineering College at the University of Iowa as well as one course each semester in Greek and Biblical literature, and my first teaching had left me with very little time for my own writing. It was the first job I'd had in years that left my hands clean, and I'd begun to wonder if I could both live on my wits and write my poetry, for I'd written much more while doing unskilled work in Detroit.

Winters's home on Portola Road was surrounded by a high redwood fence. A brief notice on the gate warned that there were dangerous dogs within; one was advised to use caution and enter at risk. I advanced gingerly. The door was answered by a tall, spare woman whom I'd interrupted at household chores; I took her to be the maid. When I explained who I was and why I'd come, she gave me a wonderful open and welcoming smile and asked me to be seated. In contrast to her strong, dark features, her voice was faint and barely audible; her hair was drawn back and largely hidden under a flowered scarf. I recalled a little magical poem by Winters's wife, the poet and novelist Janet Lewis, which depicted the slow movements of a cleaning woman, and I wondered if, like "some Elsie" of William Carlos Williams's famous poem, she were the same maid grown to womanhood.

GIRL HELP *by Janet Lewis*

Mild and slow and young,
She moves about the room,

And stirs the summer dust
With her wide broom.

In the warm, lofted air,
Soft lips together pressed,
Soft wispy hair
She stops to rest.

And stops to breathe,
Amid the summer hum,
The great white lilac bloom
Scented with days to come.

Seated, waiting for the arrival of my mentor-to-be, I
finally figured out that the woman had told me he was not
home. As the time passed slowly I could only hope he
would not be too long in returning. I noticed a photo of
Winters on a bookshelf behind the television set. (Did
Yvor Winters actually watch television?) He had aged
considerably since the famous photo of the severe young
poet I'd seen in various anthologies; it presented a grim
bespectacled fellow in shirt, tie, and leather jacket who
seemed in the throes of some terrifying moral problem.
This man was actually smiling, perhaps caught off guard,
and the woman who stood at his side in the photo was
this very housekeeper, who I realized must be Janet
Lewis.

The older man I soon met rarely smiled, but for reasons
I cannot explain I felt even on that first Friday afternoon
that there were stores of affection in him that went un-
expressed. He arrived in, of all things, a tiny red English
sports car, and, directing his gaze steadily into my eyes,
introduced himself; before I could take my seat again he
explained that the chair I'd been using was his and he
directed me to another alongside it, and thus we sat side
by side conducting one of the most awkward conversa-

tions I'd ever been a part of, but Winters was very good
at silence. Minutes passed while he stoked and puffed on
his pipe; occasionally he would issue forth a heavy sigh.
He seemed not in the least curious about me. I noticed
that every few minutes he stared into a mirror that gave
him a view of the front door to the house, which was behind him and to his left. Apparently he had never heard
Satchel Paige's dictum, "Don't look back, something
might be gaining on you," or if he had he'd discounted it.
Much to my surprise, at five that afternoon Winters
turned on the TV set to watch a rerun of a Robin Hood
serial. "Pay close attention," he said, "it may improve
your accent." So, he was not entirely without a sense of
humor.

That very night I learned he was a devotee of prizefighting. He later assured me that prizefighters and poets
had one central thing in common: pride in their abilities.
A fighter who doesn't think he can beat everyone in the
world is no good to anyone, he told me once, and a decent
poet has the same confidence. I too was a boxing fan,
and this brought us together at least once a week to
watch the "Friday Night Fights," on which we usually
bet when there was a difference of opinion. In my incredibly short career as a boxer I'd learned considerably
more about the art than Winters had. I had quit after my
marvelous coach Nate Coleman had advised me in one
pithy sentence regarding my chief strength. "Your ability
to take a punch," Nate had said, after watching me get
whacked about by a mediocre light-heavy, "is worthless
if that's all you're doing." Would that most literary
criticism went so directly to the point. I never lost a bet
to Winters, though the largest I ever won was a quarter.
I wouldn't say he was not a gambling man, for he'd taken
an enormous gamble on his talent as both critic and poet.

Like many Californians of that era, Winters was a
hater of some actual or imagined Eastern fight establishment which had managed to keep deserving West

Coast fighters permanently from glory. He especially hated Floyd Patterson and his manager Cus D'Amato, neither of whom was part of any fight establishment; they had refused to give the new California hope, Eddie Machen, a shot at the heavyweight title. (When Machen finally got his big chance he was knocked out in the first round by Ingemar Johansson, and thus it was the Swede who was given the opportunity to dethrone Patterson.) I soon came to realize that Winters felt about prizefighting exactly as he did about poetry: both were rigged by some all-powerful and invisible Eastern conspiracy, and he and his favorites would have to wait on the outside pending some miracle. For all I knew then, he was correct on both counts.

One thing was sure: he knew a lot more about poetry than he did about prizefighting. I later learned that he'd come to boxing as a young man living in what he called "the coal camps" of New Mexico, where he had gone to live on doctor's orders to combat a case of TB which he'd come down with in his early twenties in his native Chicago. In order to support himself he'd taught high school in New Mexico, and it was there he'd had to learn the fine art of boxing so as to enforce discipline on his unruly students. It was impossible for me to guess what Winters had looked like as a young man; at fifty-seven, when I met him, he had a thick sturdy body, one that in no way resembled that of the classic fighter. His shoulders were narrow, his beam broad, his arms short, and only the thickness of his neck suggested a fighting past. On Saturday nights, he told me one afternoon as we waited for the fights to come on TV, there had been public fights on the streets of his town in New Mexico; anyone and everyone was welcome to participate, and for weeks he had hoped to take part. But even then he was no fool: not being a large man or one carrying the heavy muscles of a miner, he needed to learn the finer points of the boxer's craft, and they had been taught to him by an old ex-pro.

Laying his pipe aside, he stood in his slippered feet, and showed me how his coach schooled him in the use of both right hand and left hand. He then faced an imaginary foe and pumped both hands forward and back like someone aping the movements of a cross-country skier. "Like this!" he exclaimed. "I never lost a fight."

"You were lucky," I said.

"After the first fight I had no more trouble from those big miners' sons in my classes."

"You were lucky," I repeated.

What did I mean by that? he wanted to know. I explained that the stance he'd taken was the worst possible one to assume if you were serious about not getting hurt. "Really," he said, "how should I stand?"

I'd known him some months when this exchange took place, and never before had I gotten his attention with such intensity. "Show me what I'm doing wrong," he said. I began a modified imitation of the first lesson my old coach had given me; modified because Nate always concluded that lesson with a little passage he entitled "Who's Boss," in which he'd pin back the ears of the fledgling by delivering a variety of punches that showed the student how little he knew. I had no confidence in what might happen if I were to manhandle Winters, so I merely demonstrated to him that he could move neither backward nor forward with any speed and that if I were to shove him he would land on the seat of his pants. I took the proper stance and demonstrated in slow motion that, though I could easily reach him with my left hand, he was more than a foot short of me and his entire body was open to my punching, whereas most of mine was distant and guarded. He nodded slowly, taking it all in. I then arranged him in my stance, left arm and left leg forward, and showed him how easily he could move forward or back, right leg following left forward, left following right backward. "That's the way Joe Louis always moved forward," I said. Winters asked how he moved back. "He never needed to move back."

"That was a counterpunch," Winters said and smiled. He was enjoying this, so I went on to explain that Ray Robinson didn't always follow those basics, because he was so gifted he could improvise, he could square up or cross his legs or punch off one foot, because he could get away with anything. Winters watched as I demonstrated these moves. "Louis looked like a natural," I said, "but he was someone who mastered the basics so well they looked natural. A Sugar Ray or a Wallace Stevens comes along once in a century." Winters was taking it all in, his cheeks flushed, his mouth loose and relaxed, his eyes wide. He asked me how I'd learned all this, and I told him about my great coach, who had once been the amateur-middleweight champion of the U.S. and was in training for the Olympics when World War II put them on hold for twelve years. "He was a lot like you, Mr. Winters," I said. (Yvor Winters, whose first name was actually Arthur, never encouraged me to call him anything except Mr. Winters, and I was comfortable with that name.) "Nate was a purist," I went on, "he believed in the art of boxing and at the same time he thought it was ugly to punch another person for money, so he rejected professional boxing and instead spent his evenings giving free lessons to kids like me." Once again we were seated, and I went on to describe encounters in the gym in which Nate had easily bested professionals, on one occasion a middleweight contender who'd given Graziano a tough fight. Nate had him down in less than a round; he did it all with body punches.

"Body punches?" Winters said.

"Yeah, they were wearing light bag gloves; it was a real fight. The guy wanted to hurt Nate, he wanted to take the mastery of the gym away from him. Nate couldn't let him do that, so they went at it with bag gloves, and Nate didn't want to break a hand on this guy's big hard head, so he destroyed him to the body." On previous occasions Winters had narrated some of the great West Coast matches, and I had merely listened. Now it was my turn to discover what an intense listener Winters could be. What I spoke of I'd actually seen, whereas the fights Winters related were part of a general mythology which passed from one man to another, few of whom had ever witnessed the events. When I'd finished Winters nodded. "You must be one hell of a fighter yourself."

"No," I said, "I stunk."

"You're being modest."

"No, I'm serious. My balance is mediocre and my hands aren't nearly quick enough. I fought light-heavies with quicker hands than mine. I'm strong and durable, and that may make it in poetry, but it's no good in fighting."

Winters nodded, convinced.

On the first Saturday night in Winters's house I was invited to a party he and Janet were throwing. The guests would include his former students Wesley and Helen Pinkerton Trimpi as well as the historian H. Stuart Hughes, who had left Stanford to join the History Department at Harvard. Trimpi was also just back from Harvard, where he'd gotten his doctorate. Winters stated flatly that Trimpi was now the finest Ben Jonson scholar alive and his soon-to-be-published work would prove it. The old man was pleased with this turn of events; he thought Wesley would be a finer scholar than a poet. Helen was the true poet. He'd seen almost nothing by her in years and so had no idea if she'd realized her potential. I reminded him that in one of his poems he'd urged the young poet to "write little" and do it well. Of course, he said, but he hadn't meant *that* little. I asked him why he'd ever suggested the notion of writing little; why hadn't he urged the young poet to write a great deal and write well? "You're being facetious," he said. I insisted

I was serious. Didn't every artist practice his art as much as possible so as to develop his abilities? He turned his head away from me and muttered, "You're not being serious."

Stuart Hughes, the grandson of Charles Evans Hughes, was one of the funniest-looking men I'd ever met; he had a long horse jaw and enormous teeth, and his eyes seemed set at different latitudes. He was a wonderful talker, utterly winning and charming. His wife was a dark beauty in the Jackie Kennedy mold, though lusher. The two of them moved with an ease and grace that only made Winters seem like more of the plodding bear than he was. Trimpi turned out to be a very tall, elegant young man with perfect manners. His wife was plain but handsome in a rugged way. I noticed her large, strong hands and her resemblance to the West Virginia hill women I'd worked with in Detroit and guessed her origins were far from her husband's. I immediately liked her.

Within a few minutes Winters began to bait both men. Hughes had deserted Stanford for Harvard. Trimpi had returned in triumph with his fine Eastern degree, and the old man pretended to be pleased with neither. The full force of his attack did not come until Hughes made his splendid announcement: his gorgeous wife was pregnant with their first. "You're happy about that?" Winters said.

"We're utterly delighted," said Hughes, a man in early middle age about to become a father.

"You're making a mistake," said Winters. Janet tried to shush him, but he turned to her and stated baldly that the man was old enough to hear the truth.

"And what might that be?" asked Hughes.

"Having children is the most difficult and thankless task in the world."

"Arthur," Janet said, "you know you're exaggerating."

Arthur insisted he was not. He had grown flushed and

angry and would not be stilled. Hughes shook his head back and forth and comforted his wife with small pats on the back. The room had stilled. Suddenly he turned toward me, where I sat on a bench in the corner hoping to remain invisible. "Mr. Levine," he said, "I believe Janet mentioned you had two sons who would soon be arriving."

"Yes," I said.

"Would you say that being a father is as dismal as Arthur has stated?"

"It has its problems," I said, "it can be very tough when your kids get sick." I did not look at Winters.

"All of you, wait until they grow up. Then you'll know what I'm talking about," Winters said.

The next morning all seemed forgotten, and Winters offered to make breakfast for me. I declined and helped myself to coffee and a bowl of dry cereal while he slowly downed a bowl of chili, odd fare, he admitted, for breakfast, but he claimed his pipe smoking had all but killed his sense of taste and he needed something potent to rouse himself each morning.

I was very comfortable in the Winterses' bungalow, an old stuccoed, unpretentious house that he'd added rooms to as his needs grew with the coming of children. The large backyard was dense with fruit trees Winters had planted, and at the very back, against the tall fence, stood the kennels for what remained of his famous line of show dogs, which once included a grand champion. Now there were only three aging Airedales who barked and leaped in a frenzy every time they caught sight of a stranger. Next to the garage was a large, unshaded area which Winters had transformed into a vegetable garden and where he worked several hours most summer mornings.

On this Sunday I decided to look up an old Detroit friend, the poet B. A. Uronovitz, who for some years had been a protégé of Rexroth's. I'd lost Bernie's address and so phoned Rexroth, who was listed in the phone book.

The woman who answered gave me the address. Overhearing me call, Winters remarked that I should not tell any of these people where I was staying, for they might do me harm. I told him that the man I was going to see was a very old friend. "I'm serious," he said. "Don't mention my name. Any friend of mine is their enemy." Later that day I located Bernie; when he asked me where I was staying I told him. "Winters," he said, "he's an old friend of Rexroth's; Kenneth thinks he's a great poet."

When I returned late that evening from San Francisco I was still excited by the city. Aside from New York, I'd found it the most attractive American city, and when I told Winters he told me I'd been taken in. It was not what it seemed. I believe the truth was Winters disliked cities, and in spite of his enormous intellectual curiosity he had seen very few of them. He'd spent much of his growing up in Chicago and Los Angeles, and now he found them both "dangerous": Chicago because of the violence of its population, Los Angeles because nature could easily erupt in sudden outbursts of floods and earthquakes. He hoped never to see either again. "I hate to sound nostalgic," he said, "but all of this"—and he turned his palms up in an uncharacteristic gesture—"all this 'development' has ruined this valley. When I first came here it was the most beautiful place in the world, a glorious garden. There was no traffic. You could hear the coyotes yipping at night." I asked him if they weren't a threat to his dogs. "A threat to Airedales? You don't know much about dogs. The Airedale can manage anything its size and most things larger."

One of Winters's favorite games was to take me out into his yard and quiz me on the identity of his trees, especially the fruit trees. On my second afternoon in Los Altos he'd introduced me patiently to such exotic species as apricot, fig, almond, plum, olive, lemon, loquat, and orange. Thereafter, every few weeks he would conduct an oral exam, which to his delight I would invariably flunk. Now and then I'd get one right, and he would nod solemnly to show his approval. Once I suggested we take a walk down the nearest large boulevard, El Camino Real, and we'd see how many automobiles he could identify. "Mr. Winters," I said, "I'm from Detroit, I didn't see a tree until I was in my late teens." He asked if that was true, and I explained it was meant as a joke. He did not have a great sense of humor, and yet he found very unfunny things funny. For example, his description of Chaplin's *Modern Times* (the sole movie he recalled seeing) and Kafka's "The Metamorphosis" were the same: he called each "mildly amusing."

I often missed his tone completely, especially during that first week. He owned a little female cat he indulged but was not fond of. The cat's mother had been a great favorite, but a year before she'd gotten out of the compound and been run over. Telling me this, he groaned and said in a voice that recalled W. C. Fields, "All along I assumed she would be the pet of my old age." I thought he was doing a parody of the fanatical cat lover I expected him to despise, but when I laughed he turned toward me with anger and shouted, "I'm serious, boy, this is no laughing matter!"

That same day he decided it was time to find out how closely I could read a poem. He asked me to fetch a book from his living-room shelf, opened it to a particular poem, and, handing it back, commanded me to read. The poem was the beautiful "Lullaby" by Gascoigne.

"I know it," I said.

"Read it again. It might edify you."

Written in the sixteenth century by the poet George Gascoigne, the poem had been a favorite of my Iowa friend Don Petersen, who I thought misread it exactly where Winters was most interested in it. It is a simple, repetitive lyric in what Winters called "The Plain Style," an unadorned style he admired above all others. In it the

speaker sings all his various faculties to rest as he pre-
pares to die. The poem was first published in the early
1570s, shortly before Gascoigne's death at age thirty-five.
It begins:

> Sing lullaby, as women do,
> Wherewith they bring their babes to rest,
> And lullaby can I sing too,
> As womanly as can the best.
> With lullaby they still the child,
> And if I be not much beguiled,
> Full many wanton babes have I,
> Which must be stilled with lullaby.

And so he devotes a stanza to his youthful years, another
to his gazing eyes, his wanton will, his "loving boy" addressed as his "little Robin," and in the final stanza sum-
marizes his farewells:

> Thus lullaby my youth, mine eyes,
> My will, my ware, and all that was,
> I can no mo delays devise,
> But welcome pain, let pleasure pass:
> With lullaby now take your leave,
> With lullaby your dreams deceive,
> And when you rise with waking eye,
> Remember then this lullaby.

I reread the poem certain I knew what the question
would be, but it came in a form I hadn't expected. Winters
wanted to know why, when he included the poem in
The Oxford Book of English Verse, Quiller-Couch had
omitted the penultimate stanza.

"I suppose because of the reference to 'little Robin,'"
I said. "He was a late Victorian, and it was a popular
anthology."

"What does 'My little Robin' refer to?" he asked.

"His prick," I said.

Winters was silent for a long moment. I thought he might be displeased that I'd passed his first test so easily. "What he calls 'my ware' in the final stanza," I added.

"Don't be vulgar," he said, in a quiet voice, "the word is 'penis.' " Winters turned our attention to matters of prosody. He had me read to myself Googe's little poem "On Money," which begins "Give money me, take friendship whoso list," and argues for the greater constancy of money over friendship. Winters had a curious affection for the poem, although he seemed largely unconcerned with money. We haggled in a friendly way over the scansion of the line "Believe me well, they are not to be found," which he heard as perfectly regular and which to my ear contained a substitution which allowed it to echo speech. He asked if I'd read his latest piece on prosody—which he expected to be his final word on the subject. It had appeared in a recently published collection, *The Function of Criticism*, which I didn't own. That night, when I retired, I found a fresh, cloth-bound copy of the book on my bed inscribed to me by Winters. The next morning, when I tried to thank him, he brushed my words away.

In Iowa we had been living poorly but surviving on my teaching, which paid $3,600 the second year. I'd been informed by my boss in Technical Writing that for an outstanding first year's service I was getting a $100 raise. But our rent in Iowa City had been $60 a month. Palo Alto and the surrounding communities were another world. I spent a depressing hour at the Stanford student-housing office going through their files only to discover that not a single listing was within our reach. One house that came complete with pool, gardener, and four-car garage, went for $900 a month and would have devoured three fellowships the size of the one I was getting. In

Palo Alto, near the Southern Pacific tracks, I found a second-floor apartment, unfurnished, that went for $120 a month. Janet Winters came with me to make sure it was a reasonable deal. For a moment we both stalled on the fact that I wouldn't be able to get in until the first of September, which was two weeks in the future. My wife and kids were flying out in a few days. Janet urged me to take it anyway, assuring me that she would work something out. "You don't have room for all of us," I said. She had something else in mind.

That night we went to dinner at the home of one of Janet's dearest friends, Marie Louise Koenig, who had once taught chemistry at Stanford. It was a curious evening, for both Winters and Marie Louise were terribly shy people in company and especially in each other's company. It fell to Janet and me to create whatever conversation there was. The place itself was astounding: a wild little island of several acres in the heart of neatly trimmed Los Altos Hills. The wide front porch gave onto an enormous lawn that sloped down to a thicket of young trees, weeds, underbrush, and unpruned shrubs. The area behind the house was even less tended, for Marie Louise hadn't gotten to it as yet. Wild as it all seemed, Janet assured me it was highly cultivated compared with what it had been only a few months before. To the west of the two-story mansion was a large open area covered with gravel; it was dominated by an enormous oak tree under which sat two picnic tables. It was here we sat out to have drinks before dinner.

Winters asked if I would like a highball, an expression I had never heard outside of the movies. I declined the offer. He asked if I had something against drinking. I explained that I just wasn't drinking anything stronger than wine. "Good thing," he said, "there's too much drinking in our profession." I asked which one he meant, teaching or writing. "I was thinking of teaching," he said, "but there's way too much in the other as well." It didn't stop him from having a highball, which Marie Louise brought.

It was late enough in the year that the shadows began to lengthen and darken even before we went in to dinner. In the fading light Marie Louise broke through her shyness and apropos of nothing recited the ending of a poem by Winters.

> There is no wisdom here; seek not for it!
> This is the shadow of the vast madrone.

She got the last line wrong and said "big madrone," but Winters did not correct her; he only sucked on his unlighted pipe, blushed, and nodded cordially. I thought I saw a bat circling near a side entrance to the house. Janet seemed to be watching it also, but she said nothing. Marie Louise turned her light-blue eyes on me and said in her thickly accented English, "Does that not say it exactly, Mr. Levine, just exactly?" I agreed. She went on. "I say those lines over and over to myself out loud every day at this time." She reported, " 'This is the shadow of the big madrone.' Isn't that just perfect?" There was something so genuine and infectious about her enthusiasm that I nodded in violent agreement, though in truth I had no idea what she was talking about.

The next morning Janet informed me that she and Marie Louise had worked it out. My family would spend the ten days in the mansion. Marie Louise had a separate basement apartment. She'd been thinking of renting it out, and this was an opportunity to see if it were suitable. I felt odd about accepting such generosity, but Janet assured me I'd be doing Marie Louise a favor. She had recently been abandoned by her husband, a physicist who was now in the Stanford administration; he had dumped her for a graduate student, a woman in her twenties. Since then she had been through some very rough times, but she seemed to be coming out of her depression. Janet felt that what she needed most was something to distract her, some outlet for her enormous energy. She had hoped the house would provide that, but one elderly woman in so vast a place had not answered the problem. Perhaps one elderly woman and a family of four would.

Amazingly, it worked. Marie Louise and Fran hit it off in no time, and within a day of our installation we were on a first-name basis. My two sons, Mark and John, loved her huge estate with all its overgrown nooks, its buried gazebos and duckless duck ponds. The second day John managed to fall into one of them and create a minor tragedy. Most evenings I was assigned the task of grilling a huge slab of meat outdoors. Within a few days Marie Louise's handsome second son, George, began to come around with his girlfriend, Paulette. The two of them were studying architecture at Stanford and were planning a trip to Arizona to meet their master, Frank Lloyd Wright. George was in training for the coming summer Olympics and bicycled for hours every day up and down the nearby hills. He seldom mentioned his older brother, Fred, though it was obvious that Marie Louise was proud of his record in law school and his position as editor of a prestigious Eastern law review. I gathered he was more conservative and plodding by nature than George, who, Winters had told me, except for the muscles and the tan was a ringer for their father, who was never mentioned.

Thus I was the senior male, the only father in this odd salad, and as such I was accorded the role of wise one and raconteur. Marie Louise and George urged me each evening to recite from the book of my past, to tell old family tales or describe the characters I'd met while growing up and working in Detroit. It had never occurred to me that this could be a source of interest to anyone. They seemed especially entranced by the tales of Zaydee, my tiny Russian Jewish grandfather, who at just over five feet had been a dominant character in my life. One evening, while grilling a huge steak and drinking red wine with George, I told of how even when I was in my twenties Zaydee could startle me with his moxie. We were on our way home from work in my older brother's convertible Chrysler, of which he was inordinately proud. Zaydee was in the back with his house companion, Lemon. (My grandmother had walked out on Zaydee after forty years of marriage, claiming she couldn't take another day with that man.) The old man recalled that during World War I he had hawked peaches and sweet corn on this very street. My older brother was skeptical until from the back seat came an ear-shattering cry: "Ripe freestone peaches, dollah a bushel!" The whole street had jerked to attention. "How did it sound?" asked George. But before I could do my imitation, George called his mother, and I began the tale over again for her delight.

When Marie Louise laughed she did so with all of herself. The sound would erupt in great barks from her sturdy upper body. She was a short woman and appeared even shorter than she was in her sacklike cotton dresses that fell almost to the ground, but she was very powerful. I learned this on my second day in her house, when she asked me to help her move a stone bench. The thing weighed well over two hundred pounds and I was reduced to stumbling after her and gasping for breath as she directed us effortlessly. With a single exception, the only time I ever saw her grant herself the luxury of tears was when she laughed. Her fine eyes would crinkle at the corners, and she would let go in a great flood which she wiped away with the back of one hand while the other held her abdomen as though she were capable of shaking apart. When she'd catch her breath she would ask me to stop, but as soon as I did she would ply me with wine and urge me into talk. She was, I think, the only person who enjoyed these long evenings more than I. Once George and Paulette departed and Fran went off to put the kids to bed, Marie Louise and I would do the dishes, though at first she was wary of allowing me into the kitchen. It was then we would have our most serious conversations on such themes as the young (which somehow did not include me), on poetry, on fiction, on history, on America, and, after some evenings had passed, on the subject of Germany. "I cannot go back," she would say, "I cannot."

Born into an upper-class family in Saxony during the first decade of this century, she had decided in her teens on a career in the sciences. It was while doing her university work that she met the young physicist who would become her husband. Those were the glory days of physics, and the two of them had met such notables as Heisenberg, Dirac, and Oppenheimer. Married, they moved to Leyden; Marie Louise began graduate study in chemistry, and her husband embarked on his teaching career. It was clear that Europe was drifting toward war; when a teaching offer came from America her husband accepted it. Her hands immersed in the milky dishwater, Marie Louise would shake her head back and forth and half-shout, "No, I cannot, I cannot go back!" From memory she would describe the Saxon landscape she yearned for, the small neat farms with their startlingly green fields trimmed right down to the roadsides, the narrow roads themselves which she walked or rode on her bicycle, the thick stands of oak and fir left to suggest the great forests this civilization had been cut from. "It was not like here in summer," she would repeat, "here it is burned to brown or yellow, there is no rain from June to October, but there it was a green world." She'd give me a little smile. "Yes, I came to womanhood in a green world. It makes a difference. But I cannot go back."

*   *   *

The apartment on Emerson Street, named for one of Winters's least favorite writers—which I took to be a good omen—had to be furnished. Janet sent out the word, and within no time we were picking up an assortment of abused chairs and lamps from her friends. Marie Louise offered a decent couch from the downstairs apartment, to be returned before we departed, and within a few days several trunks and cartons full of bedding, towels, and kitchen equipment arrived from Iowa by rail. We purchased some inexpensive beds, and Fran set about making curtains. We were in business. Seeing the apartment, Marie Louise declared we needed several chairs she could locate to go around the dining-room table, which was also absent. She insisted on calling the tiny space off the kitchen a dining room. She crinkled up her eyes and walked to a particular spot and announced, "The dining-room table will go here."

"Where will it come from?" I asked.

"Philip, you will make it."

When I told her I was no good with my hands, she brushed off my reservations. "With my help you will make it." I would also make, with her help, a coffee table. "You are entering the bourgeoisie, Philip, and today it is impossible to arrive without a coffee table." Back at her place, hidden away in a large storage room in the basement, she showed me two unfinished pieces of wood. One was a slab of oak about four inches thick and curiously warped; it was a long slender rectangle that vaguely suggested a coffee table. She thought for a moment and then said black was a fashionable color, black would hide the scars, and it so happened she had a can of black paint she had no use for as well as brushes. "Legs?" I asked. No problem. She knew where we could purchase short iron legs for next to nothing. The other piece was more attractive but presented greater problems: a six-foot square of plywood that was unfinished at the edges.

"We will locate thin pieces of lath and make it perfect. And the grain is very good. I have all the tools we require. Go home and dress in your worst clothes and then come back." She looked me over carefully and laughed. "Those clothes will do." And so we went off to a hardware store, which turned out to be "her" store, and bought lath, sandpaper, stain, and lacquer to finish the "dining room table." On her own she purchased wood putty, which she presented to me back at her house. "With this you will cover the few mistakes you make. Anyone who can write a poem that can please Arthur can become one of the world's great carpenters. Don't you think?"

Calling on all the skills I'd developed in my eighth-grade shop class, I worked alone for hours in her dim basement. Once things were assembled and ready, she insisted the painting and staining go on outside, behind the house, so I would not asphyxiate myself. Meantime she was working down the hill from the front of the house, using a chain saw to remove much of the underbrush that hid those trees she'd decided were her favorites. Every few hours she would appear with two beers in her hand, and we would take a break.

"I do not mean to pry, but I cannot help noticing that you sing when you do this work. I do not think," she went on, "that when you work on your poetry you can sing. I think you actually prefer this kind of work."

I told her that I'd largely done manual labor and I felt comfortable with it. "Yes," she said, "I recognized that immediately in you. I think we have this in common. Inside each of us is a peasant waiting to be allowed to live a simple, decent life, but the intellectual keeps the peasant working at all hours behind a desk. I don't know why we accept this." She smiled, her eyes reduced to mere slits in the light that filtered through the trees. Late afternoon in early September, and already an autumnal crispness was in the air. She took my empty beer bottle, and we rose to go back to our work. "Philip," she said, "this is great."

At the first meeting of Winters's graduate writing class there were three students. One was the other fellow chosen by Winters; he was an attractive young man named Francis Fike, who I had learned was also an ordained minister, though he lacked a congregation to minister to. The third was a young poet from Philadelphia who had come to Stanford on a Woodrow Wilson Fellowship. It struck me that without fellowships Winters would have no students at all. Winters had told the third poet to bring a selection of his poems so that the professor could decide if he should be admitted to the class. In Winters's place I would have grabbed at any warm body, but it was immediately clear he felt otherwise. We three students sat in silence while the old man, his face closed in a determined scowl, read slowly through the sheaf of poems. After some minutes of this Winters looked up and said, "This line doesn't make any sense."

The young poet, a short, dark-haired, neatly dressed fellow in slacks and sweater, seemed far less distressed than I would have been. "What line is that?" he said.

Winters read in his deep sonorous voice, " 'At dawn the young grass wakens on darkened legs.' The movement wouldn't be terrible if it were in the proper context of blank verse. As it is, it's set in a passage that's not verse at all, and it doesn't mean a thing."

"It is poetry," the young man said, "and it has a meaning."

Winters leaned back in his leather swivel chair behind the great oak desk. He was within easy reach of his poetry library, which was arranged alphabetically in bookshelves that reached to the ceiling on three of the walls. The three of us sat on metal chairs across the desk from him. It was a small, cozy room with a single window that opened directly onto the quad. It was easy to see why Winters spent so much time here. "Perhaps there are three lines of verse in this one, three of . . ." and he scanned the page ". . . three out of twenty-five or so, but this line means nothing." The young man began to answer, but Winters held up a palm. "I've lived with grass. I've grown every kind of grass you can possibly think of, even Jimsonweed, and I can assure you the line means nothing."

The young man repeated himself. "It's poetry, and it has a meaning."

"If it's poetry," Winters said, puffing on his pipe and shrugging his shoulders, "it's very bad poetry, but in any case it has no meaning."

The young man sat calmly and in silence. He appeared to be totally above the fray, confident in his abilities as a poet and in no way distressed by Winters's display of candor or bad manners. I thought to myself that if every class went this way I was in for one tortured year. I hoped I was just seeing Winters's version of what Nate Coleman had called his "Who's Boss" initial lesson. A few minutes passed. Outside I could see the students passing quietly down the bricked paths of the quad. Everyone seemed to behave as though we were in a library. I'd had no idea the name Stanford resonated so potently. Winters broke the silence. "You insist it has a meaning. Fair enough. Tell me what it is."

The young fellow rose from his chair, nodded first at Fike, then at me, and at last addressed Winters in a quiet, unruffled voice, reaching first across the desk to take the sheaf of poems from Winters's hand. "It means, Professor Winters, that I'm dropping this class." He padded to the door without looking back and was gone from our class forever. Perhaps feeling that some explanation was due Fike and me, Winters told us the young chap was a recent graduate of the University of Pennsylvania, an honors student with a brilliant record, but his intelligence had been wasted there, for no one on the staff of the English Department of the University of Pennsylvania had even the vaguest idea what a poem was.

Winters went on to explain that we would meet here once a week, on Tuesday afternoons, and each of us would bring at least one poem to class. In the meantime we were expected to attend his course in the English lyric poem, which met two early afternoons a week, though we were not obliged to register for it. If we wanted the credits he would certainly accept us as students. There was no text for this class save our own poems, but several anthologies of poetry were required for the other course, and we would be expected to read the relevant chapters of his own collections of criticism, *In Defense of Reason* and *The Function of Criticism*. We were dismissed.

Out in the quad I learned that Fike had taken the incident with the young poet from Philadelphia more to heart than I. For one thing they were about the same age, for another he felt Winters's attitude toward him was similar. The old man had told him that he'd chosen him for the fellowship only because "all the other applicants were worse." (I could only hope I wasn't one of the "worse" poets.) When I asked him what he'd thought of the Philadelphia poet, he smiled and said, "Gutsy guy."

Winters's class in the lyric poem was something else. It was conducted in a large airy room whose windows opened on the quad. The teacher sat at the darker end of a long wooden seminar table at which all of the registered students also sat. They numbered fewer than twenty. There were four regular auditors who sat in chairs against the wall; it was a rare meeting that did not bring one or two visitors. Winters always dressed formally. His tastes leaned toward gunmetal-gray suits, white shirts, and muted ties, the sort of outfit one expected on an All State claims adjuster circa 1957. The graduate students, who made up about half the class, also tended toward formality in dress; many were teaching fellows, and this was Stanford.

The assumptions he made concerning who was in attendance were curious. For example, during the first meeting of the class he remarked that the students would be disappointed if they expected to hear the sort of truths they'd gotten from reading the criticism of T. S. Eliot and John Crowe Ransom. All the students knew that Eliot was the most celebrated poet of the era, but I would guess that none of the undergraduates had read his criticism. Ransom was better known then than now, but he was hardly a name to conjure with. From Ransom he segued into a diatribe against the prose of Allen Tate and R. P. Blackmur, which he declared was unintelligible. He slammed a fist down on the heavy wooden table and announced that criticism was not meant to replace poetry or prose fiction; its functions were to elucidate and evaluate, and the second function was the first in importance. No one in the class had said otherwise. "I know what you're thinking," he said, "you've come from classes in which these men are regarded as the great minds of the age, and what you're hearing now is heresy." My guess was the students were wondering what the hell they were doing in his course.

He then passed out mimeographed sheets containing three poems: a sonnet by Shakespeare, a Renaissance poem entitled "Fine Knacks for Ladies," and the Googe poem "On Money." He asked the students to rate them, but only to themselves. He then read them aloud in his monumental style. Whenever he read poetry he pitched his voice at its lowest and chanted in a monotone, always coming to a heavy pause at the end of the line. His reading style was meant to underline the differences between speech and poetry, and nothing about it was meant to entertain. Poetry was a great source of moral suasion; forget that and you missed the whole point. It's possible the class did miss the whole point, for his voice and reading style so dominated the language itself that the poems sounded much alike. To my surprise he preferred the sonnet and liked least the Googe poem. "Fine Knacks for Ladies" he found delicate and lovely, a fine poem of its kind. He declared Shakespeare's rhythmic mastery far beyond the other two poets', and the poem was serious. I would later discover he could hear poetry as acutely as anyone I would ever encounter, though he did not always prefer what sounded best. How else explain his preference for Fulke Greville over Ben Jonson? When the class ended I had an inkling of how much I could learn from this man.

On the top floor of the Stanford library I found a spacious, well-lighted room that housed the university's rare-book collection. Most afternoons I used it, I was the sole customer. Here I located for the first time *The Collected Poems of Elizabeth Daryush* in four beautifully printed volumes. Daryush was the English poet who wrote the first truly successful poems in syllabics, a form she and her father had developed to escape what he, Robert Bridges, had called the "tyranny of the iamb." It was Winters, of course, who had put me on to these poems, and, ironically, at Stanford it was Winters who made the iamb's rule so tyrannical as to be called Tsarist. Winters also directed me to certain new poems by Thom Gunn in syllabics, but I felt such a powerful sympathy for these poems that I was afraid to study them for fear of falling under their spell. Most of the Daryush poems were genteel and sweet; they had very little to do with any life I knew, but they moved with such grace and poise that I fell in love with their artistry. My favorite was "Still-Life":

Through the open French window the warm sun
lights up the polished breakfast-table, laid

round a bowl of crimson roses, for one—
a service of Worcester porcelain, arrayed
near it a melon, peaches, figs, small hot
rolls in a napkin, fairy rack of toast,
butter in ice, high silver coffee-pot,
and, heaped on a salver, the morning's post.
She comes over the lawn, the young heiress,
from her early walk in her garden-wood,
feeling that life's a table set to bless
her delicate desires with all that's good,
that even the unopened future lies
like a love-letter, full of sweet surprise.

"Still-Life" was also Winters's favorite, for he had no more love for the "aristocracy" than I.

The woman who ruled over these books was firm in her refusal to allow me to withdraw them for even an hour from the room. I explained to her that I was at Stanford on a fellowship to write poetry, and I wanted the inspiration these poems could give me. She nodded perfunctorily. A tall, slender woman in her mid-thirties, in her flowered silk dress she seemed dressed for the role of tea-pourer at an English lawn party. She looked as though she were a lot closer to the world of Elizabeth Daryush than I was. She was sorry, truly, but the books did not circulate. In fact she wished there were a requirement that readers wear white gloves when they handled them. Not knowing what condition my hands were in, I considered hiding them, but finally I thrust them out. She laughed. She hadn't meant anything personal. If I was a Stanford graduate student she was sure my hands were clean at all times. I asked if that was a metaphor, and she gave me a blank look. "Do you have pencil and paper?" she asked. I had paper and pen. She was afraid a pen would not do. She gave me a # 2 pencil and pointed out a sharpener on the wall. The books could not be handled by anyone using a pen, for they might be permanently defiled. Then she took me through the exquisite nature of the binding, the paper, the print itself. These were precious books indeed, and I was welcome to copy in pencil any poem I wanted. For this I purchased a mechanical pencil called an Eversharp that promised to copy forever, and when, the next day, I showed it to the mistress of books, she smiled at my ingenuity.

Life was proving easier in California than it had been in Iowa. I was not teaching courses I had no enthusiasm for, the weather was mild, Mark's school was two blocks away, and our son John was not plagued by the childhood form of asthma that had put him in the hospital several times the winter before. But by early November it was clear we lacked the money to get us through the Christmas break and to the second check from Stanford. I applied for a temporary job with the postal service and was immediately taken on for a minimum of six weeks. Assigned a mail route in a quiet neighborhood in Palo Alto, I thought at first I was incredibly lucky, until the roving dogs got wind of me. One Sunday I told George, Paulette, and Marie Louise how Winters had given me a surefire method of dealing with dogs: fill a squirt gun with ammonia. One shot on the snout would do the job.

Marie Louise found the story very revealing. Winters, the man who raised show dogs and claimed to love them more than people for their breeding and courage, had discovered what he called a "surefire" method of dealing with his favorites. Dark clouds were scudding over the trees. The sun had dropped from sight, and the air was turning cold. It had rained much of the morning, and now it looked like it might rain again. "That man is all contradictions," Marie Louise said. We had had a very early dinner and were now gathered around the Franklin stove in Marie Louise's favorite room, a porch that had been glassed in and turned into a sort of rumpus room.

She had been in a very festive mood, especially when the rain had let up and we were able to grill. "Do you know German poetry, Philip?" she asked.

"Don't get started on that," George said.

She ignored him. "Do you know any German poetry?" she asked again.

My mind seemed to go blank for a moment. Finally I recalled that as an undergraduate I had helped a language major translate some simple lyrics by Heine.

"But you don't know German," she said.

A friend had asked me to help her translate the poems for class. She would recite them over and over and translate each word and phrase, and together we would settle on something that seemed to catch the original. I remembered being pleased with what we'd gotten. "What were they about, the poems?" asked Marie Louise. There were only three; two had been love poems, the nicest one was about a pine tree. Marie Louise began to recite in German. " '*Ein Fichtenbaum steht einsam / Im Norden auf kahler Höh'* '. . ." and then she translated haltingly, "A fir tree left alone stands / In the far northern country in the terrible winds. . . ." She stopped. "I cannot do it right," she said, "I have no talent for this. But you already know the poem." She worried a thumb across her forehead, and turned from the stove to face me. "So you think we Germans can write poetry?"

"It doesn't matter what I think. Of course gifted Germans write poetry."

"Why? Why are you so sure?" she demanded.

"For centuries they have given us great painting and perhaps the greatest music in the world, so why shouldn't they be able to write poetry?" The room was growing dark. Marie Louise had turned back to the stove; she stood ramrod-stiff, stuffing in small branches. After she stripped the leaves she crushed them to a powder, which drifted to the floor. "German is an old and great language. . . ." Finally I recalled my own reading. "Even in the versions I read, Rilke's *Duino Elegies* and his sonnets were remarkable. And the songs of Brecht . . ."

Marie Louise recited the little lyric by Heine, ending with the phrase "*Auf brennender Felsenwand.*" She repeated the last phrase. "It starts in the far north, but it ends in the burning sands. Such a little poem, it covers the whole earth. We learn these poems when we are very young, and they are always with us."

"Yes, we have poems like that. Fran can recite dozens of little poems her mother taught her." I had learned no poems as a child, but I didn't mention that.

"Once I tried to recite this little poem of the fir tree to Winters. Do you know what he did?" She had seated herself on a little stool across from me. She smoothed out her long skirt. Before I could answer she went on. "He held up a hand like a traffic policeman, just like a policeman, and told me to stop. He did not want to hear it." Why? I asked. "Because Germans are sentimental. They can praise the beauties of fir trees and clouds and then murder millions of people. Philip, what do you think? Is he right?" George tried to interrupt but she shushed him.

I didn't know how to answer, I suddenly didn't even know how I felt. I knew only that I wanted to say something that would be of comfort to this woman. "I don't think those who did the killing were those who wrote the poems."

"You don't know German poetry," she said. "How can you be sure?"

"Because it's obvious," I said, knowing at this point nothing was obvious except that this woman was a life giver. Outside the rain had started again. George switched on the porch lights, and we could see huge drops pelting off the hood of my car. He raced out the front door and clattered down the stairs. We could see him gathering up the heavy sweaters he and Paulette

had left near the grill. In a moment he was back, laughing, his fine blond hair streaming with water.

My wife even then was a far more social creature than I.
She wanted to invite Arthur and Janet to dinner as a
thanks for their many kindnesses toward us. I tried to dis-
suade her, but she is also far more stubborn than I. One
Friday night, after the fights, I asked if they would be
available. Winters nodded and said they would be if I
would provide a decent wine and enough of it. What was
enough? "Two bottles should do us. You and Janet barely
drink," he said, laughing. I confessed I didn't know a
decent wine from STP. "When you know what your wife
is preparing—I can only hope she is preparing the meal
and not you—give me a call, and I'll tell you the names
of some decent wines. And where to get them." We had
chicken tetrazzini and a Charles Krug Grey Riesling that
sold for $1.35 at the time.

Winters arrived in a fury. No one had told him we
lived on the second floor; he'd had trouble negotiating
the outside metal stairs. "They're dangerous," he said,
puffing. I was sure he was angered because even such a
short climb revealed how pitifully out of shape he was.
A highball calmed him down. The boys had been fed and
were next door watching television with our neighbors.
We sat to break bread. Winters ate slowly and methodically, trying his best to taste each mouthful. Janet praised
the meal and Italian cooking in general.

The four of us were seated comfortably around the
table Marie Louise and I had constructed; things were
going better than I could have hoped for. Winters decided that I would be the proper arbiter in a small quarrel
he and Janet had had. A look of dismay passed across
Janet's face. "I'd say it was only a disagreement," she
said. She knew what was coming. Winters put the matter
to me so formally and so precisely I had no doubt he'd

rehearsed his words in his mind. Just the day before Janet had been composing a scene in a new novel she was working on. In this scene two boys of fourteen and twelve, brothers, wrestle playfully on a large bed, their parents' bed. The play has a serious aspect, for the boys know that one day they will be rivals in important matters. "Janet," he said, "used the word 'roughhousing' to describe their play. I'd like to know what you think of the word."

I stopped eating and took a sip of wine. I could only put this off so long. Winters had put down his knife and fork. Janet and Fran went on eating. I thought the word was all wrong; for one thing it seemed terribly dated to me, but, then, Janet was twice my age. Finally I said I found the term too genteel.

"Genteel!" Winters exploded. "It's not genteel. It's far too coarse. I can't stand the word. It's simply too coarse." Janet was trying not to laugh behind her napkin, but she wasn't doing a very good job. Arthur turned to her. "You will ruin the entire scene with that one word."

Now it was Janet whose curiosity was aroused. She had stopped laughing, but it was clear she was still enjoying herself. She wanted to know if there was a word or an expression she might employ that would convey her meaning and not strike me as too genteel. She would rather be slightly coarse than genteel, but she was not up on the words young boys might use today. I considered the terms boys might actually use and immediately rejected them. One explosion from Winters was enough. "I think I would use the expression 'horsing around,' " I said, knowing perfectly well I would not use it. Janet seemed less than thrilled. She would think about it. Winters had gone back to his tetrazzini with a vengeance.

Encouragement came from an unexpected place. I had sent my friend Henri Coulette two of my syllabic poems, "Small Game" and "Night Thoughts over a Sick Child," and Coulette wrote back from Iowa City that not only he but several other poets as well were excited by them. Even Don Justice was fascinated by their movement. They were probably the first original poems I'd written. When I'd switched from traditional meters to syllabics something seemed to have been released, and without any preamble I was writing in my own voice. Coulette was anxious to learn from me how I'd managed to handle this form so quickly and with so much confidence. The truth was I had no idea. I had painstakingly copied all of the syllabic poems of Elizabeth Daryush, and then I made some tentative stabs at a few poems of my own in the form, and one day I was writing with this new authority.

"Small Game" was the first one I showed to Winters. He studied it at great length in silence. At last he looked up and said, "The rhymes are very good. The syllabic movement is fine, very fine. A poem in syllabics is seldom very good, but the details here are wonderfully observed." He paused for a puff at the unlighted pipe and said, "What is it about?"

I was caught off guard and, looking down at my own copy of the poem, improvised. "It's about the man who speaks in the poem and the life he leads and the relationship of that odd life to the life of whoever might read the poem."

Winters humphed. "You could probably say that about dozens of poems. I'm not sure you've said anything." I thought the poem was so clear it needed no explanation. I didn't dare quote the MacLeish line about poems simply being.

Before Winters handed the poem back he asked me to repeat my explanation, and I fumbled through it again. He nodded. When the quarter ended he sent me a one-page report on my progress. Again he stated that the rhymes and movement were good, the details well observed, but he could no longer figure out what the poem was about. He recalled that when I'd explained it he had half-understood me, but he no longer recalled what I'd said. He added that I might better use my new-gained skill with syllabics to write poems that were about something. I am still unsure what Winters meant by "about something." The poem was about something the way poems are about something, though it did not employ the language of abstract thought that was so dear to him. It would be too easy to say he despised the particulars of our lives and thus the language that presented them. I knew that was untrue. I had seen the man in his garden and walked with him through the dappled light that fell from his trees too many times to doubt his pride in what he grew and his love for growing things. He did not feel awkward and unlovable when he bowed to his strawberries and his tomatoes, he did not feel in any way threatened when he yanked tenderly on a branch of his favorite olive tree and spoke of the pleasure its fruit, properly cured, had given him. Calm and peaceful as it was on an afternoon in Los Altos, this was no Eden Garden; it was in the here and now, and Winters fought the grower's common pests—snails, aphids, and tomato bugs—and mostly he won. Perhaps "the mid-day air was swarming / With the metaphysical changes that occur," but the dust that rose was that of common earth worked by a man. At their best his own poems testify to what he often did not, that "the greatest poverty is not to live / In a physical world."

Even then I understood his distrust of poems in syllabics. The writing often comes in a great rush, it finds the rhymes quickly, and the poems take their own course. Winters had written a great deal of free verse, some of it gorgeous, but he had disowned the best of it and in some cases even reworked the same material into rhymed couplets. He believed in the morality of form, in the struggle of reason to discover what the imagination had gone in search of. In syllabics and even more in free verse the intuitions seize the poem and direct it, and Winters was frankly distrustful if not fearful of the intuitions. More than once he'd insisted that it was through his abiding trust in his intuitions that Hart Crane had come to his sad and watery end. It could not, he repeated, have ended any other way. According to Winters, all who wrote poetry flirted with madness and self-destruction: the more powerful the imagination, the greater the danger. To survive one practiced a heroic vigilance. All the days I knew him he lived that vigilance.

That year Winters gave his first public reading in many years. It was held in the auditorium of the San Francisco Museum of Art, and the proceeds went to the NAACP. (Much to the surprise of many of his readers and in sharp contrast to his clones today, Winters was a liberal as well as an ardent believer in equality, racial and otherwise.) A few nights before the reading he phoned and asked if I would help with his preparation. He asked me to make a list of those poems I thought essential to a final presentation. My list was modest: "The Marriage," "To the Holy Spirit," "At the San Francisco Airport," "On a View of Pasadena from the Hills," "Sir Gawaine and the Green Knight," and "By the Road to the Airbase." I'd written the names out on a piece of paper, which I handed to him. "Is that the whole list?" he said. "I'm not going to be able to fill an hour with these."

"Of course not," I said. "This is just a core of what I believe you must read." I realized I'd goofed again. "I'd like to hear you read the Theseus poems and Marie Louise's favorite, 'Manzanita.' " And then I recalled "The Journey," much of which I liked enormously. I suggested that for the sake of variety he might read the free-verse version.

"What free-verse version?" he asked, looking at me in alarm.

I explained that in an anthology in the Stanford li-

brary, a book with a title like *The American Caravan*,
I'd found an early free-verse sequence which included
passages that he'd reworked into "The Journey." He
slapped his forehead. "You found that in our library.
How did you locate it?" There'd been no trick to locating
it, for it was listed in the card catalogue under his name.
"My God," he said, "I thought all that was dead and
buried. I wrote that over thirty years ago. It was the
best I could do at the time. I shouldn't still be hounded
by it." I said truthfully that I thought it was wonderful
free verse, though I did not add that it was clearly written under the influence of Williams. "Yes, I knew what
I was doing, which is more than I can say for most poets
writing free verse."

When Winters went off to fix himself a drink I looked
at the little *Collected Poems* published in the early 1950s
by Alan Swallow. Fewer than 150 pages with notes, it is
an ugly duckling of a book. It seemed perfect for Winters. All the words were there and in the proper order,
and the binding is sturdy enough to keep things together
for a lifetime. When he returned Winters asked me to
listen to a reading of the Theseus poems, a long, brilliant
sequence full of gore and sex which traces the life of the
Athenian hero from his youthful slaughter of virgins to
his exile in old age and his final betrayal. Winters read
mainly in his familiar monotone, though now and then
the power of the blank verse would seize him and his
voice would ride out on a dazzling riff. As he read I asked
myself, Who is he talking about if not himself? I knew
the poem was written before he was forty, and yet it
read like a preparation for the end, the finale. What
chutzpah, I thought. He'd even outdone Tennyson with
his aged Ulysses. When he'd finished he sat in silence for
some time. "No," he said, "I can't read it."

"You've got to read it. It sounded marvelous." It had,
and I couldn't believe he didn't know it. "It's superb

blank verse and like nothing else." I wasn't flattering him, and he knew it.

"I couldn't read it before all those people." He went through "To the Holy Spirit," which he read in so quiet a voice I had to bend to listen. Finally he read the little poem that closes the book, "To the Moon," whom he addresses as the "Goddess of poetry." The poem, written before he was fifty, ends,

> What brings me here? Old age.
> Here is the written page.
> What is your pleasure now?

Much to the shock of his students, even in class he could not resist discussing his impending death. "That's all," he said, "I'm losing my voice." Then, before I could rise to leave, he added, "It's not much, is it?"

"I thought you read very well," I said.

"I don't mean that. I'll read well enough. I mean this little book of poems." He held it in his open palm and shook his head. "I don't think it's enough, I don't think it will last. The criticism is a solid achievement, but this is too slight. I can barely fill an hour with poetry. What do you think?" He was asking me!

"They are true poems," I said, "they will last." He shrugged and looked unconvinced.

There were curious omissions in his preparation for criticism and inconsistencies in his views. Nothing stopped him from generalizing about the greatest novels ever written, though he never mentioned the Russians, Germans, or Asians. One late Friday afternoon, before the fights came on, Janet and I were talking about one of her great loves, the historical novel, a form which she was the master of. I happened to mention my favorite, *War and Peace*. "Is it really as good as they say?" she asked.

I told her I thought it was the greatest novel I'd ever read. I turned to Arthur to get his opinion, only to learn he'd never read it. Had he given up after *Anna*? No, he had read nothing by Tolstoy. And Dostoyevsky? He'd tried *The Notes of an Underground Man* and found them mildly amusing. Chekhov? No, he didn't know Russian, and he didn't feel it was worth his time to bother with translations. He read the French, the Spanish, and the Portuguese in the original.

Janet said, "Do you think I'm missing something?"

"I think you're missing the greatest fiction ever written, but don't take my word for it," I said. "Read anything by Chekhov."

Arthur was skeptical. He hadn't the slightest doubt the work was highly overrated. Besides, there wasn't time now to learn Russian, and even if there were he had better things to do with his time.

On another occasion I discovered he had a highly selective memory. I had mentioned meeting John Crowe Ransom on two occasions and finding him a very cordial man. "You were duped," said Winters. "I know he has that reputation, but that's not Ransom." He went on to describe this curious animosity Ransom had toward him; Winters found it suggested mental instability on the part of the Kenyon critic. I remarked that if I'd been called a savage in print by Winters I might harbor some animosity toward him. "I never called him a savage," he said quite firmly. I wasn't sure quite how he'd put it. I leafed through the pages of *In Defense of Reason* until I located the passage, which I read aloud:

> Ransom's devout cultivation of sensibility leads him at times to curiously insensitive remarks. In comparing the subject of a poem by Stevens with that of a poem by Tate, he writes: "The deaths of little boys are more exciting than the sea surfaces—

a remark which seems worthy of a perfumed and elderly cannibal."

"I never wrote that," he said. I handed him the book, and he read the passage from the beginning to its brilliant conclusion. Then he burst out laughing. "Well," he said, "maybe that explains it."

I found it comforting to learn that Winters had views he never put into print that made it clear he had a wider range of appreciation than the later criticism would suggest. Once, in class, he scolded both Fike and me for the poems we'd shown him for the past several meetings. "I hate to sound Romantic," he said, "but there simply isn't enough feeling in what you've been writing. These are interesting ideas and nothing more." On another occasion he chided me for lacking imagination. When I asked him since when that had become so important, he made it clear it was central to poetry. I was miffed by his remark, which was accurate, and so I countered that he was sounding like Coleridge. "Fine," he said, "I'm in good company."

Perhaps the most interesting revelation concerned Yeats. In order to comprehend Winters's preference of the work of T. Sturge Moore to Yeats I'd been reading the two side by side. I confessed to Winters I'd found Moore small beer by comparison. He admitted that Moore had his limits. What had I been reading by Yeats? I named several of my favorites, "Lapis Lazuli," "Dialogue of Soul and Self," "The Tower," and remarked that I found enormous authority in the writing. "Of course you do," said Winters, "he was the greatest stylist of the century." He took in my stunned response. "I'm not deaf, boy, I can hear how marvelous the writing is. I hate what it's doing." His duty was not to be seduced by the enemy.

Some subjects were off limits. On several occasions I tried to get him to talk about Hart Crane, but I managed only once. Their single meeting was in Los Angeles, during a Christmas break at Stanford. Winters had gone south to visit his parents in Eagle Rock, and he and Crane had arranged a meeting. He told me it hadn't gone well, because Crane had been in bad shape. I thought by "bad shape" Winters meant he'd been out of his mind, but Winters corrected me. Crane had been or claimed to have been in a bar fight and was seriously bruised and cut about the face. As far as Winters could tell, all Crane wanted to do was drink and get in another fight. I asked him what he thought of Crane's appearance. He'd expected a slender, aesthetic-looking man, and instead he'd faced a thug. "Crane had the thick arms and shoulders of a professional boxer," he said. "There was something brutal even in the way he moved." I got the sense he'd felt intimidated by Crane.

Physical strength and its lack were very important to him. He loved to tell a story he'd gotten from J. V. Cunningham. Cunningham had told him of the enormous physical power of Robert Lowell, and to illustrate it he'd described an episode in a hotel room during which it took two strong men to subdue Lowell. The struggle had lasted five minutes. Winters wanted to know who the men were. When Winters found out they had been Cunningham and Allen Tate he'd roared out his laughter. Tate and Cunningham couldn't subdue Janet.

As the winter quarter neared its end we were once again running out of money. Out of the blue I got a call from my brother in Detroit. He wondered if I would like to work for him, purchasing bearings the government was offering for sale. He sent me long lists of what he was interested in, and I went to the Oakland Navy Yard and the huge military warehouses at Benicia. I would phone him about the accuracy of the lists and the condition of the bearings, and then enter his bid. If he got the stuff it would be my job to pack and ship it to Detroit.

I'm not sure why I hated the work so much. Each day seemed to begin well enough, usually with a spectacular drive across the Bay Bridge, where whatever fog enshrouded San Francisco lifted and the sunlight sparkled off "the chained bay waters." The drive to Benicia was lovely. I'd cross a huge old metal drawbridge north of Berkeley, turn east, and then drive through verdant hills to descend into an isolated valley with a view of an inlet of the great bay of San Francisco. From miles off I could see a huge mothball fleet of battleships, cruisers, destroyers, and even two aircraft carriers that had survived World War II. On the road to the warehouses I would pass acres of obsolete tanks, armored personnel carriers, and neat rows of 155mm howitzers that looked like toys. Everything was painted a dull olive.

If I checked in at the office early enough I would find my military contact present and sober. My brother advised me to be as inconspicuous as possible and to linger long past noon, for by lunchtime even the enlisted men would abandon all pretense of working, and I could look at whatever material I wanted, even that labeled off-limits. The bearings were sold by lot numbers, and each lot was displayed on a separate skid. With no one watching, it was easy enough to move a carton from one skid to another, to trade desirable bearings for undesirable ones. Of course, if I were free to do this, so was anyone else. I was sure my brother would be cheated. I also felt that some of the men who worked there were waiting to be bribed to look the other way or protect a purchase. My brother moved among such men with a bravado and confidence that entirely escaped me.

If he got the bid I would wait hours for a truck to arrive, usually one with an exotic name, an Iroquois or a Mohawk. An enlisted man would forklift the skid out to a loading dock, and then he and the driver would watch and smoke as I toted the cartons into the truck. If a box was unusually heavy or bulky one of the men might

suspend his sports talk to give me a hand. I'd sign the
bill of lading, fail to bribe the driver to insure a safe
voyage, and as the early darkness began to fall head
back across the valley toward the old steel bridge to
Richmond and the deepening waters of the bay. Even a
job badly done has its rewards. The ride back was still
more delicious than the ride there, and by the time I got
home all I could recall were the lovely hours from noon
until three, when the great warehouses were empty except for me and the softened California light, sifted down
from the high ceilings, turned golden in the dust. Somewhere off in the distance I'd heard music, perhaps a radio
or the songs the wind makes through raftered lofts.

The highlights of the spring quarter were visits by the
famous. I cannot now recall what Kenneth Burke spoke
on for an hour or less to a dozen graduate students in a
seminar room in the library. He had a strong profile and
beautiful white hair about which he seemed to have no
vanity. There was no one there to introduce him, so
he introduced himself, rising from the couch on which
he was seated alongside a handsome, elderly woman. I
can remember that he began by remarking that he
couldn't recall if the academic hour began like the psy-
chiatric hour, at ten after or on the hour. His relaxed and
droll manner seemed out of place at Stanford, as did the
sturdy corduroy jacket he wore, the sport shirt, and the
felt carpet slippers at which the graduate students tried
not to stare.

Frank O'Connor came next; his reading was widely
heralded and drew an audience of several hundred. To
celebrate the event, Wallace Stegner invited the entire
faculty and student body of the graduate writing program to a party at his house on Page Mill Road, which
at that time was an undeveloped prairie southwest of the
campus. That evening, much to our surprise, Winters
was there, downing a highball, when we arrived.

I was seated on a chair across from Winters when O'Connor introduced himself, and then asked was this Winters not the very Winters who preferred the work of T. Sturge Moore to that of Yeats. Winters said he was indeed the man. O'Connor, swaying above him with a drink in hand, burst into laughter. Not seeing the trap being laid for him, Winters added, "And I did it for good reasons."

"And what might they be?" said O'Connor.

"The obvious," said Winters, "he was a far better poet and a more serious man."

"Moore a serious man!" said O'Connor, almost choking on his drink. "Can't for the life of me imagine what's so serious about straining to become the last Romantic poet of the nineteenth century, especially during the twentieth century."

"There's nothing Romantic about Moore's mature poetry," said Winters.

"Perhaps you're right," said O'Connor, "you're the expert," and then he quoted the last lines of "Silence," a favorite of Winters's:

> Give me dry eyes whose gaze but looks intense!
> The dimpled lobes of unreceptive ears!
> A statue not a heart! Silence so kind,
> It answers love with beauty cleansed of mind.

O'Connor went on. "Perhaps 'Romantic' is not the right word, perhaps the word is 'adolescent.' I could accept such from a great boy poet like Keats, but in a man of our years, Professor Winters, it's unseemly."

"Keats was not a great boy poet," Winters mumbled, gnashing down on the stem of his pipe. O'Connor wanted to know if America presently boasted any poets superior to Keats, boys or otherwise, and Winters gave him the names of the two greatest living poets in English, J. V. Cunningham and Edgar Bowers. O'Connor frowned. Sad to say, he'd failed to keep up with American poetry. These names were unfamiliar to him. "They wouldn't by any chance be former students or cronies of yours?" he asked.

Winters glowered and then pointed to me. "He can tell you who they are."

I was speechless just long enough for O'Connor to lean down and whisper in my ear, "Show some cheek, lad, and tell the old man to stuff them." O'Connor then raised himself to his considerable height, staggered, and announced to Winters and all those present that he suddenly knew exactly who Winters reminded him of, to a T. Winters did not take the bait, so O'Connor went on. "You are the identical twin of Dylan Thomas. Did you ever meet him?"

"Ridiculous," said Winters. He probably loathed Thomas as a person and a poet above all his contemporaries. "Thank God I never met him."

"You would have loved him," said O'Connor. "You're exactly like Dylan. The only thing he ever loved was poetry. In no time you'd have been drunk in one another's arms reciting poetry. Take my word for it."

Flushed and trembling, Winters rose from his chair and called out, "Janet, we're going, we're going right now."

For several thousand dollars Robert Frost spent part of an April afternoon on our campus. It so happened that our writing workshop met earlier the same day, and just as Fike, Winters, and I had begun our debate on why someone ought or ought not pay two dollars to hear Frost, the good gray poet, now gone white, passed by the window of Winters's office. Winters himself whitened. Frost peered in, and the room went utterly silent. "My God," said Winters. Frost turned, and then we heard his slow steps as he continued down the walkway. Winters breathed a sigh of relief. "I never dreamed he'd seek me out," he said.

"You think he's looking for you?" Fike asked.

"Who else?" said Winters. "He'd like to get even for what I wrote about him."

"It wasn't that bad," I said.

"It was that bad, and he's read it," said Winters. "I know his reputation for wisdom, but he's a mean and spiteful man. He'd like to hurt me." When Winters asked me what I thought of the essay, I told him I'd been surprised by it, for he hadn't chosen a single one of Frost's better poems to discuss. "I wasn't trying to make him look good," said Winters.

Halfway through the Frost reading I was thinking that Winters was entirely wrong about the character of the man, for he appeared so at ease and comfortable with a huge audience he had enthralled. In the middle of a recitation of "Mending Wall," he burst out at someone in the audience, "Sit up! Where were you raised?" All twelve hundred of us unslumped. He then went back to the poem, faltered, and claimed the poem had been ruined for him. When the reading ended the audience rose in silence and filed slowly out. None of us liked being hollered at.

In December a job at Los Angeles State for the following year had looked probable, but when the Soviets launched Sputnik priorities changed, and the two sections of poetry writing I'd been offered were transformed into sections of technical writing. I decided to look elsewhere. Sacramento State interviewed me. Sequestered with their dean of humanities and his sidekick, the chair of English, in a windowless room in the Stanford Placement Office, I watched the dean give the chair the high sign. Then came the sixty-four-dollar question: "What would you do as adviser to the literary magazine if the editors

showed you an obscene story they wanted to publish?"
I answered with the wrong question: "Did the story have
any literary merit?"

Two days later it was Fresno State. Their dean was a
wiry guy with a face unfurrowed by thought. This will
go badly, I said to myself. He handed me a catalogue
which described all the courses offered by the English
Department and asked which I could and couldn't teach.
I was not up to The History of the English Language or
Beowulf. Much as I loved his work, I wasn't the right
person to teach Chaucer's poetry. I realized this was not
going well. You never got a job in Detroit by saying you
couldn't do something; if need be, you could draw
the perfect circle or load boxcars on boxcars. I amended
my remarks. In a pinch I could teach Chaucer, and
Shakespeare would be a delight. (I'd even read the
plays.) Everything since then was right up my alley,
though my specialty was creative writing. Amazingly,
they were looking for someone to teach fiction and poetry
writing.

The dean seemed delighted to have discovered a true
Renaissance man, willing and able to teach almost the
entire gamut of courses, so he began to sell me on Fresno
before Yale or Princeton discovered I was available. Since
it was located smack-dab in the middle of the San Joaquin
Valley, you could reach the Sierras in less than an hour,
the Pacific in less than two. You could have the best of
both worlds. It was unexcelled for hiking, which was his
favorite sport. Horse racing was my favorite sport, but
I made no mention of it, nor did I mention that hiking
was what we did in Detroit when the car broke down.

Winters was elated when, a week later, the chairman
of the English Department invited me down for an interview. Two of his former students were now teaching at
Fresno State, and he gave me a letter of introduction to
present to the older, a great favorite of his. I would see
beautiful country, he told me with delight, unspoiled by

development, California as it once was. I would cross the Pacheco Pass, named for the legendary Mexican bandits of the last century. Carefully he drew me a map and marked the various sights I should be on the watch for. Early the next Monday morning I headed south on 101, turned east at Gilroy, and headed for the pass. I drove beside miles of low brown fields of onions and garlic; the Ford filled with delicious perfumes. As I climbed, the hillsides burst with delicate white flowers called "mouse tails." The rains had been heavy that spring, and soon the fields were thick with lupin, wild mustard, and poppies. Cresting the pass, I saw my first magpie flash the underside of its wings. A few miles later my first Joshua tree, ancient and gnarled. Is this what it looks like east of Jerusalem? I wondered. I stopped for gas in Los Banos, where I picked up a hitchhiker, a little skinny guy who lived south of Fresno. "What you wanna go there for?" he asked. "City full of cotton pickers." On 152 we passed Berenda Slough; the fields were so flooded the water lapped at the center line of the highway. After Chowchilla I turned south on 99 toward Madera. The names were music. Winters was right; I would have to learn Spanish. My passenger asked me to drop him off at Klein's Mammoth Truck and Car Stop; I did and went on alone to find the campus. Luckily I got the job.

My school days were coming to an end. I was thirty now, and I'd had all of the student life I could take. That summer I taught poetry writing through the mails and made my last visits to the Oakland Navy Yard and Benicia. Several nights a week Marie Louise invited us over, and we began spending much of our weekends there. Janet would frequently appear. George and Paulette had gone off to meet their idol, Wright, at Taliesin West, and come back stunned and slightly disappointed. George had been reminded of Winters, for Wright was another "great man" who knew everything and tolerated no sass.

Sitting out under the oak tree one Saturday night after dinner, Marie Louise told me the story of Winters's reception of the Bollingen Award. A telegram had come, Janet had told her, and when Arthur returned from teaching she waited while he opened it. Winters read in silence and then handed the telegram to Janet with the remark, "Too little and too late." Janet wanted to go east for the award ceremony, but Arthur claimed he was too old to be traveling across country by train. He'd done it once and hated it. "Is that typical of the man?" said Marie Louise.

I said it was and it wasn't. Sometimes he was totally self-absorbed and grim, and at other times he could be as generous as anyone I'd known. "Arthur generous?" she said, disbelieving. I told her how for hours he had taken me line by line through difficult French poetry, the great work of the past hundred years, Baudelaire, Rimbaud, Corbière, Valéry. Once he discovered I was serious in my interest there was no limit to the time he would spend. It was past 8:00 p.m., the sky was still a clear blue. She poured me some red wine and asked if Janet knew of this generosity. "I must tell her," Marie Louise said, "she will be so pleased. I think she seldom sees this side of him, though I thought many times if I asked him for help he would be there. I think he is reliable, yes?"

I agreed. I was sure he wanted to be generous, but often he simply didn't know how. He was a very clumsy man. She agreed. He was clumsy in every way. "I do not know how Janet has put up with him all these years," she said. "I prefer to be alone. Do you think he is ever happy?"

"He should be. He has everything he could hope to have."

"What do you mean?" she said. "He would say he has nothing."

"He's done his writing. It's there," I said. "The criticism is original and eccentric, but it's brilliant and it's what he wanted to establish. All over the country younger poets and critics are competing for his attention."

"I'll bet he treats them like his children," she said. "I'll bet he constantly shows them his dissatisfaction."

Winters had complained to me that his son had gone into ballet dancing. He'd urged him to give it up; as far as the old man was concerned the boy was an "underpaid athlete."

Marie Louise started gathering the dessert dishes. "Yes," she said, "I know people whose sons are in jail, and they are happy they will be out soon." She laughed outrageously, holding her belly with one hand. "That is the sort of humor I have learned from you, Philip. Oh," and she dried her eyes, "tell me, have you ever seen him truly enjoy anything?"

"Yes, when he was reading those French poems to me. There were times I thought he was transported. He's the most serious lover of poetry I've ever met. Much of his pleasure was pure generosity; it came from seeing my pleasure in discovering this poetry. He already knew it all." The work Winters had done was enormous. He'd learned the Breton dialect in order to understand Corbière. One afternoon he'd spent two hours going through a particular poem so that I might follow it. I told Marie Louise that Winters had sketched out the history of a particular Christian festival the poem dealt with.

Marie Louise sat back down. "Arthur knew church history? He doesn't even believe in God."

"He believes in poetry," I said. "You can't begin to understand the poem unless you know about Saint Anne and the Pardons." I'd never heard of her, but once Winters filled me in all the pieces of the poem came together. It ends with a stunning description of a wandering rhapsodist, an ancient crone, who for a few coins will recite your favorite tale of misery. As best I could I quoted from memory the conclusion of the poem: "If you ever see her in her old army clothes it will be a holy day. Remember, she's our sister, so give her a pinch of tobacco and you'll get back her ugly smile and a true sign of the cross." Winters loved the passage; he went over it again and again to make sure I got it. I told Marie Louise that he'd been so moved I thought he might cry, but he didn't.

In the falling darkness I could see that Marie Louise was stunned by this story or perhaps by the beauty of even the slightest reflection of the poem or perhaps by our intimacy, hers and mine. I was silent for a time. The great oak tree above our heads caught the night winds, the world seemed to rock in some cradle of darkness. It was the end of a long day, and I felt perfectly at peace. "I could not believe," she said, "that he could be that happy." She wiped her eyes with her coarse cotton sleeve. "I am crying for him, that at least once he was so happy."

One morning in October of 1986 it occurred to me that I was the same age Winters had been when I studied with him. Twenty-eight years had passed. Like Winters I had become a teacher of poetry and poetry writing at a spiffy school and like him I felt like the odd man out. I lived on the ground floor of a big old house in a working-class neighborhood in Somerville, Massachusetts, with a view of the Tufts University tennis courts, which soon would be deep in snow. Except for the job I hadn't come very far. My sons had grown up, I was a grandfather twice over, and my wife and I traveled from job to job. That morning I wrote:

> 28 years ago, faithless, I
found the great bay of San Francisco where the map
said it would be and crossed the bridge from Oakland
singing "I Cover the Waterfront" into the cold winds
and the dense odor of coffee. Before I settled
in East Palo Alto among divorcees and appliance
   salesmen,

fifty yards from the Union Pacific tracks, I spent a long
    weekend
with Arthur, my mentor to be. In a voice ruined, he said,
by all-night draughts of whiskey and coffee, he praised
the nobility of his lemon and orange trees, the tang
of his loquats, the archaic power of his figs.
In a gambler's green visor and stiff Levis, he bowed
to his wounded tomatoes swelling into late summer.
Kneeling in the parched loam by the high fence
he bared the elusive strawberries, his blunt fingers
working the stiff leaves over and over. It was August.
He was almost happy.
                              Faithless, I had not found
the olive trees bursting on the hillsides west
of U.S. 99. I knew only the bitter black fruit
that clings with all its life to the hard seed.
I had not wakened to mockers wrangling in my yard
at dawn in a riot of sexual splendor or heard
the sea roar at Bondy Bay, the long fingers
of ocean running underneath the house all night
to rinse off the pain of nightmare. I had not
seen my final child, though he was on the way.
I had not become a family of five or opened
my arms to receive the black gifts of a mountain road,
of ground cinders, pebbles, rough grass.
                              At twice my age
Arthur, too, was faithless, or so he insisted
through the long sober evenings in Los Altos, once
crowded with the cries of coyotes. His face
darkened and his fists shook when he spoke
of Nothing, what he would become in that waiting blaze
of final cold, a whiteness like no other.
At 56, more scared of me than I of him,
his right forefinger raised to keep the beat,
he graveled out his two great gifts of truth:
"I'd rather die than reread the last novels

of Henry James," and, "Philip, we must never lie
or we shall lose our souls." All one winter afternoon
he chanted in Breton French the coarse poems of Tristan
    Corbière,
his voice reaching into unforeseen sweetness, both hands
rising toward the ceiling, the tears held back so long
still held back, for he was dying and he was ready.

By April I had crossed the Pacheco Pass and found
roosting in the dark branches of the Joshua tree
the fabled magpie—"Had a long tongue and a long tail;
he could both talk and do." This is a holy land,
I thought. At a Sonoco station the attendant,
wiry and dour, said in perfect Okie, "Be careful, son,
a whole family was wiped out right here
just yesterday." At Berenda the fields flooded
for miles in every direction. Arthur's blank sky
stared down at an unruffled inland sea and threatened
to let go. On the way home I cut lilacs
from the divider strip of El Camino Real.
My wife was pregnant. All night we hugged
each other in our narrow bed as the rain
came on in sheets. A family of five, and all
of us were out of work. The dawn was silent.
The black roses, battered, unclenched, the burned petals
floated on the pond beside the playhouse.
Beneath the surface the tiny stunned pike circled
no prey we could see. That was not another life.
I was 29 now and faithless, not the father of the man
I am but the same man who all this day
sat in a still house watching the low clouds massing
in the west, the new winds coming on.

A few days later I read an unfinished version of the poem
at the Blacksmith's House at Harvard, and after the reading a woman in the audience asked if Arthur was Yvor

Winters. She turned out to be the poet Linda Gregerson, who had studied at Stanford after Winters had gone into the waiting cold. No one except Fran, who was there, knew that there really was a pond and a playhouse in a warren of trees, shrubs, and weeds out behind Marie Louise's great oak. I can't recall if the carp were there or not; my imagination keeps saying they belong, and my memory keeps saying, I'm not sure.

Those were two of the great gifts of truth Winters gave me. I had not known what the soul was, and so I never used the word either in writing or in speech. I tended to shy away when others used it. Perhaps that came with listening to the radio on Sunday mornings and hearing the word bandied about by professional liars. It wasn't the sort of word the old man used loosely, and when he uttered it that afternoon I suddenly knew what it meant: the soul was that part of me that left each time I lied. That day I became a spiritual man, at least until dinner. His remark concerning Henry James was no joke: he had urged me to read *The Golden Bowl*, as had Wesley Trimpi. I got the idea that Wesley thought he was a major character in the novel. I happened to mention to Winters that I'd finished the novel the night before. He asked what I'd thought of it. I said I was glad I'd finished it, and he asked why. I admitted that I'd hated it, that I'd read it for the wrong reason, so I could say I'd read it. Then Winters gave me his great secret truth, and I learned that truth sponsors truth.

The gift of his passion for the great dead poets was the most important thing he gave me, and since he gave it out of the deepest joy it cost him nothing. "God loves a happy giver," I once read in the Abyssinian church on top of the Holy Sepulcher, so that day old Arthur was beloved of God. The last time Fran saw Winters she tried to embrace and kiss him to thank him for his many gifts to us, but he drew back, put off by such a display of affection. Perhaps in the coal camps of New Mexico he'd learned the embrace of a pregnant woman was to be feared. Perhaps not.

It's impossible to quote or paraphrase the gifts of truth I got from Marie Louise; most of them were never spoken. On occasion she could be truly eloquent even in her heavily accented English. We would pull into the gravel driveway, I would shut off the engine, my kids would leap out of the car and race toward her front porch. Behind us she would appear out of the forest of her acreage, dirt scarring her forehead, sweat running down her square, strong jaw. A hard smile would break over her face, and she would say, "This is great." All these years after, I think of her life and I think of what I caught from her, and I don't know. I do know that my friend was a woman in the deepest pain and sorrow, a woman battered by personal misfortune and by the great crimes of the century, and even on her worst days that woman was useful to me and many others. All day long she too was the happy giver God loves, the Godmother to that family of five.

That family of five was not happy with the father who in August drove them to Fresno. Large with child, my wife was grumpy all the way over the Pacheco Pass and beyond. By late summer the hills were burned to a brownish yellow, the oaks leafless and lifeless, the magpies hidden in what darkness there was. Dazed summer had arrived. The holy land I'd pictured had vanished. Berenda Slough had shrunk to the size of a swimming hole, the Fresno River wasn't even a brown trickle. I stopped at an orange-juice stand on 99; the thing was a gigantic plywood orange with a big toothless mouth for service. "A piece of Americana," I proclaimed, but no one was listening. We'd left Los Altos behind and that fairyland forlorn. Everyone was mad at me. Even the four-bedroom house I'd found for less than a hundred dollars a month failed to cheer their hearts. A bedroom for everyone! A study for the papa! No one cared.

The next morning I rose early and with Mark and John went out in search of a breakfast place and a San Francisco *Chronicle*. It was Sunday, and the town slept late. We drove back and forth down the unpeopled residential streets listening to the houses whirring, their rooftop air conditioners and swamp coolers turning over with all the life within. From each roof rose the great silver conning towers of the TV antennas. This is how you survive here, I told my boys. You close up, you grip down as hard as you can, you wait for your orders to come through the air, and you hold on. Sadly, we were back in America, we were home.

The Bread of Time Redeemed

She was born Dorothy Shaughnessy on Pingree just west of Dexter, a corner house, with lovely views from the second-story French windows. This was on Detroit's near-northwest side in late March of 1939, and she was the third child of Mary Cable Shaughnessy. At noon the day of Dorothy's birth, Mary Cable thought she had things well in hand and determined to wait for her husband, Clark, to return from work at five o'clock before taking any positive steps. Before 1:30 p.m. her water broke, things began to spin out of control, and it seemed there was no time to get to Providence. She began to panic, called a Checker Cab, and so frightened the young driver that by mistake he dropped her off around the corner, at Henry Ford Hospital, smack-dab in front of the main entrance on Grand Boulevard. That was how Dorothy came to be delivered by a Jewish doctor, Irving Schwartz, without a Sister of Mercy in sight. When Clark found out what happened he was furious, and he saw neither mother nor daughter until Mary Cable returned

home the following Monday—again in a Checker Cab—
to find Clark asleep long after noon, an empty bottle of
rye on the kitchen table, and the unmistakable odor of
another woman floating through the flat.

The war was to become part of Dorothy's mental bag-
gage. By the time she was seven her father was indulging
himself obsessively at the dinner table with tales of his
terrible winter in the Ardennes. In great detail he would
depict the strange silence that came over a glider full of
troops as they rushed noiselessly toward landing, helpless to avoid fighter planes or anti-aircraft fire. By the
time she was eight she suffered nightly through his
graphic accounts of hand-to-hand combat with the "Nips"
on Okinawa. At such times her mother would rise from
the dining-room table, carry off the empty dishes, and begin to stir up a constant clatter in the kitchen. On some
occasions she would notice her two brothers fighting to
suppress their laughter, and once—after asking permission to leave the table—the older one, Steve, had stumbled
down the stairs to the outside door howling with laughter,
while Stan, who was then only eleven and small for his
age, gritted his teeth and waited for dessert. On long
winter afternoons Dorothy loved leafing through old
copies of *Life* to study the faces of the men who survived
Dunkirk or the desert battles for Tobruk and El Alamein.
In those drawn, unshaven faces she saw something of her
father's look—the straight dark hair falling over his forehead, the sunken pale eyes that stared off into an unimaginable distance, especially on Sunday mornings,
when the rest of the family returned from mass to find
him in his favorite chair, an empty coffee cup at his feet,
a smoking cigarette dangling from his fingers, the comics
or sports section spread untouched across his lap.

She didn't get it until Clark was long gone with no
forwarding address, until she was years older, and they'd
moved in with her mother's family on the East Side. Mary
Cable Shaughnessy was working ten hours a day in a

pharmacy across the way from the Michigan Central Depot, so when Dorothy returned from St. Anthony's late in the afternoon, their two rooms on the second floor were empty. She'd pass the huge old grandfather clock on the landing without acknowledging the hour; at such times it seemed to tick with all the life that was left in the house. If her grandparents were gone and her brothers not returned from school or work, she felt the intense emptiness of the house, as though even she were not there, and—frightened—she often crawled into the bed she shared with Mary Cable and waited, hushed, for a living voice to enter downstairs, someone who might call out to see if anyone was home. On several occasions she awakened in a panic only to realize that the voice she heard was her grandmother's calling her to come down and help with dinner. There was absolutely no cause for fear. She liked her grandmother, a sober, industrious Polish woman with thick wrists and forearms of a shocking redness when she withdrew them from the steaming sink in which she felt it necessary to scald the breakfast dishes as though some danger of contagion lurked in the least smear of dried bacon fat and fried eggs. Sophie (or "Zoisha," as she called herself) had never learned more than a few hundred words in English, and though she had a powerful lilting voice, once her husband died she almost never spoke. It seemed to Dorothy that she knew all of Zoisha's sentences by heart: "you help dinner," "you come school," "me go plant." (Zoisha was a skillful, extremely eccentric gardener who practiced her own methods of folk agriculture. In season the small backyard was a profusion of roses, irises, and tulips, as well as flowering shrubs such as lilac and mock orange.)

In the winter of '51–'52 I entered Dorothy's life. She was still living in the same three-story house near Gratiot, Zoisha's house, but now Mary Cable was gone, supposedly living with a man named Randolph. They had driven off the preceding winter toward Houston, where

Randolph claimed he had a million-dollar opportunity, a once-in-a-lifetime shot he couldn't let fly by. Mary Cable had explained carefully to Dorothy that it was unfair to take her out of school where she was doing so remarkably well. It wouldn't do to upset her education at this critical moment in her coming of age. Dorothy, who always felt ill at ease in Randolph's presence, who loathed the way he stared at her, was not in the least distressed to be staying home. Her mother promised to phone once a week and to write even more often, and for several months she kept her promise. At the beginning of each month Zoisha received a postal money order for $125. Later in the year of Mary Cable's departure the money orders stopped. The phone calls had long since stopped, and soon the letters failed to show. I learned all this sitting on a kitchen chair among the yellow, pink, and blood-red roses in Zoisha's backyard, the Modern Library edition of Whitman's *Leaves of Grass* open on my lap.

There were four of us living in the house at the time. Zoisha occupied a tiny bedroom off the kitchen. Dorothy had turned the sewing room at the back of the house into her bedroom and study. Zoisha's grandson by her daughter Connie, Jon Tanzel, a philosopher, occupied both bedrooms on the second floor. He used the smaller, darker one for sleeping and working out chess problems on a little table beside his bed. The other bedroom, which looked out on the garden, he'd transformed into his study, and it was there he sat up most nights determined to complete Kant's aesthetics, which he felt the great philosopher had somehow botched. Although he was under six feet, Jon gave the impression of great size and physical power. He moved around his room in sudden unexpected bursts, talking in a barely audible voice, at intervals throwing himself down at the large wooden table that served as his desk, to dash off a few lines in one of his many imitation-leather-backed journal books. "Croce should have got it," he would say, his face fixed in a bony grimace. Then his odd, charming smile would widen, revealing tobacco-stained teeth. "Croce had it all to himself for twenty years, all of it, and never got it right." Then he would double over with laughter. "Both of them, Kant and Croce, tricked by the sublime. Levine, you can live a lifetime—you already have—and never experience the sublime. Can you imagine, men of that caliber, tricked by the sublime? Incredible." Although we'd met in a graduate aesthetics class taught by Dr. Raymond Hoekstra, a brilliant eccentric whom I worshipped, most of the time I hadn't the least notion of what Jon was talking about.

I'd been living on the third floor alone for four months. Since I paid only ten dollars a month rent, I could easily manage to support myself as a "refinisher" of bearings doing piecework for twelve hours each Saturday. ("Refinisher" was something of a euphemism. What in fact I did was transform used bearings into new ones by a variety of techniques and processes learned and mastered in various grease shops along Grand River Avenue. The stock came in as scrap metal at under twenty-five cents a pound and went out greased, glued, buffed, resurfaced to a twinkling matte finish, wrapped, sealed, and boxed to be sold at anywhere from ten dollars to forty dollars an item. I never supposed it was legal.) Jon and I had met again late the previous year under a cold, threatening sky, as, hunched in our jackets, we'd both been classified 1A and notified that Korea was somewhere in our futures. Neither of us had bothered to register for the spring semester at Wayne University, for we thought we had more important work to do. Tanzel had Kant's aesthetics to complete, and I felt I needed to leave a manuscript of adult poems behind.

* * *

Enter Teo Zoisha. For a time, exit Dorothy Slaughnessy. That warm day in March which hinted at the spring to come, Dorothy told me she was taking a step she'd been planning for close to a year. In my kitchen chair, seated among the rosebushes which were just coming into bloom, I had been musing over a line from "Song of Myself," a line that for some years was to become something of a personal anthem: "Vivas for those who have failed!" How, I was asking myself, had I so easily drifted into failure? I had no money, no car (which in Detroit was a condition unacceptable to a twelve-year-old), no girlfriend, no prospects of a career of any kind. I owned a tiny stack of books—half of them stolen by my brother and presented each year as birthday gifts—a dirty blue suede windbreaker, two pairs of heavy cotton trousers, four flannel shirts, one dress shirt, a sweater, one leather suitcase that had belonged to my grandfather, a suitcase I couldn't fill, a portable Royal typewriter, a stack of thirty-some unpublished poems and four short stories I could still bear to read. I was twenty-four years old, the holder of a B.A. degree from Wayne though diploma-less, having failed to attend graduation. Fortunately I was single. Both of my brothers were married though still childless; each was running his own auto-parts business on or near Grand River Avenue. Each was entering the life he would lead from then on, and yet I had not the least envy.

Dorothy had seated herself beside me on the damp uncut grass. She'd changed into tan army pants and a sweater, as she usually did after school, for although she never mentioned it I had the impression she despised the crested navy blazer and pleated skirt she dressed in every morning for the long walk to St. Anthony's. "What are you writing?" she said, pointing at the spiral notebook and ballpoint pen at my feet. I opened the notebook and riffled the blank pages. I explained I'd hoped a poem might come from my immersion in "Song of Myself," but I'd stalled on that particular line concerned with failure. "Is that how poems get written?" she asked. I didn't know; I'd been writing for years now, and the most powerful lesson I'd learned was that I didn't know where poems came from or how to bring them into being, but there were times I'd been so inspired by what I read that something like poetry burst from me. I'd been hoping for that.

I discovered that day that Dorothy too had ambitions to write, although she was not yet sure what. In fact she'd been writing to herself ever since her mother had gone off, even before that. She thought it had something to do with the discoveries she'd made about her father and her brothers, and that may have been why she'd shown the work to no one. And so I learned that, one afternoon in the old house on Pingree, while looking for a needle and thread to sew up a blouse she'd torn on the way home while wrestling with another girl, she'd come across a folder of old photos and documents. There was Clark Shaughnessy's draft card; in 1940 he'd been 4F. He'd never gone off to war, much less fought with Patton's tankers or wielded a flamethrower on Okinawa. And there were Steve and Stanley's birth certificates, which revealed that their father was not Clark; they were both the sons of Thaddeus Pszulborski, a name she'd never heard before. Dorothy Shaughnessy had come up against these facts one autumn afternoon in her eleventh year and realized she had no idea who her mother and father were, who her brothers were, who in fact she was.

Her first impulse had been to crawl into bed and cry. She resisted it. Instead she'd continued her search for needle and thread as though everything were exactly the same. She repaired the blouse well enough for it to go unnoticed that evening at dinner and returned all the contents of the drawers to their proper place, and said nothing to anyone. She went downstairs and finished her homework in silence and sat at the dining-room table for what seemed like hours. In the fading light of late afternoon she watched the headlights of the neighbors' cars slice through the falling darkness. She'd begun to compose something in her head, a form of speech or song or both that spoke to her solitude, her doubts, and the abrupt night falling around her like snow. I asked her if she remembered anything of what she'd written. "I didn't write it down," she said. "I didn't even say it out loud." She just began to speak in her head in this new voice. Again I asked if she remembered any of it. She smiled and shook her cap of dark curly hair. Oh, yes, she remembered it perfectly, but on that first day of confidences she had no intention of sharing her first poems—if that's what they were—with me.

However, she did tell me that she'd decided to change her name or at least publish her writing under another name. She would sign her work Theo Zoisha. I was astounded. Until that day I had no idea she'd written anything, and now she was talking about publication. Nor would I have believed she had the moxie to change her name. And where had she come up with Theo? She just didn't feel like a Shaughnessy, they'd never wanted her anyway. And while she was on the subject, she told me that she doubted her father and mother were ever married. After Clark had left for good she had accused her mother of having her out of wedlock, and all she'd gotten back was an embarrassed silence. "Where did the 'Theo' come from?" I asked. It was, she told me, the name of van Gogh's brother. Again I was stunned, to discover Dorothy had been reading Vincent's letters. More than anything else she'd ever read, they were defining for her the life of the artist.

In one way I felt slightly put down, for I had been considering taking this child, who was ten years younger than I, and physically still very much a girl, under my wing, giving her reading lists, advising her on her first struggles with language, comforting her after her first awkward steps. I saw now that she might very well be my peer. I couldn't resist correcting her pronunciation of "Theo." "It's not 'THEE-O,' " I said, "it's 'TAY-O.' "

"Oh," she said, "then I'll spell it 'Teo.' "

A few nights later Jon came bolting up the stairs, his leather-soled shoes clacking loudly up to my door, which he threw open. I had been reading *The Tempest* to myself, reciting aloud the most amazing passages and consigning some lines to memory. Standing outside the circle of light thrown by the little lamp on the bedside table, he panted a second to regain his breath, and then flung a letter at me. "I'm not going," he said in his hushed voice. I unfolded the sheet of paper to discover an induction notice. Jonathan Tanzel was ordered to report for induction at 7:00 a.m. on the morning of Monday, April 2, 1952, at the Fort Wayne Induction Center, Fort Wayne, Michigan. He pulled a chair up to the side of the bed and entered the circle of light as he lit a cigarette, his hands rock-steady. "I'm not going." I asked if he meant to flee or just pretend he'd never been notified. "Are you kidding?" he said, "if I don't show they'll be here pushing Zoisha around with their gun butts. I'm not a criminal, I don't have to run from anyone." I started to explain that it was a felony to fail to report for induction, but he cut me off abruptly. Of course he knew that, he was no moron; he would go and explain to them why he couldn't waste his time in the army.

"Jon," I said, "they don't give a shit about Kantian aesthetics. They'll think you're absolutely nuts."

Well, and he smiled, that was fine with him. He didn't care what they thought of him as long as they allowed him to complete his work. He explained that he hadn't the least animosity toward the government, that in fact he paid no attention to what it did or didn't do. He was delighted that his grandmother received Social Security; otherwise it would be difficult to run the house. If they wanted a war in Korea that was their business. Personally he did not feel threatened by Communism. In fact he was massively bored by it; he found Hegel all but unreadable, though he was pleased that the man had left aesthetics alone, and once again he was off on his Kantian quest. "Levine," he said, "I don't believe Kant ever looked at a great painting, I doubt he ever listened to a single work by Mozart or was in the least familiar with your dear Shakespeare. He was awed by mountains, he was swept away by forests, can you imagine, swept away by the Black Forest. In his own simple way, when it came to aesthetics, he was a kind of Hitler, standing on a peak moaning over the profundity of the stars." He stubbed his cigarette out and explained carefully that a single butterfly was far more astounding than a heaven of stars or the entire range of the Alps. Spitting into his palms, he rubbed his long, tapering hands together, and went on. "Consider the creature, it has a brain smaller than the head of a pin, yet it can walk, swim, fly, it can hunt, sleep on the wing, shit in various colors, change its own shape from grotesque and stumbling to dazzling and soaring. It can rebirth itself. It is millions of years older than we and has not changed in all that time because it is already far closer to perfect than we'll ever be, and it is beautiful to behold. So we crush and plaster it behind glass. The butter that flies, the fly that butters. *Mariposa*, the Spanish call it," he added, rolling the "r" perfectly.

"Jon," I said, "you're very eloquent on the beauty of butterflies, but why are you clobbering Kant for his lack of artistic appreciation?" I reminded him that, when Hoekstra had taken us to the art museum to heighten our appreciation of particular painters, Jon always managed to wander off. The one time Hoekstra had brought a phonograph to class so we might compare a Mozart quintet to a Brahms trio, Jon had fallen asleep. "Don't give me this beauty shit, Jon, you couldn't care less." Smiling, he ended the conversation: "But I have chess."

On another afternoon Dorothy asked if it bothered me to practice an art almost no one seemed to care about or was even aware of. Did I ever yearn to share my work with others the way a singer or an actor was able to? I told her that occasionally I was asked to read my poems or stories in public settings, and though it made me almost feverishly nervous I did it in the hopes that sooner or later I would master the art of performance. In fact each spring Wayne celebrated poetry with a week of readings: the faculty, the students, the alumni all presented their work, and one "famous" poet was brought to the campus for the big reading of the year. Last year it had been John Berryman and this year it would be Louise Bogan. Dorothy was very curious about what the students' writing would be like, and so I invited her to accompany me to their reading the following week.

I was surprised by the way she dressed for the event. There she was waiting for me in the hated blazer, a white pleated, short, very full skirt, white buck shoes, and white socks. In this ensemble she looked even younger than she was. Already she was over five feet four inches tall, so she gave the impression of a teenager trying to pass for a little kid, the sort of character one saw in the awful high-school comedies of the day. I had assumed she would try to appear as inconspicuous as possible, but if that had been her hope she'd failed miserably. In truth she seemed to take no notice of the impression she made. When we entered the room on the first floor of the student union it was crowded with adults of all ages sitting in chairs or on the floor, most of them casually dressed.

We had arrived late. The poet Walter Rousek had already begun reading. Wally, as his friends called him, had been something of a boy wonder when we first came across him, a high-school kid of sixteen who seemed to have read everything, but whose aspirations had stalled on Hart Crane and Rimbaud. His face flushed from excitement or the previous night's drinking, Wally stared off into the future, and although he held a typed page in his shaking hand, he recited from memory a poem he always presented at readings, "Phoenix," which ended:

> I, too, am consumed in these fires
> Of my breath, made holy as the calyx
> Of memory cries upward to the stars.

I had placed one hand on Dorothy's shoulder and was steering her toward two empty seats in the back row. I could feel her body trembling as though the words or the images were too much for her, and she'd been overwhelmed by her emotions. She'd removed a small, crumpled hankie from her purse and covered her mouth and nose. Seated beside her at last, I turned to see if she was okay and realized that she was choking with hilarity.

Rousek looked up as though to locate some minor disturbance, but he was too nearsighted even to recognize me, a friend of some years, at a distance greater than ten feet. A squat, overdressed woman in the front row now began to applaud and the audience—largely composed of the poets who would read and their families and friends—picked it up. Walter's left hand moved slowly across the face of some imaginary waters as though in the hope of calming them. "I'm touched," he said in his breathless tenor, "duly and deeply touched." His voice quivered with genuine emotion as he began again with a second chestnut, "When in a Mirror":

> When in a mirror love redeems
> My eyes and lets me climb
> into the rags and baggage of despair,
> I do so eagerly knowing that time

> Dulls the edges of the ragged air
> That haloes my breath. . . .

Dorothy turned her shaking, tearstained face toward me and whispered, "Please." We left the room as quietly as possible. I was thankful the audience was so rapt that no one seemed to notice our departure.

Once outside I turned to Dorothy. "He's my friend."

"I'm sorry, Philip, I just couldn't help it. I had no idea what to expect. Honest, if I'd known this would happen I swear I never would have come. Really, I didn't mean it." I had no choice but to believe her. In truth I'd always felt that Walter overplayed the role of the *poète maudit*, that, like so many of the young Detroit poets—myself included—he cultivated the role of the writer too sensitive for the world. In Wally's case I felt there was a legitimate claim to his behavior. Physically fragile, emotionally delicate, he'd come into the world as the son of Polish working-class parents who early on realized his intellectual gifts and tried to steer him toward one of the more lucrative professions. He had discovered French Symbolist poetry by the age of fifteen and embarked on a career of rebellion. I could only hope he never discovered my early departure from his reading.

As the bus bobbed over the railroad tracks on East Forest, I finally forgave Dorothy her little outburst. After all, she was merely a kid. I recalled that the first time I'd heard a poetry reading at Wayne—it too had been given by students, one of whom was Wally—I'd been stunned by how seriously these young people took themselves and their writing and how totally opaque and uninteresting I'd found most of the poems. Dorothy had taken the window seat, and she was staring out silently at the rail yards behind the old Packard plant. She'd said nothing since we'd left the student union; she'd waited by my side at the bus stop at Forest and Woodward unwilling or unable to meet my eyes. Finally, I decided one of us should speak and end it. "Listen," I said, "it's no big deal. Wally is a very self-conscious guy. I suppose all of us are. You get up there to read, and the temptation is to cover your inadequacy or your stage fright with some sort of presentation or act you think is poetic. I mean none of us really knows what a poet is supposed to be like." Dorothy nodded. I could see she was holding her mouth shut very firmly, as though she was afraid to say a word for fear of what might tumble out. This time she buried her face in her hands, and again her shoulders shook. Now I was really angry, but by the time we reached our stop I cooled off, though I made no show of helping her off the bus. On the long walk home she explained it all. It hadn't been the performance. She'd never seen a poetry reading and had no idea what to expect. "I would have been ten times more scared than he was," she said, "but that wasn't it. It was the writing, Philip, the writing was simply so . . ." I waited for the judgment. ". . . Inept."

"You think it's that easy?" I said. I had some idea how seriously Walter took poetry, how much it meant to him to write well.

"I didn't say it was easy," she said, "but I was expecting something better from a university poet, something far better than I could write."

"Let's just see you try!"

"If I couldn't do better," she said, "I wouldn't try."

Two days later I wakened to a strange dream of home. I'd somehow lost my glasses when they slipped off my nose and fell into the closet of the room I once shared with my twin brother, Eddie. In the dream I couldn't find them because without them I saw so poorly and Eddie wouldn't help me. Instead he sat at the room's one desk drawing World War II fighter planes engaged in daring combat. He kept trying to show me the drawings, which I also couldn't see, but he merely bowed his head to his drawing and said nothing. I wakened to what I took to be my own shouting. The room was very still. Downstairs I could hear Zoisha running water in the kitchen sink, perhaps into the huge black kettle for that day's coffee. She was a great believer in the virtues of coffee, which was all she took for breakfast, whitened with milk and sweetened with sugar cubes she let dissolve between her teeth. How odd, it seemed to me, to feel such affection for a person with whom speech was almost impossible. Perhaps, I considered, it wasn't odd at all. I came from a family that talked far too much, that seemed to believe that without speech and more speech there could be no understanding and that without an intellectual agreement there could be no happiness. Only my tiny grandfather obviously felt otherwise. Behind a cloud of cigarette smoke he withdrew from all arguments. Often on Sundays I chauffeured him around the city in his long black Packard straight eight—a driver's test had at last revealed he couldn't read English, and thus in his sixties he was suddenly, after thirty years of driving, denied a license, much to the relief of his neighbors. Instead of speaking, Zaydee and I sang songs back and forth to each other, mainly show tunes, which he adored and invariably got wrong. Neither of us could carry a tune, but we didn't let that discourage us.

"If you knew Solly," he would belt out, "like I knew Solly, oye, oye, oye, veh, what a girl . . ." He incanted with verve and style and—for a man under five feet two—a thunderous voice.

I caught the first whiffs of the coffee perking below and rose to dress. It was then I noticed a sheet of lined paper on the table beside my bed, a sheet that had not been there when I'd turned off the light at 2:00 a.m. exhausted by my own efforts to revise a poem which refused to go anywhere. The sheet bore the following untitled poem printed neatly in a firm script that leaned neither to the right nor the left.

Where is the bread of time redeemed?
Does it sleep on the palm
Of a hand opened to the rain?

Who eats the bread of time,
Of time to come? Hard as stone,
The bread I eat and call my own

Is coarse, cross-grained, born
Of an old woman's sighs and groans.
It sleeps within me like a stone.

The dawn's light wakens the world
Scattering the hardness I slept upon
While into the old rain the rain comes down.

It was signed "Teo Zoisha."

Jon seemed to take his new classification as the inevitable outcome of the candor he had expressed at the induction center. I regarded it as an amazing stroke of luck. "Why luck?" he said. "I merely explained to the doctor that my first duty was not to the nation but to Kantian aesthetics." He actually seemed to believe that they'd sympathized with the conflict his allegiances to philosophy and nation had involved him in, or perhaps he didn't and was merely acting. I could never read Jon. We'd sat up all the night before as he downed cup after cup of coffee, chain-smoked, and discussed his obligations to philosophy—to Kantian aesthetics, to be more precise. Each time I tried to explain that in refusing to accept the government's version of his duty he was acting on the strongest moral principles, he'd wave me away. "Levine," he'd say, as patiently as possible, "I don't care about their war, they're welcome to it. I am not a moral philosopher, I am an aesthetician. I've read Thoreau and found him tedious.

I'm simply not interested in how ants construct their abodes or the changing seasons in New England. To you he's a great writer, to me he's a vain wordsmith." As the night wore on and I began to drift in and out of sleep, I picked up a quality of hysteria in his voice. His movements about the room grew still more unexpected and sudden. At times he would even stumble into a chair. Once he scattered the chess pieces on the board beside his bed, and as he stopped to retrieve them I could see he was close to total exhaustion, but he was putting up a marvelous front. In the first light of dawn I walked him down to the bus stop in the chilly April air. He'd put on only a thin cotton windbreaker over his white shirt, and I could see he was shivering, whether from cold or the massive dose of caffeine in his system I couldn't tell. As the bus approached we shook hands and I wished him well. "Don't worry," was all he said, and he waved from the back window of the empty bus.

Late that afternoon he awakened me to tell me the news: he was 4F. The doctors had completely understood his position; they had accepted his greater duty toward philosophy. "On what grounds did they classify you 4F?" I asked. "You're strong as an ox even if you're full of nicotine and coffee and your heart is probably beating faster than a wren's." His blood pressure had been abnormally high, but they'd assured him this was common among inductees, many of whom were scared half to death at the prospect of being shot at in the near future. And he'd told them he'd been up all night; he didn't want them to think he was ordinarily so frantic. They had felt he was clearly psychotic. He'd seen the doctor write the word slowly on his papers, "4F, psychotic."

"Why would that bother me, Levine? I'm not planning to run for public office or become a commercial pilot. Since I was in the seventh grade everyone has thought I was crazy. You think I'm crazy." I insisted that I didn't. Certainly he was eccentric, and no doubt the croakers at the induction center had mistaken his eccentricity for madness. "Don't play games with me, Levine. By their lights I'm mad. What is this 'eccentric' stuff? As I said, you think I'm mad." I insisted I didn't, but he was right about one thing; I'd never met anyone like Tanzel, and I very much doubted they'd taken his philosophical rant seriously. They'd thought they had a genuine lunatic on their hands, and the Jon they were seeing was the true Jon; maybe raised to the second power by circumstances. "Jon," I said, "can you imagine how long you'd have to sit at an induction center hearing why young men did not want to die in Korea before someone told you he had to complete Kant's aesthetics?" Jon mused over the question. "I think you could construct a formula for solving it, but I don't have a paradigm. An educated guess would be eternity minus seven minutes."

Richard Werry was one of two practicing poets who taught at Wayne. The other, George Feldman, was a pleasant man who worked mainly as an adviser to returning World War II vets. Now and then he taught a course in the Humanities Program, one of the poorest in the school, in which he insinuated his own work, which at its best resembled—at least on the page—the less interesting work of e. e. cummings. When he read his poetry in public, he half fell away from the finale of each poem, as though overwhelmed by his own inspiration or moral force. He would have been well advised to patent his *shtick*, but he had no way of knowing that leading poets of the generations to come would adapt it to their own ends. At least he had the good taste never to combine it with hair tossing—he was almost bald—or discreet weeping to crown the performance, so it was up to those brave little warriors only just born to achieve the apotheosis he merely suggested. Werry was something else again. A modest and restrained man who dressed like a United Automobile Workers lawyer, he formed powerful friendships with his students, loaned them money, bought them drinks, consoled them when their lovers betrayed them. He may have been one of a kind. Because of his cool exterior, I found it impossible to express my affection for him, and I believe the other Wayne poets felt the same. But when I needed advice of any kind he was there, a listening ear that seemed attached to no agenda but mine.

Werry welcomed me into his office and rose to shake my hand. "What can I do for you, sport?" As I reached into my shirt pocket for the folded page of Dorothy's poem, I was certain he expected to see something of mine. I explained that I hadn't written what I was about to show him, that a friend had, and I was eager to get his appraisal. He hunched his shoulders and slumped in his chair as he read, and then looked up. "Very interesting and more than a little familiar," he said. I asked what he meant. He pushed a hand through his brown hair, which was cut in the military fashion that some World War II vets still clung to, and then rose from his swivel chair and stalked to the bookcase. For a man of over six feet with a thick, strong-looking body, he moved with surprising grace. "I think I've read something similar in Stevens, something very similar, but not the same. I know it's not in *Harmonium*, but I'm not sure where it *is* from." He began rummaging through anthologies and literary magazines and old books. He handed me several. "See if Stevens is in any of them." The writing hadn't reminded me of Stevens at all, but I was not as well read as he.

"I'm very good at this detective work. I seem to get the worst students, and so many of them cheat. I once caught a fraternity kid who thought he could slip an essay by Elia by me. Flunked him. Told him I didn't like my Lamb served cold." Werry did not have a doctorate, his publications were largely thriller novels and popular short stories, so he had been frozen at the rank of associate professor and required to teach Freshman Comp. "Ah," he said, "our search is all ended," and he read the following, mocking the voice of his current favorite, Dylan Thomas.

> Here is the bread of time to come,
>
> Here is the actual stone. The bread
> Will be our bread, the stone will be
>
> Our bed and we shall sleep by night.
> We shall forget by day, except
>
> The moment when we choose to play
> The imagined pine, the imagined jay.

It was Stevens. Werry wanted to know who had written the poem I'd brought, and so I told him. "A thirteen-year-old? I'd call it utterly amazing. I haven't met a thirteen-year-old who could tell Stevens from Groucho Marx. She got the tune in her head and went from there. We all do it, only we older farts learn to hide it better. She probably genuinely doesn't know what she's doing. This is terrific for a kid that age. This is terrific for a kid my age."

"You wouldn't call this plagiarism?" I asked.

He leaned back in his chair, blinked his eyes several times, a mild tic he had when he was thinking of how to say something with exactitude. "Let me be professorial," he said, and lit his pipe. "If I called this plagiarism, I'd have to call all of us plagiarists. I'm doing this with Thomas, Wally is doing it with Crane, Bill Leach is doing it with George Barker, Petrie is stuck back with Shelley, and you're robbing Yeats. You guys are still young, you're learning your craft. I'm too old to be writing in the voice of another poet, but I don't have the talent this kid has. Look what she's done with the original. She takes a cadence, a few key terms, adds a dramatic situation, her own 'local habitation and a name,' manages to avoid totally the worst phrases in the original, and completes a tribute to Stevens that is also a poem of her own. Teo Zoisha, 'A name to conjure with.' "

On the way back to the bus stop I was of two minds. I wanted to jump and shout for Dorothy's true talent, and I was also disappointed that she hadn't made it up totally out of her own imagination. I felt the wonder of someone from nowhere who seemed born with this amazing natural gift for poetry; I wanted to believe in the possibility of a Dorothy, a Teo Zoisha. And there was another question that was part of the problem: why hadn't I been this natural wonder?

Before the week ended it was my turn to receive an induction notice. I'd known it was coming, but, sitting on my bed in the late afternoon and staring at it, I realized I was totally unprepared not only for that specified Monday at the beginning of May, I was also unprepared for the future, any future I might venture into. I could not say in all candor, as Jon had, "Without me the great work will not go forward." I did not believe in my particular powers as a poet as Jon believed in his as an aesthetician. I no longer believed in my singular gifts as a poet with the same assurance I'd had even a month before. I remember that I went to the window with a cigarette in hand and a wooden match I'd learned to strike with my thumbnail, a gesture toward the world that a fellow worker at Mavis-Nu-Icy Bottling Company had helped me master. I was going to look down on the little world of Zoisha's garden and then let my gaze wander across fence lines and streets, take in the entire neighborhood, until in the distance I beheld the great smokestacks near the river, and then I was going to sigh with a world-weariness that came directly out of John Garfield's Depression-era films. But I didn't. Instead I turned to the mirror above the dark-green chifforobe that held my few belongings, for after some months of living in this house I'd finally unpacked. I barely recognized the young man I saw, yet I knew he was Philip Levine, though I had no idea why that might be important to anyone, I had no idea where he was going or why. I knew he wanted to say something dramatic and memorable like a character in a movie, something about "destiny," a word that had fascinated me when I was a child and heard my father first use it, but "destiny" was a concept that involved the grown men and women of a previous era, those who had crossed Europe and an ocean to set up housekeeping in America or venture again across other seas to seek their fortune. I was not yet in the habit of speaking to myself; curiously, it would have embarrassed me. I would have been shamed before my own eyes, as though I were actually two men, one who acted and another who held up certain standards of behavior with which to judge the first. So I said nothing, nothing at all, even inside my head. I went back to the bed, lay down, and did not cry.

Dylan Thomas was one of my heroes, to some degree for his outrageous behavior and his brilliant unwillingness to bow down to any authority. After his reading at Wayne two years before these events, he had gone to a reception attended by no students (none had been invited), although the student poets had been his most excited audience. Dick Werry thanked him for coming and added that it meant a great deal to the students. Thomas, the story went, roared back, "Yes, I came for the students, fuck the faculty."

I knew all of Thomas's published poetry and had consigned several of the best poems to memory; I recited them often to myself when the boredom of work threatened to do me in. I might have inferred from the poems not only his refusal to mourn the death of a child by fire in wartime London but also his refusal to participate in any form in that war, the war we have come to regard as "The Good War." Had I known his letters or had an occasion to talk politics with him, I might have gained a measure of solace or courage. In his long journal letter written to Pamela Hansford Johnson, he goes on about war:

> This is written on Armistice Day, 1933, when the war is no more than a memory of privations and the cutting down of the young. . . . The state was a murderer, and every country in this rumor-ridden world . . . is branded like Cain across the forehead. What was Christ in us was stuck with a bayonet to the sky, and what was Judas we fed and sheltered, rewarding at the end, with thirty hanks of flesh. Civilisation is a murderer.

When the war actually came in '39 he was no longer the unknown beginner, the nineteen-year-old bard just breaking into print, but his politics were intact. Just before hostilities broke out he wrote to his fellow poet Henry Treece, "What are you doing for your country? I'm letting mine rot." And once it began he wrote his friend Desmond Hawkins: "I've no wish to propagandise, nor to do anything but my own work. . . . What have we got to fight for or against? To prevent Fascism coming here? It's come. To stop shit by throwing it? To protect our incomes, bank balances, property, national reputations? I feel sick. All this flogged hate again." And to his old friend Bert Trick, a few days later, "I've only my own feelings to guide me, & they are my own, and nothing will turn them savage against people with whom I have no quarrel. There's a need now for some life to go on, strenuously & patiently, outside the dictated hates & pettinesses of War. . . ." In 1939 Thomas had been only one year older than I was in '52, but he had the advantage of being a genius, and so saw things with a clarity I lacked. As we put it back in those "innocent" times, "it was all Greek to me."

Yes, it was all Greek to me. For some weeks I lived in a Sophoclean conflict. I felt my country had embarked on a career of empire building on the Asian mainland, as well as a suppression of "freethinking" here at home, which it had sold to a cowed populace as anti-Communism. I did not see Communism as the great threat to my freedom. I had no fears that the forces of the Soviet Union were massed at the Mexican or Canadian border, or that they had infiltrated the State Department. What I feared politically was what soon came to be known as the "Power Elite." I knew enough American history to recognize how successfully the government and the wealth that controlled it could waste any movement for social equality. I had no intention of giving my life to perpetuate a system that despised me. Yet many of my friends were being called and were answering the call. I did not relish the notion of forming a nation of two along with Jon Tanzel.

In 1952 I did not know that one way or another the dilemma would pass into the scrap heap of past dilemmas to be replaced by others. I had no idea how many options were open to me. I saw only refusal or acquiescence at the induction center. I could have taken a bus downtown, crossed the huge vacant square known as Campus Martius to reach the small navy-and-marine recruiting center that crouched between Sam's Discount Drugs and Ruby's Clothiers, purveyors of sharp-schmutter (see my poem "The Suit"), and there, by a series of examinations and oaths, enlisted in the marines. My friend Martin did that during the third week of May; I could have joined him and later been transported by submarine to the coast of North Korea with forty-one other marines to perform a daring, useless operation and for my troubles received one small round hole in my forehead and a monumental ringing in my ears for eternity. Or I could have driven instead to the West Coast alone in a '48 Pontiac sedan bought at an estate sale for four hundred dollars, the one car of millions of such advertised cars driven by a retired junior-high-school teacher the few miles back and forth to work. In Long Beach I could have married an overweight, gentle woman in sales, a woman from Laredo with two small sons and a sense of humor. Her financial dependency could have rendered me unacceptable to the Selective Service. I could have remembered that Batista's Havana was eighty-nine dollars from the Miami airport and returned to that haven of pornographers, drug pushers, whores, and weapons salesmen, where I'd spent my twentieth summer, and there taken up a career in reportage of things Latin and revolutionary. Or I could have done nothing save fret over endless cigarettes and glasses of cheap red wine until I lost the knack of sleep and wound up babbling in the mental ward at Detroit's Receiving Hospital, where I would have gone unnoticed until hostilities were suspended. I could have simply crossed the Ambassador Bridge to Canada on foot and kept on walking north until I turned into Wallace Stevens's snow man with a mind of winter and marveled over the "junipers shagged with ice" or the spruces "rough in the distant glitter" of the Canadian sun. Or I could have remained absolutely still, breathing the heady air of self-abandonment, the way a poet suspends all motion as the first words make their entry.

In July of 1957 I was jogging on the track at the University of Michigan when I spotted a familiar figure as it streaked lightly past me. At the time I was living in an upstairs two-bedroom flat in Ann Arbor, I was the father of two sons, and, much to my own surprise and that of my friends, I was married to a beautiful woman. We'd moved here for the summer only to escape the damp heat of Iowa City, where I'd been teaching Technical Writing and The Bible as Literature, courses for which I was wondrously unqualified. In Ann Arbor I was near friends from my college days who'd transferred to Michigan to do graduate work, and the wiry chap who had whizzed by me was none other than Jon Tanzel. I started to chase him but thought better of it and let him circle the track and catch me. "Levine," he said, pulling even with me and slowing down, his voice no more breathless than it had ever been, "you still fooling with the poetry shit?" I told him I was. He had another two miles to go and then we could take a cigarette break. I learned he was in graduate school at Michigan and expected to get his Ph.D. the following spring, when he completed his dissertation on "The Moral Imperative." When I asked if he'd completed Kant's aesthetics he looked at me as though I were mad. "All human behavior, behavior period, is moral," he assured me. As for aesthetics, we had the work of Bentham; we didn't need anything else. Did I have any idea what General Motors and the American government were doing to the human environment? Was I aware of the erosion of civil liberties under Truman and Eisenhower? Was I aware of the threat to the future of the planet posed by the military-industrial complex? His last disclosure was the most surprising and may have been the basis for the others. Tanzel, who never seemed to notice the presence of a woman, was now married, in thrall to an extraordinary woman, "big in body and in spirit," he said. (He was certainly right about the former.)

"How is Dorothy?" I asked.

"You mean Teo," he said. She'd changed her name to Teo Zoisha.

"Legally?"

As far as he knew the change was legal. He hadn't

kept close track of her. He thought she was no longer living with his grandmother, though he wasn't sure. It was all vague to him. He seldom got into Detroit; there wasn't any reason, because the library in Ann Arbor was so much better, and since Hoekstra's retirement the philosophers at Wayne were all hopeless, Logical Positivists who denied the moral factor in behavior.

"Does she still write poetry?"

"Who, Dorothy? She never wrote poetry." Before he left he invited me over to meet his wife and sample her cooking. "Bring some red wine," he called back over his shoulder as he sprinted off, "and bring your wife if you want to."

I was pleased and more than a little surprised that Zoisha remembered me. I had so much trouble locating the house in the changing Detroit that I considered forgetting the whole thing. I asked myself if I'd dreamed that year and knew immediately I hadn't. I drove back to Woodward Avenue and traced the bus route, and there it was. Zoisha looked the same, and the house still smelled of lard and cabbage, smells that at first had offended me but which I had come to delight in the way I delighted in the perfume of chicken schmaltz at my great-aunt Tsipie's. When Zoisha answered the door, she leaned way back and squinted so as to get a better look; she then leaped forward and grasped my shoulders in her strong hands. "Philip," she said, putting the accent on the second syllable, "Philip, look good," and the tears started from her eyes. The moment I asked about Dorothy, I unleashed a flood. "Dorothy go," she told me, and the going seemed final, for Dorothy had not returned, not even once in more than a year; she was not sure how long. She tried drying her eyes on the sleeve of her coarse cotton blouse, but the tears kept coming. She shook her head slowly from side to side, for there was more sad news. Jon had

gone to "Hen Habor" with his wife, and he too did not
return, not even for a short visit. She invited me into the
kitchen for a cup of scalding-hot coffee. After the familiar
sugar cube dissolved between her teeth, we sat in a
silence so profound I could hear the great clock ticking
on the landing to the second floor. When at last I rose to
leave, she rose and embraced me, and this time with her
clear blue eyes dry she said, "Zoisha okay."

It was from my old maestro Dick Werry that I learned
that Dorothy—that is, Teo Zoisha—had started Wayne
and during her first semester had enrolled in his creative-
writing class. She'd rarely shown up, and when she did
she'd sat in the back of the classroom, smoked sullenly,
and kept her own counsel. "She just never tried to become part of the class," Dick said, which was a shame
because it had been a good class with some very interesting older people in it. During the course of the semester
she'd handed in two poems, the best two poems he'd seen
from a student in many years. No, she was no longer writing like Stevens. "Both of the poems suggested García
Lorca," he recalled, "the Lorca of *Poet in New York*,
only they were much more interesting than the Rolf
Humphrey translations." He assured me Miss Zoisha
wrote a stunning English, whereas Humphrey had butch-
ered the originals by preferring to write in his own style.
He began a search for the poems, copies of which he'd
kept because they were so remarkable, but this time the
search came to nothing. He sat back behind his desk,
removed his glasses, placed a hand over his eyes, and
announced he would quote the simpler one, which dealt
with a broken jar. "No, it was a jug. It went, 'The jug
that stood so high here / Broke and fell away, fell
into . . .' She managed to get birds into the next line.
Goddamnit, what kinds of birds were they? The poem
rhymed. Phil, I tell you the damn Dewar's is doing me in.

How's that for alliteration?" And he gave up, disgusted with himself, and offered to give me some Keats instead, knowing he was my favorite poet.

He did remember that she'd said her intention was to major in Spanish and that she had read Lorca in the original and found him "massive." That had been her word for it. "An unusual term, don't you think, but, then, she had a very original way with language. She may be a genius. I teach here twenty years, get one genius, and lose her halfway through the first semester. What does that tell you, Levine? Genius is going elsewhere." Even though she'd stopped attending he'd given her an A.

I checked with the registrar's office. There was no longer a Teo Zoisha attending Wayne. She'd completed one semester. They were not at liberty to tell me if she'd taken any incompletes or had applied for a second semester. They were not at liberty to tell me where her residence had been. Yes, the grades had been sent to her address and had not been returned.

Dorothy Shaughnessy or Teo Zoisha, whatever her name now is, meant far more to me than I to her. Meeting her as I did in my twenty-fifth year was one of the most valuable lessons of my life, so valuable that at times I've mythologized it, I've turned Dorothy into some sort of poetic angel sent by the muse to transform my youthful arrogance into the humility I required if I were ever to become even a decent poet. As the years passed I saw her in my imagination not as the slightly awkward girl-woman in white pleated skirt worn above raw knees, but as a powerful spiritual presence hiding in the body of a girl, a superhuman spirit that took this unlikely shape. I once heard Stanley Kunitz declare that if one spent enough years struggling with poetry—he had been at it over sixty-five years when he made the remark—one was almost certain to mythologize one's self. My penchant for this sort of thing is clearly greater than Stanley's, for by the age of thirty-five I had turned Teo Zoisha into a mysterious force in my life, one largely responsible for whatever success I've had.

In truth Dorothy was the most precocious child I'd ever met, one who possessed a dazzling gift for language, a gift far greater than my own. But she was only the first of many poets I would meet whose innate gift was far greater than my own. In 1953 I met Donald Justice, a few years later Peter Everwine. In 1965, at the age of thirty-eight, I met the eighteen-year-old Larry Levis, who was writing poems that were light-years beyond anything I'd written at his age. Three years later it was David St. John, also eighteen, then Ernesto Trejo, who could do it in both Spanish and English. By the time I was twenty-four I'd learned that there was nothing democratic about the way these natural gifts are parceled out. I'd also learned the most essential lesson of my writing life: if I were to make poems that would outlast my own body, I'd have to devote myself with an unequaled ferocity. Not believing in the power of prayer, I had only one alternative: to learn what work is.

Dorothy would enter my life again. On the evening of my first reading for the Academy of American Poets in the spring of 1967, Betty Kray, who then directed the Academy, handed me an envelope when I showed up for a sound test at the auditorium of the Guggenheim Museum. I was quite nervous, never having read in New York City and believing then that such a reading could be important. Fortunately I read first before my co-reader could put most of the audience to sleep—including me— with a presentation of a fable by Robert Louis Stevenson. Later that evening, in my hotel room, while preparing for my second sleep of the night, I discovered the letter crammed into a back pocket. It was addressed to me care of the Academy and had been mailed from New York City. It read:

Dear Philip,

I had planned on staying here until your reading, but I've been deprived of that opportunity. I wanted to see you so much and to hear you read your poetry. I wanted to thank you for remaining faithful to poetry as I did not, though I have lived usefully. I'll keep looking for your poems.

As ever, Dorothy S.

It was handwritten on very thin blue paper and bore no return address.

In the spring of 1980, after a reading at the Folger Shakespeare Library in D.C., there was a small, awful party in my honor. I say "awful" because a particularly ugly woman pursued me shamelessly from room to room through the downstairs of the guest house. I do not think her intentions were sexual, for there were younger and more nearsighted men there. During my lifetime I have encountered perhaps a dozen people who are identical twins of this woman—I shall call her Mary Betty—men and women who live by robbing others of breath. They put their mouths so close to yours as they speak that you begin to feel the oxygen abandoning your lungs, your heart sputtering to a standstill, your kidneys stalling before they can prime your emotions. You know you must flee or die. I snatched Mary Betty's drink from her hand and told her to remain rooted exactly where she was while I went to refresh it. Instead I passed through the kitchen and out a rear door, where, uninhibited, I could breathe in the chill air and feel my life returning. Within less than a minute I saw I was not alone; a woman I could barely make out was smoking in silence. She turned to face me; she was tall, very slender, with dark curls falling to her shoulders. Moments passed before either of us spoke. "Do you remember Dorothy Shaughnessy?" she asked. For the second time that evening I felt my heart stutter. While working in the Bolivian Andes, she had met Dorothy. She had been with the Peace Corps; Dorothy had been there on her own, had lived there for years, ever since she'd first graduated from Berea College in Kentucky, where she'd studied Andean arts and crafts.

"Is there any way I could get in touch with her?" I asked. The woman wrote out Dorothy's address on a check stub, a bed-and-breakfast place in Washington where Dorothy stayed when she returned periodically to the States. "What was she like the last time you saw her?" I asked.

"Just the same," the woman said. "You know Dorothy. Everything else changes and she stays the same."

Over the years I've written the address several times and received no answer.

April 12, 1952. Wakening to the rain, I hear this old house creak. The wind comes in from the west heavy with the smell of the new year; the spring that never was will be. The first flags will stream in the open fields between the car barns on Rivard and the parking lots behind the old Packard plant, and then will come the tulips Zoisha planted in her dark little garden between the house and garage no one uses. She'll bury fish bones in the gray soil, she'll part the crumbs of earth with her strong fingers and tamp down small balls of cornmeal and lard she rolled late at night in the kitchen. Then the rosebushes that just a few weeks ago were dull, black spines along the fence will spring into reddened new thorns so light at their tips I can see through them, and then the fine white buds about to darken, rolled up so tight I can hear the suspended breath kept back the way a newborn child holds its breath before it takes the one plunge into the only world it will know. Now the house is quiet and I close my eyes in the darkness. The clock stops on the

landing, the world ceases its whirling toward my womanhood. I open my eyes and they are still closed, for I see
nothing and I hear nothing, not even the steady breathing
of an old woman who worked all this day to exhaustion.
Time holds still as I know it never will again, and I open
my hands to receive the rain and the benedictions of rain,
and what falls into them is more like dust than the round
beads of wet wonder, more like the tiny hard stones of
wheat that Zoisha cracks each morning into bread. At
last I am happy, for now I know that before time eats me
I shall eat time like bread, and like bread time will sleep
within me. My time is coming, I carry it here in my heart,
a holy stone that takes and receives the gifts of light.
Slowly my hands close, I hear the winds again beating
wetly on dark wings against the windows, and together—
my grandmother, my sleeping brothers, this house full
of memories forgotten and stored—we whirl into the
single journey that will take us into morning or into
mourning. Is this the just-born day come for the first time
to whiten the windows? Do I wake or sleep?

A NOTE ON THE TYPE

This book was set in Monticello, a Linotype revival of the original Roman No. 1 cut by Archibald Binny and cast in 1796 by the Philadelphia type foundry Binny & Ronaldson. The face was named Monticello in honor of its use in the monumental fifty-volume *Papers of Thomas Jefferson*, published by Princeton University Press. Monticello is a transitional type design, embodying certain features of Bulmer and Baskerville, but it is a distinguished face in its own right.

Composition by Heritage Printers,
Charlotte, North Carolina
Printed and bound by
Fairfield Graphics, Fairfield, Pennsylvania
Designed by Harry Ford